# Raising an

# Emotionally

# Intelligent

# Child

## John Gottman, Ph.D.,

## with Joan DeClaire

SIMON & SCHUSTER PAPERBACKS
NEW YORK    LONDON    TORONTO    SYDNEY

Simon & Schuster Paperbacks
Rockefeller Center
1230 Avenue of the Americas
New York, NY 10020

Previously published as *The Heart of Parenting*.

Simon & Schuster Paperbacks and colophon are registered trademarks of Simon & Schuster, Inc.

For information about special discounts for bulk purchases, please contact Simon & Schuster Special Sales: 1-800-456-6798 or business@simonandschuster.com.

Designed by Barbara M. Bachman

Manufactured in the United States of America

20   19

The Library of Congress has cataloged the hardcover edition as follows:
Gottman, John Mordechai.
    The heart of parenting : how to raise an emotionally intelligent child / John Gottman with Joan DeClaire.
        p.   cm.
    Includes bibliographical references.
    1. Emotions in children.   2. Emotions in adolescence.   3. Child rearing.
4. Parenting.   I. DeClaire, Joan.   II. Title.
BF723.E6G67   1997
649'.1—dc 20                    96-38947
ISBN-13: 978-0-684-80130-8
ISBN-10:    0-684-80130-2
ISBN-13: 978-0-684-83865-6 (Pbk)
ISBN-10:    0-684-83865-6 (Pbk)

# ACKNOWLEDGMENTS

THE IDEA FOR THIS RESEARCH ON "META-EMOTION" WAS conceived in 1984 when John Gottman was on leave, visiting Robert Levenson in Paul Ekman's laboratory in San Francisco. The research could not have progressed without the support of Robert Levenson, who built Gottman's first psychophysiology laboratory. This was the first study we did in that lab. The research has also received a great deal of support from Dr. Michael Guralnick, director of the Center for Human Developmental Disabilities (CHDD), and CHDD's core facilities, particularly the Instrument Development Laboratory at the University of Washington. The research was supported by National Institute of Mental Health research grants MH42484, titled "Marital discord, parenting, and child emotional development," MH35997, titled "Friendship formation among children," an NIMH Merit Award to extend research in time, and Research Scientist Award K2MH00257 awarded to John Gottman. Gottman wishes to acknowledge the great love, help, and intellectual companionship of his wife, Julie Schwartz Gottman, who coleads parent training groups at their Seattle Marital and Family Institute and who has been a true partner in parenting. Gottman also wishes to acknowledge the great love, patience, and teaching skill of his daughter, Moriah. Thanks to Mark Malone for his comments as a careful reader and devoted dad. Thanks also to writer Sondra Kornblatt for her insightful feedback on our manuscript.

*To the work and memory*

*of Dr. Haim Ginott*

# CONTENTS

# RAISING AN EMOTIONALLY INTELLIGENT CHILD

# FOREWORD

THESE ARE HARD TIMES FOR CHILDREN, AND SO FOR PARENTS.
There has been a sea change in the nature of childhood over the
last decade or two, one that makes it harder for children to learn the
basic lessons of the human heart and one that ups the ante for parents who used to pass these lessons on to the children they love.
Parents have to be smarter about teaching their children basic emotional and social lessons. In this practical guide for good parenting,
John Gottman shows how.

The need may never have been more pressing. Consider the statistics. Over the last few decades the number of homicides among
teenagers has quadrupled, the number of suicides has tripled,
forcible rapes doubled. Beneath headline-grabbing statistics like
these lies a more general emotional malaise. A nationwide random
sample of more than two thousand American children, rated by
their parents and teachers—first in the mid-1970s and then in the
late 1980s—found a long-term trend for children, on average, to be
dropping in basic emotional and social skills. On average, they become more nervous and irritable, more sulky and moody, more depressed and lonely, more impulsive and disobedient—they have
gone down on more than forty indicators.

Behind this deterioration lie larger forces. For one, the new economic realities mean parents have to work harder than earlier generations to support their families—which means that most parents
have less free time to spend with their children than their own parents had to spend with them. More and more families live far from
relatives, often in neighborhoods where parents of young children
are afraid to let them play on the streets, let alone visit a neighbor's

house. And more and more hours in children's lives are spent staring at a video screen—whether watching TV or looking at a computer monitor—which means they are not out playing with other children.

But in the long spread of human history, the way children have learned basic emotional and social skills has been from their parents and relatives, from neighbors, from the rough-and-tumble of play with other children.

The consequences of failing to learn the basics of emotional intelligence are increasingly dire. Evidence suggests, for example, that girls who fail to learn to distinguish between feelings like anxiety and hunger are most at risk for eating disorders, while those who have trouble controlling impulses in the early years are more likely to get pregnant by the end of their teen years. For boys, impulsivity in the early years may augur a heightened risk of delinquency or violence. And for all children, an inability to handle anxiety and depression increases the likelihood of later abusing drugs or alcohol.

Given these new realities, parents need to make the best use of the golden moments they have with their children, taking a purposeful and active role in coaching their children in key human skills like understanding and handling troubling feelings, controlling impulse, and empathy. In *Raising an Emotionally Intelligent Child*, John Gottman offers a scientifically grounded, eminently practical way for parents to give their children an essential tool kit for life.

—Daniel Goleman, author of
*Emotional Intelligence*

# PREFACE

BEFORE I BECAME A FATHER, I HAD SPENT NEARLY TWENTY years working in the field of developmental psychology, studying the emotional lives of children. But it was not until our daughter, Moriah, arrived in 1990 that I began truly to understand the realities of the parent-child relationship.

Like so many parents, I could not have imagined the intensity of feeling I would have for my child. I had no idea how thrilled I would be when she first learned to smile, to talk, to read a book. I did not anticipate how much patience and attention she would require from me minute by minute. Nor did I know how willing I would be to give her all the attention she needed. On the other hand, I was surprised at how frustrated, disappointed, and vulnerable I could sometimes feel. Frustrated when she and I couldn't communicate. Disappointed when she misbehaved. Vulnerable when I had to acknowledge how dangerous the world could be; how losing her would mean losing everything.

At the same time that I was learning about my own emotions, I was making related discoveries in my professional life. As a Jew whose parents escaped Austria to survive the Holocaust, I had respected the efforts of other theorists who rejected authoritarianism as a way to raise morally healthy children. They proposed that the family operate as a democracy and that children and parents act as rational, equal partners. But my years of investigation into family dynamics were beginning to yield new evidence that *emotional interactions* between parent and child could have an even greater impact on a child's long-term well-being.

Surprisingly, much of today's popular advice to parents ignores the world of emotion. Instead, it relies on child-rearing theories that address children's misbehavior, but disregard the feelings that underlie that misbehavior. However, the ultimate goal of raising children should not be simply to have an obedient and compliant child. Most parents hope for much more for their children. They want their children to be moral and responsible people who contribute to society, who have the strength to make their own choices in life, who enjoy the accomplishments of their own talents, who enjoy life and the pleasures it can offer, who have good relationships with friends and successful marriages, and who themselves become good parents.

In my research I discovered that love by itself wasn't enough. Very concerned, warm, and involved parents often had attitudes toward their own and their children's emotions that got in the way of them being able to talk to their children when they were sad or afraid or angry. But while love by itself was not enough, channeling that caring into some basic skills that parents practiced as if they were coaching their children in the area of emotion *was* enough. The secret lay in how parents interacted with their children when emotions ran hot.

We have studied parents and children in very detailed laboratory studies and followed the children as they developed. After a decade of research in my laboratory my research team encountered a group of parents who did five very simple things with their children when the children were emotional. We call these five things "Emotion Coaching." We discovered that the children who had Emotion-Coaching parents were on an entirely different developmental trajectory than the children of other parents.

The Emotion-Coaching parents had children who later became what Daniel Goleman calls "emotionally intelligent" people. These coached children simply had more general abilities in the area of their own emotions than children who were not coached by their parents. These abilities included being able to regulate their own emotional states. The children were better at soothing themselves when they were upset. They could calm down their hearts faster. Because of the superior performance in that part of their physiology that is involved in calming themselves, they had fewer infectious illnesses. They were better at focusing attention. They related better to other people, even in the tough social situations they encountered in middle childhood like getting teased, where being overly emotional is a liability, not an asset. They were better at understanding people. They had better friendships with other children. They were also better at situations in school that required academic performance. In short, they had developed a kind of "IQ" that is about people and the world of feelings, or emotional intelligence. This book will teach you the five steps of Emotion Coaching so that you can raise an emotionally intelligent child.

My emphasis on the emotional bond between parent and child has emerged from my longitudinal research. To my knowledge, this is the first research to confirm the work of one of our most brilliant child clinicians, the psychologist Dr. Haim Ginott, who wrote and taught in the 1960s. Ginott understood the importance of talking to children when they were emotional, and he understood the basic principles of how parents should do this.

Emotion Coaching gives us a framework based on emotional communication. When parents offer their children empathy and help them to cope with negative feelings like anger, sadness, and fear, parents build bridges of loyalty and affection. Within this context, although Emotion-Coaching parents do effectively set limits, misbehavior is no longer the major concern. Compliance, obedience, and responsibility come from a sense of love and connectedness the children feel within their families. In this way, emotional interactions among family members become the foundation for instilling values and raising moral people. Children behave according to family standards because they understand with their hearts that good behavior is expected; that living right is all part of belonging to the clan.

Unlike other parenting theories that offer a scattered hodge-podge of strategies for trying to control children's behavior, the five steps of Emotion Coaching provide a framework for maintaining a close personal relationship with our children as they develop.

The news of this book is that through scientific investigation, my colleagues and I have evidence that emotional interactions between parent and child are of utmost importance. We now know with certainty that when mothers and fathers practice Emotion Coaching it makes a significant difference in their children's success and happiness.

Our work will put our approach to children's emotions into a context that makes sense for today's parents, things that Ginott never addressed in the 1960s. With increasing divorce rates and concerns over problems like youth violence, raising emotionally intelligent kids becomes more crucial than ever. Our studies shed surprising light on how parents can protect their kids from the proven risks associated with marital conflict and divorce. They also show in new ways how an emotionally connected father, whether married or divorced, influences the well-being of his children.

The key to successful parenting is not found in complex theories, elaborate family rules, or convoluted formulas for behavior. It is based on your deepest feelings of love and affection for your child, and is demonstrated simply through empathy and understanding. Good parenting begins in your heart, and then continues on a moment-to-moment basis by engaging your children when feelings run high, when they are sad, angry, or scared. The heart of parenting is being there in a particular way when it really counts. This book will show you that way.

John Gottman, Ph.D.

## NOTE

We find the terminology "he or she" or "he/she" to be awkward. Traditionally, authors have avoided this awkwardness by using masculine pronouns exclusively. We believe this practice perpetuates gender bias. We have chosen instead to alternate masculine and feminine pronouns throughout the book. We hope our book will be equally useful to parents of daughters and parents of sons.

# Chapter 1

# EMOTION COACHING:

## *The Key to Raising*

## *Emotionally Intelligent Kids*

DIANE IS ALREADY LATE FOR WORK AS SHE TRIES TO COAX three-year-old Joshua into his jacket so she can take him to daycare. After a too-quick breakfast and a battle over which shoes to wear, Joshua is tense too. He doesn't really care that his mom has a meeting in less than an hour. He wants to stay home and play, he tells her. When Diane tells him that's not possible, Joshua falls to the floor. Feeling sad and angry, he starts to cry.

Seven-year-old Emily turns to her parents in tears just five minutes before the baby-sitter's arrival. "It's not fair to leave me with somebody I don't even know," she sobs. "But Emily," her dad explains, "this sitter is a good friend of your mother's. And besides, we've had tickets to this concert for weeks." "I still don't want you to go," she cries.

Fourteen-year-old Matt tells his mom he just got kicked out of the school band because the teacher smelled somebody smoking pot on the bus. "I swear to God it wasn't me," Matt says. But the boy's grades have been falling and he's running with a new crowd. "I don't believe you, Matt," she says. "And until you bring your grades up, you're not going out." Hurt and furious, Matt flies out the door without a word.

Three families. Three conflicts. Three kids at different stages of development. Still, these parents face the same problem—how to deal with children when emotions run high. Like most parents, they want to treat their kids fairly, with patience and respect. They know the world presents children with many challenges, and they want to be there for their kids, lending insight and support. They want to teach their kids to handle problems effectively and to form strong, healthy relationships. But there's a big difference between *wanting* to do right by your kids and actually having the wherewithal to carry it off.

That's because good parenting requires more than intellect. It touches a dimension of the personality that's been ignored in much of the advice dispensed to parents over the past thirty years. Good parenting involves *emotion*.

In the last decade or so, science has discovered a tremendous amount about the role emotions play in our lives. Researchers have found that even more than IQ, your emotional awareness and ability to handle feelings will determine your success and happiness in all walks of life, including family relationships. For parents, this quality of "emotional intelligence"—as many now call it—means being aware of your children's feelings, and being able to empathize, soothe, and guide them. For children, who learn most lessons about emotion from their parents, it includes the ability to control impulses, delay gratification, motivate themselves, read other people's social cues, and cope with life's ups and downs.

"Family life is our first school for emotional learning," writes Daniel Goleman, psychologist and author of *Emotional Intelligence*, a book that describes in rich detail the scientific research that has led to our growing understanding of this field. "In this intimate cauldron we learn how to feel about ourselves and how others will react to our feelings; how to think about these feelings and what choices we have in reacting; how to read and express hopes and fears. This emotional schooling operates not just through the things parents say and do directly to children, but also in the models they offer for handling their own feelings and those that pass between husband and wife. Some parents are gifted emotional teachers, others atrocious."

What parental behaviors make the difference? As a research psychologist studying parent-child interactions, I have spent much of the past twenty years looking for the answer to this question. Working with research teams at the University of Illinois and the University of Washington, I have conducted in-depth research in two studies of 119 families, observing how parents and children react to one another in emotionally charged situations. We have been following these children from age four to adolescence. In addition, we are in the process of tracking 130 newlywed couples as they become parents of young infants. Our studies involve lengthy interviews with parents, talking about their marriages, their reactions to their children's emotional experiences, and their own awareness of the role emotion plays in their lives. We have tracked children's physiological responses during stressful parent-child interactions. We have carefully observed and analyzed parents' emotional reactions to their kids' anger and sadness. Then we have checked in with these families over time to see how their children developed in terms of health, academic achievement, emotional development, and social relationships.

Our results tell a simple, yet compelling story. We have found that most parents fall into one of two broad categories: those who give their children guidance about the world of emotion and those who don't.

I call the parents who get involved with their children's feelings "Emotion Coaches." Much like athletic coaches, they teach their children strategies to deal with life's ups and downs. They don't object to their children's displays of anger, sadness, or fear. Nor do they ignore them. Instead, they accept negative emotions as a fact of life and they use emotional moments as opportunities for teaching their kids important life lessons and building closer relationships with them.

"When Jennifer is sad, it's a real important time for bonding between us," says Maria, the mother of a five-year-old in one of our studies. "I tell her that I want to talk to her, to know how she's feeling."

Like many Emotion-Coaching parents in our studies, Jennifer's dad, Dan, sees his daughter's sad or angry moments as the time she needs him most. More than any other interaction he has with his daughter, soothing her "makes me feel like a dad," Dan says. "I have to be there for her . . . I have to tell her it's all right. That she'll survive this problem and probably have lots more."

Emotion-Coaching parents like Maria and Dan might be described as "warm" and "positive" toward their daughter, and indeed they are. But taken alone, warm, positive parenting does not teach emotional intelligence. In fact, it's common for parents to be loving and attentive, yet incapable of dealing effectively with their children's negative emotions. Among these parents who fail to teach their kids emotional intelligence, I have identified three types:

1. Dismissing parents, who disregard, ignore, or trivialize children's negative emotions;

2. Disapproving parents, who are critical of their children's displays of negative feelings and may reprimand or punish them for emotional expression; and

3. Laissez-Faire parents, who accept their children's emotions and empathize with them, but fail to offer guidance or set limits on their children's behavior.

To give you an idea of how differently Emotion-Coaching parents and their three noncoaching counterparts respond to their children, imagine Diane, whose little boy protested going to daycare, in each of these roles.

If she was a Dismissing parent, she might tell him that his reluctance to go to daycare is "silly"; that there's no reason to feel sad about leaving the house. Then she might try to distract him from his sad thoughts, perhaps bribing him with a cookie or talking about fun activities his teacher has planned.

As a Disapproving parent, Diane might scold Joshua for his refusal to cooperate, telling him she's tired of his bratty behavior, and threatening to spank him.

As a Laissez-Faire parent, Diane might embrace Joshua in all his anger and sadness, empathize with him, tell him it's perfectly natural for him to want to stay home. But then she'd be at a loss for what to do next. She wouldn't want to scold, spank, or bribe her son, but staying home wouldn't be an option, either. Perhaps in the end, she'd cut a deal: I'll play a game with you for ten minutes— then it's out the door with no crying. Until tomorrow morning, that is.

So what would the Emotion Coach do differently? She might start out like the Laissez-Faire parent, empathizing with Joshua, and letting him know that she understands his sadness. But she would go further, providing Joshua with guidance for what to do with his uncomfortable feelings. Perhaps the conversation would go something like this:

*Diane:* Let's put on your jacket, Joshua. It's time to go.

*Joshua:* No! I don't want to go to daycare.

*Diane:* You don't want to go? Why not?

*Joshua:* Because I want to stay here with you.

*Diane:* You do?

*Joshua:* Yeah I want to stay home.

*Diane:* Gosh, I think I know just how you feel. Some mornings I wish you and I could just curl up in a chair and look at books together instead of rushing out the door. But you know what? I made an important promise to the people at my office that I'd be there by nine o'clock and I can't break that promise.

*Joshua* (starting to cry): But why not? It's not fair. I don't want to go.

*Diane:* Come here, Josh. (Taking him onto her lap.) I'm sorry, honey, but we can't stay home. I'll bet that makes you feel disappointed doesn't it?

*Joshua* (nodding): Yeah.

*Diane:* And kind of sad?

*Joshua:* Yeah.

*Diane:* I feel kind of sad, too. (She lets him cry for a while and continues to hug him, letting him have his tears.) I know what we can do. Let's think about tomorrow, when we don't have to go to work and daycare. We'll be able to spend the whole day together. Can you think of anything special you'd like to do tomorrow?

*Joshua:* Have pancakes and watch cartoons?

*Diane:* Sure, that would be great. Anything else?

*Joshua:* Can we take my wagon to the park?

*Diane:* I think so.

*Joshua:* Can Kyle come, too?

*Diane:* Maybe. We'll have to ask his mom. But right now it's time to get going, okay?

*Joshua:* Okay.

At first glance, the Emotion-Coaching parent may seem much like the Dismissing parent because both directed Joshua to think

about something other than staying home. But there is an important distinction. As an Emotion Coach, Diane acknowledged her
son's sadness, helped him to name it, allowed him to experience his
feelings, and stayed with him while he cried. She didn't try to distract his attention away from his feelings. Nor did she scold him for
feeling sad, as the Disapproving mother did. She let him know that
she respects his feelings and thinks his wishes are valid.

Unlike the Laissez-Faire mother, the Emotion-Coaching parent
set limits. She took a few extra minutes to deal with Joshua's feelings, but she let him know that she wasn't going to be late for work
and break her promise to her co-workers. Joshua was disappointed
but it was a feeling both he and Diane could deal with. And once
Joshua had a chance to identify, experience, and accept the emotion, Diane showed him it was possible to move beyond his sad feelings and look forward to fun the next day.

This response is all part of the process of Emotion Coaching that
my research colleagues and I uncovered in our studies of successful
parent-child interactions. The process typically happens in five
steps. The parents:

1. become aware of the child's emotion;

2. recognize the emotion as an opportunity for intimacy and
teaching;

3. listen empathetically, validating the child's feelings;

4. help the child find words to label the emotion he is having; and

5. set limits while exploring strategies to solve the problem at hand.

---

## THE EFFECTS OF EMOTION COACHING

---

WHAT DIFFERENCE DOES it make when children have Emotion-
Coaching parents? By observing and analyzing in detail the words,
actions, and emotional responses of families over time, as we have
done in our studies, we have discovered a truly significant contrast.

Children whose parents consistently practice Emotion Coaching have better physical health and score higher academically than children whose parents don't offer such guidance. These kids get along better with friends, have fewer behavior problems, and are less prone to acts of violence. Over all, children who are Emotion-Coached experience fewer negative feelings and more positive feelings. In short, they're more healthy emotionally.

But here's the result I find most surprising: When mothers and fathers use a coaching style of parenting, their children become more resilient. The kids who are Emotion-Coached still get sad, angry, or scared under difficult circumstances, but they are better able to soothe themselves, bounce back from distress, and carry on with productive activities. In other words, they are more emotionally intelligent.

Indeed, our research shows that Emotion Coaching can even protect kids from the proven harmful effects of an increasingly common crisis for American families—marital conflict and divorce.

With more than half of all marriages now ending in divorce, millions of children are at risk for problems many social scientists have linked to family dissolution. These problems include school failure, rejection by other children, depression, health challenges, and antisocial behavior. Such problems can also affect children from unhappy, conflict-ridden homes even when their parents don't divorce. Our own research shows that when a couple constantly fights, their conflict gets in the way of their child's ability to form friendships. We also found that marital conflict affects a child's schoolwork and increases the child's susceptibility to illness. We now know that a major result of the epidemic of ailing and dissolving marriages in our society is an increase in deviant and violent behavior among children and teenagers.

But when the Emotion-Coaching parents in our studies experienced marital conflict, or were separated or divorced, something different happened. With the exception of the fact that these kids were generally "sadder" than the other children in our study, Emotion Coaching seemed to shield them from the deleterious effects suffered by so many who have this experience. Previously proven effects of divorce and marital conflict, such as academic failure, aggression, and problems with peers, did not show up in the Emotion-Coached kids; all of which suggests that Emotion Coaching offers children the first proven buffer against the emotional trauma of divorce.

While such findings are obviously relevant for families who are currently struggling with marital problems and the aftermath of divorce, we expect that further research will reveal that Emotion Coaching can buffer children against a whole host of other conflicts, losses, and heartaches as well.

Another surprising discovery from our research has to do with fathers. Our studies found that when dads adopt an Emotion-Coaching style of parenting, it has an extremely positive impact on their children's emotional development. When fathers are aware of their kids' feelings and try to help them solve problems, children do better in school and in relationships with others. In contrast, an emotionally distant dad—one who is harsh, critical, or dismissing of his children's emotions—can have a deeply negative impact. His kids are more likely to do poorly in school, fight more with friends, and have poor health. (This emphasis on dads does not mean that a mother's involvement doesn't affect children's emotional intelligence as well. The effects of her interactions with her children are significant. But our studies indicate that a father's influence can be much more *extreme*, whether that effect is good or bad.)

At a time when an alarming 28 percent of American children are growing up in mother-only households, the significance of a father's presence in a child's life cannot be overlooked. We shouldn't assume, however, that any father is better than no father. An emotionally present dad can be a tremendous benefit in a child's life, but a cold and cruel father can do great harm.

While our research shows that Emotion-Coaching parents can help their kids develop into healthier, more successful adults, the technique is by no means a cure for serious family problems that require the help of a professional therapist. And unlike proponents of many other parenting theories, I will not promise that Emotion Coaching is a panacea for all the normal problems of family life. Practicing Emotion Coaching does *not* mean all family arguments will cease, that there will be no more harsh words, no more bruised feelings, no more sadness or stress. Conflict is a fact of family life. Still, once you start using Emotion Coaching, you will probably feel yourself growing closer to your children. And when your family shares a deeper intimacy and respect, problems between family members will seem lighter to bear.

And finally, Emotion Coaching does *not* mean an end to discipline. Indeed, when you and your children are emotionally close, you are even more invested in their lives and can therefore assert a stronger influence. You're in a position to be tough when toughness is called for. When you see your children making mistakes or slacking off, you call them on it. You're not afraid to set limits. You're not afraid to tell them when they've disappointed you, when you know they can do better. And because you have an emotional bond with your children, your words matter. They care about what you think and they don't want to displease you. In this way, Emotion Coaching may help you guide and motivate your kids.

Emotion Coaching requires a significant amount of commitment and patience, but the job is essentially the same as that of any other coach. If you want to see your kid excel at baseball, you don't avoid the game; you get out in the yard and start working with him. Likewise, if you want to see your child handle feelings, cope with stress, and develop healthy relationships, you don't shut down or ignore expressions of negative emotion; you engage with your child and offer guidance.

While grandparents, teachers, and other adults can serve as Emotion Coaches in a child's life, as a parent, you're in the best spot for the job. After all, you're the one who knows what rules you want *your* child to play by. And you're the one who's going to be there when life gets tough. Whether the challenge is infant colic, potty training, sibling warfare, or broken prom dates, your child looks to you for signals. So you might as well put on the coach's cap and help your child win the game.

## How Coaching Can Reduce Your Child's Risks

THERE'S LITTLE DOUBT that parents today face challenges those of previous generations did not. While parents in the 1960s may have fretted about alcohol on graduation night, today's parents worry daily about cocaine sales at middle school. Yesterday's parents worried that their teenage daughters might turn up pregnant; today's parents are teaching their fifth-graders about AIDS. A generation ago, turf battles between rival youth gangs erupted only in tough, urban areas and ended with fistfights or an occasional stabbing. Today, youth gangs spring up even in middle-class neighborhoods. And with the proliferation of the drug trade and firearms, gang fights often end in fatal shoot-outs.

Violent crimes against young people have been rising at an alarming rate. Between 1985 and 1990, homicide rates among fifteen- to nineteen-year-old youths rose 130 percent in nonwhite males, 75 percent in white males, and 30 percent in females of all races. At the same time, young American males have been committing more violent crimes at younger ages than ever before. From 1965 to 1991, the juvenile arrest rate for violent crime more than tripled. Between 1982 and 1991, the number of juveniles arrested for murder increased 93 percent, and for aggravated assault, 72 percent.

Parents have to do more today than provide kids with basic nurturing, a good education, and a strong moral ethic. Today's families must also concern themselves with some of the most basic survival issues. How can we immunize our children from an epidemic of violence that is infesting youth culture in our country? How can we persuade them to postpone sexual activity until they are mature enough to make responsible, safe choices? How can we infuse them with enough self-regard that they steer clear of drug and alcohol abuse?

Over the years, social scientists have proven that children are drawn into antisocial, delinquent behavior as a result of problems in their family environment—problems like marital conflict, divorce, the physical or emotional absence of a father, domestic violence, poor parenting, neglect, abuse, and poverty. The solutions, then, should be to build better marriages and see that parents have the economic and social support they need to take good care of their children. The problem is, our society appears to be headed in the opposite direction.

In 1950, only 4 percent of new mothers were unmarried; today some 30 percent are. While most of today's unmarried mothers eventually wed, a high divorce rate—now more than half of all new marriages—keeps the number of mother-only households high.

Right now, it's around 28 percent, with about half of these families living in poverty.

Many children from divorced families lack the financial or emotional support they need from fathers. Figures from the 1989 U.S. Census show that just over half the mothers entitled to child support receive the full amount; a quarter received partial payment, and a fifth received nothing at all. One study of children from disrupted families found that two years after a divorce, a majority of children had not seen their fathers for a year.

Remarriage, if it happens, brings its own problems. Divorce is more common in second marriages than in first marriages. And while studies show that stepfathers often bring a more reliable income, the relationship often brings more stress, confusion, and sadness into a child's life. Child abuse occurs more frequently in stepfamilies than in natural families. According to one Canadian study, preschool children in stepfamilies are forty times more likely than those who live with biological parents to suffer physical and sexual abuse.

Children in emotional pain don't leave their problems at the schoolhouse door. As a result, schools nationwide have reported dramatic increases in behavior problems over the past decade. Our public schools—many already drained from antitax initiatives—are being called upon to provide an increasing number of social services for children whose emotional needs are not met at home. In essence, schools are becoming emotional buffering zones for the growing number of children hurt by divorce, poverty, and neglect. Consequently, there are fewer resources available to fund basic education, a trend that's reflected in declining academic scores.

In addition, families of all kinds are stressed by changes that have occurred in the workforce and the economy over the past few decades. Effective income has been eroded over the past two decades, which means that many families need double paychecks to stay afloat. More women have entered the paid workforce. And for many couples, the power shift that happens as the male partner loses his role as the sole breadwinner brings added stresses. At the same time, employers are demanding more of workers' time. According to Harvard economics professor Juliet Schor, the typical American family now works one thousand more hours each year than it did twenty-five years ago. One survey showed that Americans have a third less free time than they did in the 1970s. As a result, people say they are spending less time on basics like sleeping, eating, and playing with their kids. Between 1960 and 1986, the time parents had available to spend with their children fell by more than ten hours a week. Short on time, Americans are participating less in community and religious activities that uphold the family structure. And as our society becomes more mobile, moving from city to city for economic reasons, an increasing number of families live without the support of nearby family and lifelong friends.

The net effect of all these social changes is that our children face increased risks to their health and well-being. Meanwhile, the support systems that aid families in protecting kids are getting weaker.

Still, as this book shows, we as parents are far from helpless. My research tells me that the answer to keeping our children safe from many risks lies in building stronger emotional bonds with them, thus helping them to develop a higher level of emotional intelligence. Evidence is mounting that kids who can feel their parents' love and support are better protected from the threats of youth violence, antisocial behavior, drug addiction, premature sexual activity, adolescent suicide, and other social ills. Studies reveal that children who feel respected and valued in their families do better in school, have more friendships, and live healthier, more successful lives.

Now, with more in-depth research into the dynamics of families' emotional relationships, we are beginning to understand how this buffering effect happens.

## EMOTION COACHING AS AN
## EVOLUTIONARY STEP

AS PART OF OUR research into the emotional lives of families, we ask parents to tell us about their responses to their preschoolers' negative feelings. Like many fathers, Mike tells us that he finds his four-year-old daughter, Becky, comical when she's angry. "She says, 'Gosh darn it!' And then she walks away like some little midget human," he says. "It's just so funny!"

And indeed, on at least one level, the contrast of this tiny girl expressing such a big emotion would make many people smile. But just imagine for a moment what would happen if Mike reacted this way to his wife's anger. Or, what if Mike's boss responded to him this way when he was mad? It probably wouldn't amuse Mike at all. Yet, many adults think nothing of laughing in the face of a raging preschooler. Many well-meaning parents dismiss children's fears and upsets as though they didn't matter. "There's nothing to be afraid of," we tell a five-year-old who wakes up crying from a nightmare. "Then you obviously didn't see what I saw," might be an appropriate reply. Instead, the child in such situations begins to accept the adult's estimation of the event and learns to doubt her own judgment. With adults constantly invalidating her feelings, she loses confidence in herself.

Thus, we have inherited a tradition of discounting children's feelings simply because children are smaller, less rational, less experienced, and less powerful than the adults around them. Taking children's emotions seriously requires empathy, keen listening skills, and a willingness to see things from their perspective. It also takes a certain selflessness. Behavioral psychologists have observed that preschoolers typically demand that their caretakers deal with some kind of need or desire at an average rate of *three times a minute*. Under ideal circumstances, a mom or dad might respond cheerfully. But when a parent is stressed or otherwise distracted, a child's incessant, and sometimes irrational demands can drive that parent wild.

And so it has been for centuries. While I believe parents have always loved their children, historical evidence shows that, unfortunately, past generations did not necessarily recognize the need for patience, restraint, and kindness in dealing with kids. Psychiatrist Lloyd deMause, in his 1974 essay "The Evolution of Childhood," paints a horrifying picture of neglect and cruelty that children of the Western world have endured through the ages. His work shows, however, that throughout the nineteenth and early twentieth centuries, the plight of children gradually improved. With each generation, parents generally became better than the last at meeting the physical, psychological, and emotional needs of children. As deMause describes it, raising a child "became less a process of conquering a child's will than training it, guiding it into proper paths, teaching it to conform, and socializing it."

Although Sigmund Freud would promote theories in the early 1900s that children were highly sexualized, aggressive creatures, observational research later in the century would prove otherwise. Social psychologist Lois Murphy, for example, who conducted extensive observations and experiments with toddlers and preschoolers in the 1930s, showed that most small children are, by nature, primarily altruistic and empathetic toward one another, particularly toward another child in distress.

With this growing belief in the intrinsic goodness of children, our society has been evolving since mid-century into another new era of parenting, one that deMause described as "the helping mode." It is a period in which many parents are letting go of strict, authoritarian models by which they themselves may have been raised. Instead, more parents now believe their role is to assist children to develop according to their own interests, needs, and desires. To do this, parents are adopting what psychological theorist Diana Baumrind first referred to as an "authoritative" style of parenting. While *authoritarian* parents characteristically impose many limits and expect strict obedience without giving children explanations, *authoritative* parents set limits but are considerably more flexible, providing their children with explanations and lots of warmth. Baumrind also describes a third style of parenting she calls *permissive*, whereby parents are warm and communicative toward their children, but exert few limits on behavior. In studies of preschool children in the 1970s, Baumrind found that children of *authoritarian* parents tended to be conflicted and irritable, while children of *permissive* parents were often impulsive, aggressive, low in self-reliance, and low in achievement. But children of *authoritative* parents were most consistently cooperative, self-reliant, energetic, friendly, and achievement-oriented.

Movement toward this less authoritarian, more responsive mode of parenting has been fueled by tremendous growth in our understanding of child psychology and the social behavior of families in the past twenty-five years. Social scientists have discovered, for example, that infants have an amazing ability to learn social and emotional cues from their parents, beginning at birth. We now know that when caregivers respond sensitively to babies' cues—engaging in eye contact, taking turns at "baby talk," and allowing babies to rest when they seem overstimulated—the babies learn early how to regulate their own emotions. These babies still get excited when that's called for, but they are able to calm themselves down afterward.

Studies have also shown that when infants have caretakers who don't pay attention to these cues—say, a depressed mom who doesn't talk to her baby, or an anxious dad who plays with the baby too hard and too long—the baby doesn't develop the same knack for regulating his emotions. The baby may not learn that babbling gets attention, so he becomes quiet and passive, socially disengaged. Or, because he's constantly stimulated, he may not get the chance to learn that sucking his thumb and stroking his blanket are good ways to calm down.

Learning to calm down and focus attention become increasingly important as the baby matures. For one, these skills allow a child to be attentive to social cues from parents, caregivers, and others in their environment. Learning to be calm also helps the child to concentrate in learning situations and to focus on the achievement of specific tasks. And, as a child grows, it's extremely helpful for learning how to share toys, pretend, and otherwise get along with playmates. Eventually, this so-called self-regulation skill can make a big difference in a child's ability to enter new play groups, make new friends, and handle rejection when peers turn away.

Awareness of this link between parents' responsiveness and children's emotional intelligence has grown in the past two or three decades. Countless books have been written for parents telling them how crucial it is that they provide distressed infants with affection and comfort. Parents are urged to practice positive forms of discipline as their children grow; to praise their kids more than they criticize them; to reward rather than punish; to encourage rather than discourage. Such theories have taken us a long way, thankfully, from the days when parents were told that sparing the rod would spoil the child. We now know that kindness, warmth, optimism, and patience are far better tools than the hickory stick for raising well-behaved, emotionally healthy children.

And yet, I believe we can go even further in this evolutionary process. Through our work in family psychology labs, we can now see and measure the benefits of healthy emotional communication between parent and child. We are beginning to understand that parents' interactions with their infants can affect children's nervous systems and emotional health throughout life. We now know that the strength of a couple's marriage affects the well-being of their children and we can see tremendous potential when fathers become more emotionally involved with their children. And finally, we are able to document that parents' awareness of their own feelings is at the heart of improving children's emotional intelligence as well. Our program of Emotion Coaching—outlined in detail in Chapter 3—is our blueprint for parenting based on this research.

MUCH OF TODAY's popular literature on parenting seems to sidestep the dimension of emotional intelligence, but it was not always so. That's why I must acknowledge an influential psychologist, teacher, and author who has contributed much to our understanding of the emotional lives of families. He is Haim Ginott, who wrote three popular books in the 1960s, including *Between Parent and Child*, before his premature death from cancer in 1973.

Writing long before the words "emotional" and "intelligence" were ever fused, Ginott believed that one of our most important responsibilities as parents is to listen to our children, hearing not only their words, but the feelings behind their words. He also taught that communication about emotions can serve as a way for parents to teach their children values.

But for this to happen, parents must show genuine respect for their children's feelings, Ginott taught. They must attempt to empathize with their kids—that is, feel what their children are feeling. Communication between parent and child must always preserve both parties' self-respect. Statements of understanding should precede statements of advice. Ginott discouraged parents from telling children what they ought to feel, because that simply makes children distrust their feelings. He said kids' emotions do not disappear when parents say, "Don't feel that way," or when parents tell kids there is no justification for their emotions. Ginott believed that while not all behavior is acceptable, all feelings and wishes are acceptable. Therefore, parents should set limits on acts, but not emotions and desires.

Unlike many parent educators, Ginott did not disapprove of getting angry with children. Indeed, he believed that parents should honestly express their anger, provided that it is directed at a specific problem and does not attack the child's personality or character. Used judiciously, he believed parental anger can be part of a system of effective discipline.

Ginott's regard for emotional communication with children has been an important influence for others, including Adele Faber and Elaine Mazlish, who were his students and who wrote important, practical books for parents based on his work, including *Liberated Parents/Liberated Children*, *Siblings Without Rivalry*, *How to Talk so Kids Will Listen and Listen so Kids Will Talk* , and *How to Talk so Kids Can Learn*.

Despite these contributions, however, Ginott's theories had never been proven using empirically sound, scientific methods. But I am proud to say that with the help of my research associates, I can provide the first quantifiable evidence to suggest that Ginott's ideas were essentially correct. Empathy not only matters; it is the foundation of effective parenting.

## HOW WE DISCOVERED EMOTION COACHING

WE BEGAN OUR studies in 1986 with fifty-six married couples in Champaign, Illinois. Each couple had a child age four or five at the time. Members of our research team spent fourteen hours with each family, administering questionnaires, conducting interviews, and observing behavior. We gathered a rich, deep pool of information about each couple's marriage, their children's peer relationships, and the family's ideas about emotion.

In one audiotaped session, for example, couples talked about their experiences with negative emotion, their philosophies of emotional expression and control, and their feelings about their children's anger and sadness. These interviews were then coded for the parents' awareness and regulation of emotions, and their ability to recognize and coach their children's negative feelings. We determined whether or not these parents showed respect for their children's feelings, and how they talked to their kids about emotions when the kids were upset. Did they try to teach their children rules for appropriate expression of emotion? Did they share strategies children can use to soothe themselves?

To get information about the children's social competence, audiotapes were made of each child during a thirty-minute play period at home with a best friend. Researchers coded these interactions for the amount of negative emotion the child expressed during the session as well as the overall quality of the child's play.

In another audiotaped interview, each couple spent up to three hours answering open-ended questions about the history of their marriage. How did they meet? What was their dating period like? How did they decide to get married? How had their relationship changed over the years? Couples were encouraged to talk about their philosophy of marriage and what it takes to make marriage work. These tapes were then coded for several factors including how much fondness or negativity the couple expressed toward each other, how much they talked in terms of togetherness or separateness, and how much they glorified the struggles they've faced together.

While such interviews and observations are important to our understanding of these families, the unique aspects of our research involved collecting data about the participants' physiological responses to emotion. Our aim was to measure the way our participants' autonomic, or involuntary, nervous systems responded to emotion. For example, we asked each family to collect urine samples from their children over a twenty-four-hour period of time. These samples were then analyzed for traces of stress-related hormones. Other measures of the autonomic nervous system were taken in our labs where we could monitor participants' heart rates, respiration, blood flow, motor activity, and how much their hands sweat.

Studying these physiological processes and observing families provides more objective data than relying solely on questionnaires, interviews, and observation. It's difficult, for obvious reasons, to get parents to honestly answer questions like, "How often do you harshly criticize your child?" And even when social scientists observe their subjects' habits using "candid camera" methods such as two-way mirrors, it's hard to determine how much one person's behavior touches another's feelings. Keeping track of autonomic responses to stress is much easier. Stethoscope-like electrodes hooked up to the chest can monitor heart rate; electrodes can also track how much hands sweat by measuring the electricity conducted via salt in perspiration.

Such technology is considered reliable. Indeed, law enforcement officials routinely use it to conduct lie detector tests. Police have an advantage over family researchers, however—their study subjects can be intimidated into sitting still. Working with four- and five-year-olds requires craftier measures. That's why we built a mock space capsule for children participating in one of our major experiments. The kids donned space suits and crawled inside the contraption, where they were hooked up to various electrodes so we could measure their physiological responses to activities designed to elicit emotion. We showed them film clips like the flying monkey scene from *The Wizard of Oz*, for example. We also invited their parents to stand nearby and teach their children a new video game. Having such captive participants allowed us to record the research sessions on videotape so we could systematically observe and code each family member's words, actions, and facial expressions, considering factors such as content of the spoken word, tone of voice, and gesture.

We used this same type of monitoring equipment (minus the space motif) for another set of sessions that measured the physiological and behavioral responses of the children's parents as they discussed high-conflict topics like money, religion, in-laws, and child-rearing. These marital interaction sessions were coded for both positive expressions (humor, affection, validation, interest, joy) and negative expressions (anger, disgust, contempt, sadness, stonewalling).

To find out how different styles of parenting serve children over time, we revisited the families from our 1986 study three years later. We were able to reach 95 percent of the study participants at a time when their children were seven to eight years old. Once again, we audiotaped a play session between each child and his or her best friend. Teachers were asked to complete questionnaires regarding the children's levels of aggression, withdrawal, and social competence in the classroom. In addition, teachers and mothers filled out surveys regarding the children's academic performance and behavior. Each mother provided information about her child's health, as well as monitoring and reporting the total number of negative emotions expressed by her child over the course of one week.

We gathered information about the couples' marriages as well. Parents told us in telephone interviews whether they had separated or divorced during the intervening three-year period or seriously considered separation or divorce. In individually administered questionnaires, each parent also told us about his or her current satisfaction with the marriage.

Results of this follow-up study showed us that, indeed, children with Emotion-Coaching parents were better off in areas of academic performance, social competence, emotional well-being, and physical health. Even controlling for IQ, their math and reading scores were better. They were getting along bett_r with their friends, they had stronger social skills, and their mothers reported these children had fewer negative and more positive emotions. Several measures also indicated that the Emotion-Coached kids were experiencing less stress in their lives. For example, they had lower levels of stress-related hormones in their urine. They had a lower resting heart rate. And, according to their mothers' reports, they were getting fewer infectious illnesses, such as colds and flu.

## EMOTION COACHING AND SELF-REGULATION

MANY OF THE positive outcomes we found in these emotionally intelligent, Emotion-Coached children at age seven and eight are the result of a characteristic we refer to as "high vagal tone." The term comes from the vagus nerve, which is a large nerve originating in the brain and supplying impulses for functions throughout the upper body such as heart rate, respiration, and digestion. The vagus nerve is responsible for many functions of the parasympathetic branch of the autonomic nervous system. While the sympathetic branch accelerates functions such as heart rate and breathing when a person is under stress, the parasympathetic branch acts as a regulator, putting the brakes on these involuntary functions, keeping the body from speeding its systems out of control.

We use the term "vagal tone" to describe a person's ability to regulate the involuntary physiological processes of the autonomic nervous system. Just as kids with good muscle tone excel at sports, kids with high vagal tone excel at responding to and recovering from emotional stress. The heart rates of such autonomic athletes will temporarily accelerate in response to some alarm or excitement, for example. But as soon as the emergency is over, their bodies are able to recover quickly. These children are good at soothing themselves, focusing their attention, and inhibiting action when that's what's called for.

First-graders with high vagal tone would have no problem during a fire drill, for instance. They'd be able drop everything and get out of the school in an orderly, efficient manner. Once the fire drill was over, these kids would be able to settle down and focus on their math lessons in fairly short order. Kids with low vagal tone, on the other hand, would be more likely to get confused during the drill. ("What? Leave now? It's not even time for recess.") Then, upon returning to the classroom, they'd have a hard time getting over all the excitement and getting back to work.

In our video game experiment, kids with Emotion-Coaching parents demonstrated that they were indeed the autonomic athletes in our sample. When compared to kids whose parents were not Emotion Coaching, they showed more physiological responsiveness to stress, followed by quicker recovery. Ironically, the events that usually induced stress in these kids were criticism or mockery from their fathers, behavior that doesn't happen that often in these Emotion-Coaching families. Perhaps that's why the children reacted so strongly. Still, the Emotion-Coached kids recovered from stress more quickly than others in our sample, despite the fact that they had much stronger physiological responses to stress in the first place.

This ability to respond and bounce back from stress can serve kids well throughout childhood and beyond. It's a dimension of emotional intelligence that allows them to focus their attention and concentrate on schoolwork. And because it gives kids the emotional responsiveness and self-control needed to relate to other children, it's also useful in forming and maintaining friendships. Kids with high vagal tone are quick on the uptake, noticing and reacting to emotional cues from other kids. They can also control their own negative responses in high-conflict situations.

These qualities were evident in one of the thirty-minute play sessions we recorded between two four-year-olds as part of our research. The two children—a boy and a girl—got into an argument because the boy wanted to play Superman and the girl wanted to play house. After shouting their wishes back and forth a few times, however, the boy calmed down and suggested a simple compromise: They would pretend they were at Superman's house. The girl thought this was a great idea and the two moved forward to enjoy a creative period of pretend play for the next half hour.

Such creative compromise between two four-year-olds takes a lot of social skill, including the ability to listen to each other, to empathize with each other's position, and to solve problems together. But what children learn from Emotion Coaching goes far beyond such social skills to encompass a broader definition of emotional intelligence. This is demonstrated later in middle childhood (ages eight to twelve), when peer acceptance is often measured by a child's ability to be "cool" and emotionally unflappable among friends. Psychologists have observed that expressing feelings, as parents and children do in Emotion Coaching, can actually be a social liability for children in this age group. What matters instead is the child's ability to observe, to pick up on social cues that will allow the child to assimilate without drawing too much attention to himself. What we found in our research was that children who are Emotion-Coached in early childhood do indeed develop this sort of social skill later on, which helps them to be accepted by peers and form friendships.

Children's emotional intelligence is determined to some degree by temperament—that is, the personality traits with which a child is born—but it's also shaped by the child's interactions with his parents. This influence begins in the earliest days of infancy, when a child's immature nervous system is being formed. The experience children have with emotion while their parasympathetic nervous systems are still under construction may play a big part in the development of their vagal tone—and consequently their emotional well-being—later in life.

Parents have a tremendous opportunity, therefore, to influence their kids' emotional intelligence by helping them learn self-soothing behaviors from infancy on. As helpless as babies are, they can learn from our response to their discomfort that emotion has a direction; that it is possible to go from feelings of intense distress, anger, and fear, to feelings of comfort and recovery. Babies whose emotional needs are neglected, on the other hand, don't get the chance to learn this lesson. When they cry out of fear, sadness, or anger, they experience only more fear, more sadness, more anger. As a result, they may become passive and nonexpressive much of the time. But when they do get upset, they lack any sense of control. They've never had a guide to take them from distress to comfort, so they can't self-soothe. Instead, they experience negative emotion as a black hole of anxiety and fear.

It's interesting to watch small children who have had emotional guidance gradually begin to incorporate their caretakers' soothing responses into their own behavior. Perhaps you've seen it in your own children's play. Whether they are pretending with a real live playmate, a doll, or an action figure, kids often fantasize situations where one character is scared and the other takes on the role of soother, comforter, or hero. Such play gives them experience they can call upon when they are alone and upset; it helps them establish and practice patterns for regulating emotion and calming down. It helps them to respond to one another in an emotionally intelligent way.

The first step parents can take toward raising emotionally intelligent children is to understand their own style of dealing with emotion and how that affects their kids. This is the subject of Chapter 2.

# Chapter 2

## ASSESSING YOUR

## PARENTING STYLE

THE CONCEPT OF EMOTION COACHING IS A SIMPLE ONE THAT'S based on common sense and rooted in our deepest feelings of love and empathy for our children. Unfortunately, however, Emotion Coaching doesn't come naturally to all parents simply because they love their children. Nor does it automatically flow out of a parent's conscious decision to take a warm and positive approach to dealing with a child. Rather, Emotion Coaching is an art that requires emotional awareness and a specific set of listening and problem-solving behaviors—behaviors my colleagues and I identified and analyzed in our observation of healthy, well-functioning families—families that can be described as emotionally intelligent.

I believe that almost any mom or dad can become an Emotion Coach, but I also know that many parents must overcome certain obstacles first. Some of these barriers may be the result of the way emotions were handled in the homes where parents grew up. Or, parents may simply lack the skills they need to be good listeners for their kids. Whatever the source, such obstacles can keep them from being the kind of strong, supportive mothers and fathers they want to be.

The path to becoming a better parent—like most every road to personal growth and mastery—begins with self-examination. That's where the research we have been conducting in family labs can help. Obviously, we can't offer every family the kind of in-depth analysis we did with the families in our studies. But we can offer the following self-test to help you evaluate your own style of parenting. At the end of the test, you'll find descriptions of the four distinct parenting styles our research uncovered. There we will tell you how the different styles of parenting affected the children we studied.

A SELF-TEST: WHAT STYLE OF PARENT ARE YOU?
This self-test asks questions about your feelings regarding sadness, fear, and anger—both in yourself and in your children.
For each item, please circle the choice that best fits how you
feel. If you're not sure, go with the answer that seems the closest. While this test requires you to answer lots of questions, try
to stick with it. The lengthy design ensures that we cover most
aspects of each parenting style.
T = True    F = False

1. Children really have very little to be sad about.
T    F

2. I think that anger is okay as long as it's under control.
T    F

3. Children acting sad are usually just trying to get adults to
feel sorry for them.    T    F

4. A child's anger deserves a time-out.    T    F

5. When my child is acting sad, he turns into a real brat.
T    F

6. When my child is sad, I am expected to fix the world and
make it perfect.    T    F

7. I really have no time for sadness in my own life.
T    F

8. Anger is a dangerous state.    T    F

9. If you ignore a child's sadness it tends to go away and take
care of itself.    T    F

10. Anger usually means aggression.    T    F

11. Children often act sad to get their way.    T    F

12. I think sadness is okay as long as it's under control.
T    F

13. Sadness is something one has to get over, to ride out, not
to dwell on.    T    F

**14.** I don't mind dealing with a child's sadness, so long as it doesn't last too long.    T    F

**15.** I prefer a happy child to a child who is overly emotional. T    F

**16.** When my child is sad, it's a time to problem-solve. T    F

**17.** I help my children get over sadness quickly so they can move on to better things.    T    F

**18.** I don't see a child's being sad as any kind of opportunity to teach the child much.    T    F

**19.** I think when kids are sad they have overemphasized the negative in life.    T    F

**20.** When my child is acting angry, she turns into a real brat. T    F

**21.** I set limits on my child's anger.    T    F

**22.** When my child acts sad, it's to get attention.    T    F

**23.** Anger is an emotion worth exploring.    T    F

**24.** A lot of a child's anger comes from the child's lack of understanding and immaturity.    T    F

**25.** I try to change my child's angry moods into cheerful ones.    T    F

**26.** You should express the anger you feel.    T    F

**27.** When my child is sad, it's a chance to get close. T    F

**28.** Children really have very little to be angry about. T    F

**29.** When my child is sad, I try to help the child explore what is making him sad.    T    F

**30.** When my child is sad, I show my child that I understand. T    F

31. I want my child to experience sadness.     T     F

32. The important thing is to find out why a child is feeling sad.     T     F

33. Childhood is a happy-go-lucky time, not a time for feeling sad or angry.     T     F

34. When my child is sad, we sit down to talk over the sadness.     T     F

35. When my child is sad, I try to help him figure out why the feeling is there.     T     F

36. When my child is angry, it's an opportunity for getting close.     T     F

37. When my child is angry, I take some time to try to experience this feeling with my child.     T     F

38. I want my child to experience anger.     T     F

39. I think it's good for kids to feel angry sometimes.     T     F

40. The important thing is to find out why the child is feeling angry.     T     F

41. When she gets sad, I warn her about not developing a bad character.     T     F

42. When my child is sad I'm worried he will develop a negative personality.     T     F

43. I'm not really trying to teach my child anything in particular about sadness.     T     F

44. If there's a lesson I have about sadness it's that it's okay to express it.     T     F

45. I'm not sure there's anything that can be done to change sadness.     T     F

46. There's not much you can do for a sad child beyond offering her comfort.     T     F

**47.** When my child is sad, I try to let him know that I love him no matter what.     T     F

**48.** When my child is sad, I'm not quite sure what she wants me to do.     T     F

**49.** I'm not really trying to teach my child anything in particular about anger.     T     F

**50.** If there's a lesson I have about anger it's that it's okay to express it.     T     F

**51.** When my child is angry, I try to be understanding of his mood.     T     F

**52.** When my child is angry, I try to let her know that I love her no matter what.     T     F

**53.** When my child is angry, I'm not quite sure what he wants me to do.     T     F

**54.** My child has a bad temper and I worry about it.
T     F

**55.** I don't think it is right for a child to show anger.
T     F

**56.** Angry people are out of control.     T     F

**57.** A child's expressing anger amounts to a temper tantrum.
T     F

**58.** Kids get angry to get their own way.     T     F

**59.** When my child gets angry, I worry about his destructive tendencies.     T     F

**60.** If you let kids get angry, they will think they can get their way all the time.     T     F

**61.** Angry children are being disrespectful.     T     F

**62.** Kids are pretty funny when they're angry.     T     F

**63.** Anger tends to cloud my judgment and I do things I regret.     T     F

**64.** When my child is angry, it's time to solve a problem.
T   F

**65.** When my child gets angry, I think it's time for a spanking.
T   F

**66.** When my child gets angry, my goal is to get him to stop.
T   F

**67.** I don't make a big deal of a child's anger.   T   F

**68.** When my child is angry, I usually don't take it all that seriously.   T   F

**69.** When I'm angry, I feel like I'm going to explode.
T   F

**70.** Anger accomplishes nothing.   T   F

**71.** Anger is exciting for a child to express.   T   F

**72.** A child's anger is important.   T   F

**73.** Children have a right to feel angry.   T   F

**74.** When my child is mad, I just find out what is making her mad.   T   F

**75.** It's important to help the child find out what caused the child's anger.   T   F

**76.** When my child gets angry with me, I think, "I don't want to hear this."   T   F

**77.** When my child is angry I think, "If only he could just learn to roll with the punches."   T   F

**78.** When my child is angry I think, "Why can't she accept things as they are?"   T   F

**79.** I want my child to get angry, to stand up for himself.
T   F

**80.** I don't make a big deal out of my child's sadness.
T   F

**81.** When my child is angry I want to know what she is thinking.    **T    F**

## How to Interpret Your Scores

*Dismissing:*

Add up the number of times you said "true" for the following items:
1, 2, 6, 7, 9, 12, 13, 14, 15, 17, 18, 19, 24, 25, 28, 33, 43, 62, 66, 67, 68, 76, 77, 78, 80.
Divide the total by 25. This is your *Dismissing* score.

*Disapproving:*

Add up the number of times you said "true" for the following items:
3, 4, 5, 8, 10, 11, 20, 21, 22, 41, 42, 54, 55, 56, 57, 58, 59, 60, 61, 63, 65, 69, 70.
Divide the total by 23. This is your *Disapproving* score.

*Laissez-Faire:*

Add up the number of times you said "true" for the following items:
26, 44, 45, 46, 47, 48, 49, 50, 52, 53.
Divide the total by 10. This is your *Laissez-Faire* score.

*Emotion-Coaching:*

Add up the number of times you said "true" for the following items:
16, 23, 27, 29, 30, 31, 32, 34, 35, 36, 37, 38, 39, 40, 51, 64, 71, 72, 73, 74, 75, 79, 81.
Divide the total by 23. This is your *Emotion-Coaching* score.

Now compare your four scores. The higher you scored in any one area, the more you tend toward that style of parenting. Then look at the bulleted lists on pages 50–52, which summarize behaviors typical of each parenting style and explain how each style affects children.

Following the lists, you'll find deeper descriptions of each of the various styles. Most of these profiles were taken from our research interviews with parents of children ages four or five, and from stories told by mothers and fathers in parenting groups I've conducted based on this research. As you read, think about interactions with your own children, noting those that seem similar or different from your style of parenting. You may also want to think about childhood experiences with your own parents. Such memories may be helpful in assessing your strengths and weaknesses as a mom or dad. Think about the way emotions were perceived in the house where you grew up. What was your family's philosophy of emotion? Did they treat sad and angry moments as natural occurrences? Did they lend an ear when family members felt unhappy, fearful, or angry? Did they use such moments to show each other support, offer guidance, and help one another solve problems? Or was anger always viewed as potentially destructive, fear as cowardly, sadness as self-pitying? Were feelings concealed or dismissed as unproductive, frivolous, dangerous, or self-indulgent?

Keep in mind that many families have a mixed philosophy of emotion; that is, their attitude toward emotional expression may vary depending on what emotion is being expressed. Parents may believe, for example, that it's fine to be sad once in a while, but expressions of anger are inappropriate or dangerous. On the other hand, they may value anger in their children because they see it as assertiveness, but they think of fear or sadness as cowardly or babyish. In addition, families may hold different family members to different standards. Some may believe, for example, that it's okay for a son to show his temper and for a daughter to be depressed, but not vice versa.

If, after reading about the different styles of parenting, you identify aspects of your relationship with your child that you'd like to change, you'll probably find the advice in Chapter 3 helpful. This chapter offers detailed information about the five steps that constitute Emotion Coaching.

## Four Styles of Parenting

### THE DISMISSING PARENT

- treats child's feelings as unimportant, trivial
- disengages from or ignores the child's feelings
- wants the child's negative emotions to disappear quickly
- characteristically uses distraction to shut down child's emotions
- may ridicule or make light of a child's emotions
- believes children's feelings are irrational, and therefore don't count
- shows little interest in what the child is trying to communicate
- may lack awareness of emotions in self and others
- feels uncomfortable, fearful, anxious, annoyed, hurt, or overwhelmed by the child's emotions
- fears being out-of-control emotionally
- focuses more on how to get over emotions than on the meaning of the emotion itself
- believes negative emotions are harmful or toxic
- believes focusing on negative emotions will "just make matters worse"
- feels uncertain about what to do with the child's emotions
- sees the child's emotions as a demand to fix things
- believes negative emotions mean the child is not well adjusted
- believes the child's negative emotions reflect badly on their parents
- minimizes the child's feelings, downplaying the events that led to the emotion
- does not problem-solve with the child; believes that the passage of time will resolve most problems

**Effects of this style on children:** They learn that their feelings are wrong, inappropriate, not valid. They may learn that there is something inherently wrong with them because of the way they feel. They may have difficulty regulating their own emotions.

## THE DISAPPROVING PARENT

- displays many of the Dismissing Parent's behaviors, but in a more negative way
- judges and criticizes the child's emotional expression
- is overaware of the need to set limits on their children
- emphasizes conformity to good standards or behavior
- reprimands, disciplines, or punishes the child for emotional expression, whether the child is misbehaving or not
- believes expression of negative emotions should be time-limited
- believes negative emotions need to be controlled
- believes negative emotions reflect bad character traits
- believes the child uses negative emotions to manipulate; this belief results in power struggles
- believes emotions make people weak; children must be emotionally tough for survival
- believes negative emotions are unproductive, a waste of time
- sees negative emotions (especially sadness) as a commodity that should not be squandered
- is concerned with the child's obedience to authority

*Effects of this style on children:* Same as the Disapproving style.

## THE LAISSEZ-FAIRE PARENT

- freely accepts all emotional expression from the child
- offers comfort to the child experiencing negative feelings
- offers little guidance on behavior
- does not teach the child about emotions
- is permissive; does not set limits
- does not help children solve problems
- does not teach problem-solving methods to the child
- believes there is little you can do about negative emotions other than ride them out
- believes that managing negative emotions is a matter of hydraulics; release the emotion and the work is done

*Effects of this style on children:* They don't learn to regulate their emotions; they have trouble concentrating, forming friendships, getting along with other children.

## THE EMOTION COACH

- values the child's negative emotions as an opportunity for intimacy
- can tolerate spending time with a sad, angry, or fearful child; does not become impatient with the emotion
- is aware of and values his or her own emotions
- sees the world of negative emotions as an important arena for parenting
- is sensitive to the child's emotional states, even when they are subtle
- is not confused or anxious about the child's emotional expression; knows what needs to be done
- respects the child's emotions
- does not poke fun at or make light of the child's negative feelings
- does not say how the child should feel
- does not feel he or she has to fix every problem for the child
- uses emotional moments as a time to
  —listen to the child
  —empathize with soothing words and affection
  —help the child label the emotion he or she is feeling
  —offer guidance on regulating emotions
  —set limits and teach acceptable expression of emotions
  —teach problem-solving skills

*Effects of this style on children:* They learn to trust their feelings, regulate their own emotions, and solve problems. They have high self-esteem, learn well, get along well with others.

## THE DISMISSING PARENT

ROBERT WOULD PROBABLY be surprised to hear himself described as a Dismissing parent. After all, in interviews with our research staff, it was obvious that he adores his daughter Heather and spends a great deal of time with her. Whenever she's sad, he does his best to "pamper her," he says. "I carry her around and ask her if she needs anything. 'Do you want to watch television? Can I get you a movie? Do you want to go outside and play?' I just work with her to see if I can correct things."

One thing Robert doesn't do, however, is to confront his child's sadness head-on. He doesn't ask questions like, "How do you feel, Heather? Are you kind of sad today?" That's because he believes that focusing on uncomfortable feelings is like watering weeds. It just makes them grow bigger and more noxious. Like many parents, he fears that feelings of anger or sadness can take over your life, something he doesn't want for himself, and something he certainly doesn't want for his precious daughter.

I have observed many Dismissing parents like Robert, both in my research and in everyday life. Perhaps the most publicized recent example is the mother of Jessica Dubroff, the seven-year-old whose single-engine Cessna crashed in April 1996, during her attempt to be the youngest pilot to fly across the United States. According to *The New York Times,* Jessica's mother did not let her daughter use negative words like "scared," "fear," and "sadness." "Children are fearless," she told reporters. "That's their natural state until adults ingrain fear in them." Following her daughter's fatal accident, the mother told *Time* magazine, "I know what people want. Tears. But I will not do that. Emotion is unnatural. There is something untruthful about it."

Whether Jessica or her flight instructor was in control of the plane when it crashed after taking off into a Wyoming thunderstorm may never be determined. But perhaps if the child had been allowed to express fear—an emotion that prevented seasoned pilots from taking off during that same storm—adults around Jessica would have stopped and questioned the wisdom of their actions. Perhaps the tragedy might have been avoided.

Shutting the door on negative feelings is a pattern of behavior many Dismissing parents learned in childhood. Some, like Jim, were raised in violent households. Jim remembers his parents' arguments thirty years ago, and how he and his siblings would scatter to separate rooms, each quietly struggling to cope. They were never allowed to talk about their parents' problems or how they were feeling because to do so would risk more of their father's rage. And now that Jim's married and has his own children, he continues to duck and cover whenever there's a hint of conflict or emotional pain. He's even found it hard to talk to his six-year-old son about problems the boy has been having with a schoolyard bully. Jim would like to be closer to his son, listening to his troubles and helping him work out solutions, but he's had little practice talking about matters of the heart. Consequently, he rarely initiates such conversations, and his son, sensing his dad's discomfort, isn't about to bring up such matters either.

Adults who were raised by needy or neglectful parents may also have problems facing their kids' emotions. Accustomed to taking a rescuer role since childhood, these parents assume too much personal responsibility for fixing their children's every hurt, righting every injustice. It's a superhuman job that soon becomes overwhelming; parents lose perspective about what their children really need. One mom in our studies, for example, appeared mystified and distraught with her inability to soothe her preschooler after he had broken his favorite toy tractor. If she couldn't fix the trinket—i.e., make the world perfect for him again—she wasn't sure how to help him with his sadness. All she heard in his sadness was the demand that she make the world better. She didn't hear his need for comfort and understanding.

Over time, such parents may begin to see all their kids' expressions of sadness or anger as impossible demands. Feeling frustrated or manipulated, these parents react by disregarding or minimizing their children's distress. They try to shrink the problem down to size, encapsulate it, and put it away so it can be forgotten.

"If Jeremy comes in and says one of his friends took his toy, I just say, 'Well, don't worry about it; he'll bring it back,' " explains Tom, a dad we studied. "Or if he says, 'This kid hit me,' I say, 'It was probably an accident.' . . . I want to teach him to roll with the punches and get on with his life."

Jeremy's mom, Mariann, says she takes a similar attitude toward her son's sadness. "I give him ice cream to cheer him up, make him forget about it," she says. Mariann voices a belief common among Dismissing parents: Children are not supposed to be sad, and if they are, something is psychologically amiss with the child or with the parents. "When Jeremy is sad it makes me sad because you want to think that your kids are happy and well adjusted," she says. "I just don't want to see him upset. I want him to be happy all the time."

Because Dismissing parents often value smiles and humor over darker moods, many become masters at "making light" of their children's negative emotions. They may attempt to tickle a sad child, for example, or poke fun at an angry child's bad feelings. Whether their words are offered in a good-natured way ("Where's that precious smile?") or in a humiliating way ("Oh, Willie, don't be such a baby!") the child hears the same message: "Your assessment of this situation is all wrong. Your judgment is off-base. You can't trust your own heart."

Many parents who trivialize or discount their kids' emotions feel justified in doing so, because their offspring are, after all, "just children." Dismissing parents rationalize such indifference with the belief that kids' concerns over broken toys or playground politics are "petty," especially when compared to adult-size worries about things like job loss, the solvency of one's marriage, or what to do about the national debt. Furthermore, they reason, children can be irrational. Asked how he responds to his daughter's sadness, one perplexed father answers that he doesn't respond at all. "You're talking about a four-year-old," he says. Her feelings of sadness are often "based on lack of understanding of how the world works," and therefore not worth much in his estimation. "Her reactions are not *adult* reactions," he explains.

This is not to suggest that all Dismissing parents lack sensitivity. In fact, many feel quite deeply for their children, and are simply reacting out of parents' natural urges to protect their offspring. They may believe that negative emotions are somehow "toxic" and they don't want to "expose" their children to harm. They believe it's unhealthy to "dwell on" emotions for very long. If they engage in problem solving with their children at all, they focus on what it will take to "get over" the emotion rather than focusing on the emotion itself. Sarah, for example, was worried about her four-year-old daughter's reaction to the death of a pet guinea pig. "I was afraid that if I sat down and got all emotional with Becky, that was just going to upset her even more," she explains. So instead, Sarah played it low-key. "I told her, 'That's okay. Things like this happen, you know? Your guinea pig was getting old. We'll get a new one.'" While Sarah's nonchalant response may have spared her the anxiety of dealing with Becky's grief, it probably didn't help Becky feel understood or comforted. Indeed, Becky may have wondered, "If this is no big deal, why am I feeling so lousy? I guess I'm nothing but a big baby."

And finally, some Dismissing parents seem to deny or ignore their kids' emotions out of a fear that getting emotional inevitably leads to "losing control." You're likely to hear such parents using metaphors that equate negative emotions with elements like fire, explosives, or storms. "He's got a short fuse." "She blew up at me." "He stormed out of here."

These are parents who may have had little help as children learning to regulate their own emotions. Consequently, as adults, when they feel sadness, they fear they'll slide into unending depression. Or, when they feel anger, they're afraid they'll fly off the handle and hurt someone. Barbara, for instance, feels guilty about letting her own temper flair in front of her husband and children. She believes that expressing anger is "being selfish" or dangerous, "like those killer bees." Besides, she says, her anger "doesn't accomplish anything . . . I raise my voice to a loud extreme and . . . make them disgusted with me."

With this unflattering picture of her own anger as a backdrop, Barbara uses humor to deflect her daughter's temper. "When Nicole gets angry I just kind of smile," she says. "There are times when Nicole is being completely ridiculous and I point that out to her. I just say, 'Can it,' or 'Lighten up.'" Whether Nicole thinks the situation is comical doesn't seem to matter to Barbara; an angry Nicole just makes her laugh. "She's so little and her face gets all red," says Barbara. "I tend to see her as this little doll and think, 'Isn't that funny?'"

Barbara also does whatever she can to deflect Nicole's attention away from negative feelings. She recalls an incident where Nicole was mad at her brother and his friends for excluding her from their play. "So I sat her on my lap and played this little game," Barbara explains proudly. She pointed to Nicole's crimson winter tights and asked, "What happened to your legs? You've turned all red and fuzzy!" This time, the teasing made Nicole giggle. Nicole could probably feel her mother's warmth and attention, which made her forget about her anger and move on to other pursuits. Barbara feels she handled the incident successfully: "I deliberately do things like that because I've learned . . . that's a really good way of handling her," she says. What Barbara missed however, was an opportunity to talk to Nicole about feelings like jealousy and exclusion. This incident could have been a chance for Barbara to empathize with Nicole, help her to identify her emotions. She could have even given Nicole pointers for resolving the conflict with her brother. Instead, Nicole got the message that her anger isn't very important; best just to swallow it and look the other way.

## THE DISAPPROVING PARENT

DISAPPROVING PARENTS HAVE much in common with parents who dismiss their kids' emotions, with a few distinctions: They are noticeably critical and lacking in empathy when they describe their children's emotional experiences. They don't just ignore, deny, or trivialize their kids' negative emotions; they disapprove of them. Consequently, their children are often reprimanded, disciplined, or punished for expressing sadness, anger, and fear.

Rather than trying to understand a child's emotions, Disapproving parents tend to focus on the behavior surrounding the emotions. If a child stamps her feet in anger, for example, her mother might spank her for her unpleasant, defiant display without ever acknowledging what made the girl so angry in the first place. A father might scold his son for his annoying habit of crying at bedtime without ever addressing the connection between his son's tears and his fear of the dark.

Disapproving parents can be quite judgmental of their children's emotional experiences, sizing up extenuating circumstances before deciding whether a situation warrants comfort, criticism—or in some cases—punishment. Joe explains it this way: "If Timmy is *genuinely* in a bad mood for a good reason—like he misses his mom because she went off for the night—I can understand that, have empathy for him, and try to cheer him up. I give him a hug or whatever; toss him around, try to get him out of that mood." But if Timmy is upset for a reason Joe doesn't like—"Say I told him to go take a nap or something"—Joe responds harshly. "He's being sad just because he wants to be a little brat, so I ignore him or tell him to shape up." Joe justifies this distinction as a form of discipline. "Timmy's got to learn not to do that [get sad for the wrong reason], so I tell him, 'Hey, moping is not going to get you anywhere.' "

Many Disapproving parents see their children's tears as a form of manipulation and this disturbs them. As one mother put it: "Whenever my daughter cries and pouts, she's doing it for attention." Framing children's tears or tantrums this way turns emotional situations into power struggles. Parents may think, "My child is crying because he wants something from me and I must give it to him or I have to put up with more crying, more tantrums, more sulking." Feeling thus cornered or blackmailed, the parent responds with anger and punishment.

Like many Dismissing parents, some Disapproving parents fear emotional situations because they are afraid of losing their grip on emotions. "I don't like to be angry because I feel like it takes away my self-control," says Jean, mother to five-year-old Cameron. Facing off against a rebellious child, these parents feel themselves careening toward emotions and behavior they distrust in themselves. Under these circumstances, they may feel justified in punishing their children for "making me angry." Explains Jean: "If Cameron starts yelling, I just say, 'I won't put up with that!' Then if he continues to act that way, he gets a spanking."

Linda, who is married to a man with a violent temper, fears that her four-year-old son, Ross, will grow up "just like his dad." Desperate to save him from that fate, she reacts violently herself. When Ross gets upset, "he kicks and hollers, so I spank him to calm him down," she explains. "Maybe that's the wrong thing to do, but I really don't want him to have a bad temper."

Similarly, some parents reprimand or punish their children for emotional displays in order to "toughen them up." Boys who show fear or sadness are particularly vulnerable to this kind of treatment from Disapproving fathers who believe it's a hard world and their sons had better learn not to be "wimps" or "cry-babies."

In the most extreme cases, some parents seem determined to teach their children to express no negative feelings at all. "So Katy's sad," says one dad sarcastically of his daughter. "What am I going to do? Tickle her chin? I don't think that's what you need to do. I think people need to work out their own problems." This father takes an eye-for-an-eye approach to his daughter's anger—when she gets mad, he gets mad. If Katy "flies off the handle," Richard reacts by "slapping her bottom" or "smacking her on top of the head."

Of course, we found such blanket disapproval and harsh responses to be rare, even among the Disapproving parents. It was more common for parents to be Disapproving only under certain circumstances. For example, some parents appear tolerant of negative emotions—as long as the episode is limited to an amount of time the parent can accept. One dad in our studies actually pictures an alarm clock in his head. He says he'll put up with his son's bad moods "until that alarm goes off." Then "it's time to bring Jason out of it" by meting out his punishment, which is isolation from the rest of the family.

Some parents disapprove of their children's experience with negative emotions—especially sadness—because they see it as a "waste" of energy. One father, who described himself as a "cold-hearted realist," says he objects to his child's sadness as "useless time" and "doing nothing constructive whatsoever."

Some view sadness as a precious and finite commodity; use up your allotment of tears on trivial matters and you won't have any left to spend on life's major sorrows. But whether Disapproving parents measure sadness in tears shed or minutes spent, the problem is still the same—children who waste it. "I tell Charley to save his sadness for major things like dead dogs," says Greg. "Losing a toy or tearing a page in a book is not something you should waste your time being sad on. But the death of a pet—now that's something that's worth getting sad over."

With this metaphor operating in a family's life, it's easy to see how a child might be punished for squandering sadness on "frivolous matters." And if his parents were emotionally neglected as children themselves, they may be even more likely to see the child's sadness as a "luxury" only the emotionally "privileged" can afford. Karen, a mother in our studies who was abandoned by her parents and raised by a string of relatives, comes to mind. Deprived of emotional comfort as a child, Karen now has low tolerance for her daughter's "dark moods."

There is a considerable amount of overlap between the behavior of Dismissing and Disapproving parents. Indeed, the same parents who identify themselves as Dismissing one day may find they act more like Disapproving parents the next.

The children of Dismissing parents and Disapproving parents also have much in common. Our research tells us that children from both groups have a hard time trusting their own judgment. Told time and time again that their feelings are inappropriate or not valid, they grow up believing there is something inherently wrong inside themselves because of the way they feel. Their self-esteem suffers. They have more difficulty learning to regulate their own emotions and to solve their own problems. They have more trouble than other children concentrating, learning, and getting along with peers. In addition, we can assume that children who are reprimanded, isolated, spanked, or otherwise punished for expressing their feelings get a strong message that emotional intimacy is a high-risk proposition; it can lead to humiliation, abandonment, pain, and abuse. If we had a scale with which to measure emotional intelligence, these children, unfortunately, would probably score quite low.

The tragic irony of these results is that parents who dismiss or disapprove of their children's emotions usually do so out of the deepest concerns for their children. In attempts to protect their kids from emotional pain, they avoid or terminate situations that might bring about tears or tantrums. In the name of building tough men, they punish their sons for expressing their fears or sorrows. In the name of raising kindhearted women, they encourage their girls to swallow their anger and turn the other cheek. But in the end, all of these strategies backfire, because children who aren't given the chance to experience their emotions and deal with them effectively grow up unprepared to face life's challenges.

## THE LAISSEZ-FAIRE PARENT

UNLIKE DISAPPROVING AND Dismissing parents, some of our study subjects proved to be accepting of their children's emotions, eager to embrace unconditionally whatever feelings their children expressed. I refer to this style of parenting as "Laissez-Faire." Such parents are filled with empathy for their kids and they let them know that whatever they're going through, it's okay by mom and dad.

The problem is, Laissez-Faire parents often seem ill-equipped or unwilling to offer their children guidance on how to handle negative emotions. These parents have a hands-off philosophy about their kids' feelings. They tend to see anger and sadness as a matter of letting off steam: Let your child express emotions and your work as a parent is done.

Laissez-Faire parents seem to have little awareness of how to help their children learn from emotional experiences. They don't teach their children how to solve problems and many have a hard time setting limits on behavior. Some might call these parents overpermissive because, in the name of unconditional acceptance, they let their children get away with inappropriate and/or unfettered expressions of emotion. An angry child turns aggressive, hurting others with her words or actions. A sad child cries inconsolably with no awareness of how to calm and comfort himself. While such negative expression might be acceptable to the parent, for the small child who has far less life experience, it can be frightening, like entering a black hole of painful emotion with no knowledge of how to escape.

Our research revealed that many Laissez-Faire parents seem unsure of what to teach children regarding emotion. Some say they've never given it much thought. Others express a vague sense that they'd like to give their children "something more." But they seem genuinely puzzled about what a parent can offer beyond unconditional love.

Louann, for example, expresses genuine concern for her son, Toby, when another child is mean to him. "He gets upset over it and that hurts me, too," she says. But when asked how she responds to him, she can only add, "I try to let him know that I love him no matter what; that we think the world of him." While this is certainly good information for Toby to have, it probably won't go far in helping him repair the relationship with his playmate.

Like the Disapproving and Dismissing parents, the Laissez-Faire parents' style may be a response from their own childhood. Sally, whose father was physically abusive, wasn't permitted to vent her anger and frustration as a child. "I want my kids to know they can scream and yell all they want," she explains. "I want them to know it's all right to say, 'I've been put upon and I don't like it.' "

Still, Sally admits she's often frustrated by parenthood and her patience runs thin. "When Rachel does something wrong, I'd like to be able to say, 'That wasn't a very good idea; maybe we should try something different.' " Instead, she often finds herself "screaming and yelling" at Rachel—even slapping her at times. "I find I'm at the end of my rope and that's all that works," she laments.

Another mom, Amy, remembers feeling a great sense of melancholy as a child—an experience she now suspects was clinical depression. "I think it came from fear," she recalls, "and maybe it was a fear of just having the emotion." Whatever its foundation, Amy can't remember any adult in her life willing to talk to her about her feelings. Instead, she heard only the demand to change her tune. "People were always telling me, 'Smile!,' which I just hated." As a result, she learned to hide her sadness, to withdraw. As she grew older, she also became an avid runner, finding solace from her depression in solitary exercise.

Now that Amy has her own two children, she's aware that one of her sons experiences this same type of recurrent sadness and she empathizes with him deeply. "Alex describes it as 'a funny feeling,' which is exactly how I felt when I was a kid." Determined that she won't demand smiles from Alex when he's feeling down, she tells him, "I know what you're feeling because I felt that way, too."

Still, Amy has a hard time staying with Alex when he's despondent. Asked how she reacts when Alex expresses sadness, she says, "I go for a run." In effect, then, she withdraws, leaving her son in much the same predicament she was in as a child. Alex drifts alone with his anxiety and fear; his mother is not available to offer him an anchor of emotional support.

What effect do such accepting but noncoaching Laissez-Faire parents have on their children? Unfortunately, not a positive one. With such little guidance from adults, these children don't learn to regulate their emotions. They often lack the ability to calm them-selves when they are angry, sad, or upset, and that makes it hard for them to concentrate and to learn new skills. Consequently, these children don't do as well in school. They also have a harder time picking up on social cues, which means they may experience diffi-culty making and keeping friends.

Again, the irony is clear. With their all-accepting attitude, Lais-sez-Faire parents intend to give their children every opportunity for happiness. But because they fail to offer their kids guidance on how to handle difficult emotions, their kids end up in much the same po-sition as the children of Disapproving and Dismissing parents—lacking in emotional intelligence, unequipped for the future.

## THE EMOTION COACH

IN SOME WAYS, Emotion-Coaching parents aren't that different from Laissez-Faire parents. Both groups appear to accept their children's feelings unconditionally. Neither group tries to ignore or deny their kids' feelings. Nor do they belittle or ridicule their children for emo-tional expression.

There are significant differences between the two groups, how-ever, in that Emotion-Coaching parents serve as their children's guides through the world of emotion. They go beyond acceptance to set limits on inappropriate behavior and teach their kids how to regulate their feelings, find appropriate outlets, and solve problems.

Our studies showed that Emotion-Coaching parents have a strong awareness of their own emotions and those of their loved ones. In addition, they recognize that all emotions—even those we generally consider negative, such as sadness, anger, and fear—can serve useful purposes in our lives. One mom, for example, talked about how anger with a bureaucracy motivates her to write letters of protest. Another dad talked about his wife's anger as a creative force that energizes her to tackle new projects around the house.

Even melancholy feelings are portrayed in a positive light. "Whenever I'm feeling sad I know it means I have to slow down and pay attention to what's going on in my life, to find out what's miss-ing," says Dan. This idea extends to his relationship with his daughter. Rather than disapproving or trying to smooth over Jennifer's feelings, he sees her sad moments as opportunities to be close to her. "It's a time when I can just hold her, and talk to her, and let her say what's on her mind." Once dad and daughter are on the same wavelength, it's also a chance for Jennifer to learn more about her emotional world and how she relates to others. "Nine times out of ten, she doesn't really know where her feelings are coming from," says Dan. "So I try to help her identify her feelings. . . . Then we talk about what to do next time, how to handle this or that."

Many Emotion-Coaching parents talked about their appreciation for their children's emotional expression as an indication that parent and child share the same values. One mom described how gratified she felt watching her five-year-old daughter grow teary-eyed over a sad television program. "I liked it because it made me feel like she's got a heart, that she cares about things other than herself; she cares about other people."

Another mother told how proud (but also surprised) she was the day her four-year-old snapped at her after a scolding. "I don't like that tone of voice, Mommy!" the little girl told her. "It hurts my feelings when you talk like that!" Once the mother got over her shock, she marveled at her daughter's assertiveness and felt pleased that the girl would use her anger to command respect.

Perhaps because these parents can see value in their children's negative emotions, they have more patience when their children are angry, sad, or fearful. They seem to be willing to spend time with a crying or fretful child, listening to their worries, empathizing with them, letting them vent their anger, or just "cry it out."

After listening to her son Ben when he's upset, Margaret says she often tries to show empathy for him by telling "when I was a kid" stories. "He loves those stories because they let him know it's okay to have his feelings."

Jack says he makes a concerted effort to tune in to his son, Tyler's, perspective, especially if the boy is upset over an argument he's had with his dad. "When I really listen to Tyler's point of view, it makes him feel a lot better because we can resolve things on terms he can accept. We can settle our differences like two people, rather than a guy and his dog."

Emotion-Coaching parents encourage emotional honesty in their children. "I want my children to know that just because they're angry doesn't mean they are bad or that they necessarily hate the person they're angry with," says Sandy, mother of four girls. "And I want them to know that good things can happen from the things that make them angry."

At the same time, Sandy sets limits on her daughters' behavior and tries to teach them to express their anger in ways that are not destructive. She'd like to see her girls grow to be lifelong friends, but she knows that in order for this to happen, they must be kind to one another and nurture their relationships. "I tell them it's okay to be mad at your sister, but it's not okay to make mean remarks," she says. "I tell them that your family members are the people you can always turn to no matter what, so you don't want to alienate them."

Such limit setting is common among Emotion-Coaching parents, who can accept all feelings but not all behavior. Consequently, if these children act in ways that might be harmful to themselves, to others, or to their relationships with others, Emotion-Coaching parents are likely to put a quick stop to the offensive behavior and redirect their children to an activity or mode of expression that's less harmful. They don't go out of their way to shield their kids from emotionally charged situations; they know kids need such experiences in order to learn how to regulate their feelings.

Margaret, for example, has been working on options for her son Ben, a four-year-old whose personality has been volatile since infancy. Left on his own with his anger, "he often grinds his teeth and screams and throws things," Margaret explains. "He takes it out on his little brother or breaks a toy." Rather than trying to eradicate Ben's angry feelings—a fruitless effort, Margaret believes—she is trying to teach him better ways to express his feelings. When she sees his tension starting to build, she steers him toward activities that will allow some physical relief. She sends him outdoors to run hard or down to the basement where he can pound on a drum set she recently bought for just this purpose. Although Margaret worries about Ben's temperament, she says she recognizes a positive side to his stubborn, hard-driving personality, as well. "He's not a quitter. If he's working on a drawing and he doesn't like the way it's turning out, he just keeps working on it, even if that means throwing it out five and six times. But once he gets it right, his frustration is gone."

Although it can be unsettling for parents to watch from a distance as kids grapple with problems, Emotion-Coaching parents don't feel compelled to fix everything that goes awry in their kids' lives. Sandy, for example, says her four girls often complain when she tells them they can't buy all the new toys and clothes they'd like. Rather than trying to placate them, Sandy simply listens to their frustration and tells them it's perfectly natural to feel letdown. "I figure if they learn to handle little disappointments now, they will know how to cope with bigger disappointments later on in life, if they need to."

Maria and Dan also hope their patience will pay off later on. "Ten years down the road, I hope Jennifer will have dealt with these feelings enough times that she'll know how to react," says Maria. "I hope she'll have the self-confidence to know it's okay to feel this way, and there is something she can do about it."

Because Emotion-Coaching parents value the power and purpose of emotions in their lives, they are not afraid to show their own emotions around their children. They can cry in front of their kids when they're sad; they can lose their tempers and tell their children why they're angry. And most of the time, because these parents understand emotion and trust themselves to express their anger, sadness, and fear constructively, they can serve as models for their children. In fact, parental displays of emotion can speak volumes to a child about ways to handle feelings. For example, a child who sees his parents engage in a heated argument and then resolve their differences amicably, learns valuable lessons about conflict resolution and the staying power of loving relationships. By the same token, a child who sees his parents extremely sad—over a divorce or the death of a grandparent, for example—can learn important lessons about how to deal with grief and despair as well. This is particularly true if there are supportive, loving adults around who offer comfort and assistance to one another in their sadness. The child learns that sharing sadness can lead to a greater level of intimacy and bonding.

When Emotion-Coaching parents say or do hurtful things to

their children—which, of course, happens at times in all families—
they are not afraid to apologize. Under stress, parents may react
without thinking, calling a child an unkind name or raising their
voice in a threatening way. Regretting such actions, the parents
then tell their kids they're sorry and look for ways to learn from the
incident. In this way, the incident can become yet another opportunity for intimacy—especially if the parent is willing to tell the child
how he was feeling at the moment and talk about how he might
handle such situations better in the future. This allows the parent,
again, to demonstrate for his child ways to deal with uncomfortable
feelings like guilt, regret, and sadness.

Emotion Coaching works well alongside positive forms of discipline that rely on providing children with clearly understood consequences for misbehavior. In fact, parents who practice Emotion
Coaching may find that behavior problems decrease as the family
becomes more comfortable with the coaching style. This may happen for many reasons.

One, Emotion-Coaching parents consistently respond to their
children when feelings are still at a low level of intensity. In other
words, emotions don't have to escalate before the child gets the attention he's after. Over time, these children get the clear sense that
their parents understand them, empathize with them, and care
deeply what happens in their lives. They don't have to act out in order to feel their parents' concern.

Two, if children are Emotion-Coached from a young age, they
become well practiced at the art of self-soothing and they can stay
calm under stress, which also makes them less likely to misbehave.

Three, Emotion-Coaching parents don't disapprove of their children's emotions, so there are fewer points of conflict. In other
words, children aren't reprimanded simply for crying over a disappointment or expressing anger. Emotion-Coaching parents do set
limits, however, and give their children clear and consistent messages about what behavior is appropriate and what behavior is not.
When children know the rules and understand the consequences
for breaking them, they are less likely to misbehave.

And finally, this style of parenting makes the emotional bond between parent and children strong, so children are more responsive

to their parents' requests. These children see their parents as their confidants and allies. They want to please their folks; they don't want to disappoint them.

One mom tells how this phenomenon played out with her eight-year-old daughter during an episode of lying. Suzanne had found a mean-spirited note about another child among her daughter's school papers. Although the note didn't have her daughter, Laura's, name on it, it was obviously written in Laura's handwriting. When Suzanne confronted the girl about it, she balked and insisted she hadn't written it, but Suzanne knew that Laura was lying. The incident bothered Suzanne for days, as she felt her perception of Laura's innocence and her own trust in her daughter slipping away. Finally, she knew she had to confront the girl again, this time sharing her own feelings about the situation.

"I know you are lying about the note," Suzanne said, clearly and firmly, "and it makes me feel very disappointed in you, very sad. I believe you are an honest person but now I know you are lying. I want you to know that when you are ready to tell me the truth, I will listen and I will forgive you."

Two minutes passed in silence before Laura's eyes welled up in tears. "I lied about the note, Mama," she sobbed. That said, Suzanne gave her a hug and the pair had a long talk about the content of the note, the child for whom it was intended, and how Laura could resolve her conflict with the girl. Suzanne also reiterated to her daughter how important she felt honesty was to their relationship. To Suzanne's knowledge, Laura hasn't lied to her again.

When children feel emotionally connected to their parents and the parents use this bond to help kids regulate their feelings and solve problems, good things happen. As stated earlier, our studies show that children who are Emotion-Coached do better in terms of academic achievement, health, and peer relationships. They have fewer behavior problems, and are better able to bounce back from distressing experiences. With emotional intelligence, they are well prepared to handle the risks and challenges that lie ahead.

*Chapter 3*

---

# THE FIVE KEY STEPS

# FOR EMOTION COACHING

---

I REMEMBER THE DAY I FIRST DISCOVERED HOW EMOTION Coaching might work with my own daughter, Moriah. She was two at the time and we were on a cross-country flight home after visiting with relatives. Bored, tired, and cranky, Moriah asked me for Zebra, her favorite stuffed animal and comfort object. Unfortunately, we had absentmindedly packed the well-worn critter in a suitcase that was checked at the baggage counter.

"I'm sorry, honey, but we can't get Zebra right now. He's in the big suitcase in another part of the airplane," I explained.

"I want Zebra," she whined pitifully.

"I know, sweetheart. But Zebra isn't here. He's in the baggage compartment underneath the plane and Daddy can't get him until we get off the plane. I'm sorry."

"I want Zebra! I want Zebra!" she moaned again. Then she started to cry, twisting in her safety seat and reaching futilely toward a bag on the floor where she'd seen me go for snacks.

"I know you want Zebra," I said, feeling my blood pressure rise. "But he's not in that bag. He's not here and I can't do anything about it. Look, why don't we read about Ernie," I said, fumbling for one of her favorite picture books.

"Not Ernie!" she wailed, angry now. "I want Zebra. I want him *now!*"

By now, I was getting "do something" looks from the passengers, from the airline attendants, from my wife, seated across the aisle. I looked at Moriah's face, red with anger, and imagined how frustrated she must feel. After all, wasn't I the guy who could whip up a peanut butter sandwich on demand? Make huge purple dinosaurs appear with the flip of a TV switch? Why was I withholding her favorite toy from her? Didn't I understand how much she wanted it?

I felt bad. Then it dawned on me: I couldn't get Zebra, but I could offer her the next best thing—a father's comfort.

"You wish you had Zebra now," I said to her.

"Yeah," she said sadly.

"And you're angry because we can't get him for you."

"Yeah."

"You wish you could have Zebra *right now*," I repeated, as she stared at me, looking rather curious, almost surprised.

"Yeah," she muttered. "I want him *now*."

"You're tired now, and smelling Zebra and cuddling with him would feel real good. I wish we had Zebra here so you could hold him. Even better, I wish we could get out of these seats and find a big, soft bed full of all your animals and pillows where we could just lie down."

"Yeah," she agreed.

"We can't get Zebra because he's in another part of the airplane," I said. "That makes you feel frustrated."

"Yeah," she said with a sigh.

"I'm so sorry," I said, watching the tension leave her face. She rested her head against the back of her safety seat. She continued to complain softly a few more times, but she was growing calmer. Within a few minutes, she was asleep.

Although Moriah was just two years old, she clearly knew what she wanted—her Zebra. Once she began to realize that getting it wasn't possible, she wasn't interested in my excuses, my arguments, or my diversions. My validation, however, was another matter. Finding out that I understood how she felt seemed to make her feel better. For me, it was a memorable testament to the power of empathy.

## Empathy: The Foundation of Emotion Coaching

Imagine for a moment what it would be like to grow in a home without empathy. Imagine it as a place where your parents expect you always to be cheerful, happy, and calm. In this home, sadness or anger are taken as a sign of failure or an indication of potential disaster. Mom and Dad get anxious whenever they encounter you in one of your "dark moods." They tell you they prefer you to be content and optimistic, to "look on the bright side," never to complain, never to speak ill of anyone or anything. And you, being just a kid, assume that your parents are right. A bad mood is the sign of a bad child. So you do your best to live up to their expectations.

The trouble is, things keep happening in your life that make it nearly impossible to keep up this happy front. Your baby sister gets into your room and destroys your comic book collection. You get in trouble at school for something you didn't do and your best friend lets you take the rap. Each year, you enter the science competition, and each year, your project bombs. Then there was that godawful family vacation Mom and Dad had been touting for months. Turned out to be little more than one interminable car ride, listening to Mom gasp at "gorgeous" scenery while Dad lectured incessantly about "fascinating" historic sites.

But these things are not supposed to bother you. If you call your baby sister a rotten pest, your mother says, "Of course you don't mean that!" Talk about the incident at school and your dad says, "You must have done *something* to provoke your teacher." Science project disasters? "Forget it. You'll do better next year." And the family vacation? Don't even mention it. ("After all the money your dad and I spent to take you kids to Utah . . .")

So after a while, you learn to keep your mouth shut. If you come home from school with a problem, you just go to your room and put on your happy face. No need to upset Mom and Dad. They hate problems.

At dinner your dad says, "How was school today?"

"Fine," you answer with a halfhearted smile.

"Good, good," he replies. "Pass the butter."

And what do you learn growing up in this make-believe home? Well, first you learn that you are not at all like your parents because they don't seem to have all the bad and dangerous feelings that you do. You learn that because you have these feelings, you're the problem. Your sadness is a fly in the ointment. Your anger is an embarrassment to the clan. Your fears are an obstacle to their progress. Their world would probably be perfect if it weren't for you and your emotions.

Over time, you learn that it makes little sense to talk to your folks about your true inner life. And that makes you lonely. But you also learn that as long as you feign cheerfulness, everybody gets along *just fine*.

Of course, this can be confusing—especially as you grow older and see mounting evidence that life really is a drag sometimes. Your birthday comes and you don't get that one toy you wished for. Your best friend finds a new best friend and you're left standing in the cafeteria line alone. You get braces. Your favorite grandma dies.

And still, you're not supposed to feel all these bad feelings. So you become a master at covering up. Better yet, you do your best not to feel. You learn to avoid situations that lead to conflict, anger, and pain. In other words, you steer clear of intimate human bonds.

Denying your own emotions isn't always easy, but it can be done. You learn to come up with distractions, diversions. Eating sometimes helps to quash uncomfortable feelings. TV and video games are a great way to get your mind off your troubles. And just wait a couple years; then you'll be old enough to get your hands on some *real* distractions. In the meantime, you'll do your best to keep up a good front, keep your folks satisfied, keep everything under control.

But what if things were different? What if you grew up in a home where, instead of cheerfulness, your family's primary goal was empathetic understanding? Imagine if your parents asked "How are you?" because they really wanted to know the truth. You might not feel compelled to answer "Just fine" every time because you'd know they could handle it if you said, "I had a rough day today." They wouldn't jump to conclusions, nor would they assume that every problem was a catastrophe they needed to fix. They would simply listen for what you had to say next and they would do their best to understand and help you.

If you said you had an argument with your buddy at school, your mom might ask you how that came about, how it made you feel, and whether she could help you find a solution. If you had a misunderstanding with your teacher, your parents wouldn't automatically take the teacher's side; they would listen carefully as you told your story and they would believe you because they trusted you to tell the truth. If your science project failed, your dad would tell you that he had had an experience like that when he was a boy; he knew how it felt to stand there nervous in front of the class while the damn thing fizzled. If your baby sister ruined your comic book collection, your mom would put her arms around you and say, "I can see why you're so angry. You cared a lot about those books. You've been collecting them for years."

Chances are, you wouldn't feel so lonely. You'd feel that your parents were there for you no matter what happened. You'd know that you could turn to them for support because you'd know that they would understand what was happening inside you.

In its most basic form, empathy is the ability to feel what another person is feeling. As empathetic parents, when we see our children in tears, we can imagine ourselves in their position and feel their pain. Watching our children stamp their feet in anger, we can feel their frustration and rage.

If we can communicate this kind of intimate emotional understanding to our children, we give credence to their experience and help them learn to soothe themselves. This skill puts us, as river rafters might say, "in the chute." No matter what rocks or rapids lie ahead in our relationships with our children, we can stay in the flow of the river, guiding them forward on course. Even if the course becomes extremely treacherous (as in adolescence it often does), we can help our children steer past obstacles and risks to find their way.

How is it that empathy can be so powerful? I believe it's because empathy allows children to see their parents as allies.

Imagine, for a moment, a situation where eight-year-old William comes in from the yard, looking dejected because the kids next door have refused to play with him. His dad, Bob, looks up from his paper just long enough to say, "Not again! Look, William, you're a big kid now, not a baby. Don't get upset every time somebody gives you the cold shoulder. Just forget about it. Call one of your buddies from school. Read a book. Watch a little TV."

Because children usually believe their parents' assessments, chances are William's thinking: "Dad's right. I'm acting like a baby. That's why the guys next door don't want to play with me. I wonder what's wrong with me. Why can't I just forget it like Dad says? I'm such a wimp. Nobody wants to be my friend."

Now imagine how William might feel if his father responds differently when he comes in. What if Bob puts down his newspaper, looks at his son, and says: "You look kind of sad, William. Tell me what's going on."

And if Bob listens—*really* listens with an open heart—perhaps William will come up with a different assessment of himself. The conversation might continue like this:

> *William:* "Tom and Patrick won't let me play basketball with them."
> *Bob:* "I'll bet that hurt your feelings."
> *William:* "Yeah it did. It made me mad, too."
> *Bob:* "I can see that."
> *William:* "There's no reason why I can't shoot baskets with them."
> *Bob:* "Did you talk to them about it?"
> *William:* "Nah, I don't want to."
> *Bob:* "What do you want to do?"
> *William:* "I don't know. Maybe I'll just blow it off."
> *Bob:* "You think that's a better idea?"
> *William:* "Yeah, 'cuz they'll probably change their minds to-morrow. I think I'll call one of my friends from school, or read a book. Maybe I'll watch some TV."

The difference, of course, is empathy. In both scenarios, Bob is concerned about his son's feelings. Perhaps he's been worried for a long time that William is "oversensitive" to his playmates' rejec-tions; he wants his son to get tougher. In the first scenario, however, Bob makes the common mistake of letting his own goals for William get in the way. Instead of empathizing, he criticizes, gives a mini-lecture, offers unsolicited advice. As a result, his well-in-tended efforts backfire. William walks away feeling more hurt, fur-ther misunderstood, and more like a wimp than ever.

By contrast, Bob in the second scenario takes time to listen to his son, makes it clear that he understands William's experience. This helps William feel more comfortable, more sure of himself. In the end William comes up with the same solutions his father might have offered (find another playmate, go read a book, etc.). But the boy owns the solutions and walks away tougher, with his self-respect intact.

That's how empathy works. When we seek to understand our children's experience, they feel supported. They know we're on their side. When we refrain from criticizing them, discounting their feelings, or trying to distract them from their goals—they let us into their world. They tell us how they feel. They offer their opinions. Their motivations become less mysterious, which in turn leads to further understanding. Our children begin to trust us. Then, when conflicts crop up, we've got some common ground for solving problems together. Our kids may even risk brainstorming solutions with us. Indeed, the day may come when they are willing to actually hear our suggestions!

If I have made the concept of empathy sound simple, that's because it is. Empathy is simply the ability to put yourself in your child's shoes and respond accordingly. Just because empathy is a simple concept, however, doesn't mean it's always easy to practice.

In the following pages, you'll read about the five steps of Emotion Coaching, steps parents commonly use to build empathy into relationships with their children, enhancing the children's emotional intelligence. As mentioned in Chapter 1, these steps include:

1. Being aware of the child's emotion;

2. Recognizing the emotion as an opportunity for intimacy and teaching;

3. Listening empathetically and validating the child's feelings;

4. Helping the child verbally label emotions; and

5. Setting limits while helping the child problem-solve.

In Chapter 4 you'll find additional strategies for Emotion Coaching, as well as descriptions of common parenting situations in which Emotion Coaching is not appropriate. In addition, you'll find two self-tests in the following pages—one in this chapter that gauges your emotional awareness and another in Chapter 4 to test your skills as an Emotion Coach.

## STEP NO. 1: BEING AWARE OF THE
## CHILD'S EMOTIONS

OUR STUDIES SHOW that for parents to feel what their children are feeling, they must be aware of emotions, first in themselves and then in their kids. But what does it mean to become "emotionally aware"? Does it mean "wearing your heart on your sleeve"? Letting your guard down? Revealing parts of yourself you'd just as soon keep under wraps? If so, naturally reserved or stoic fathers may wonder what's to become of the cool, masculine image they've been perfecting since junior high school. Will they suddenly be expected to cry at Disney movies, to hug the other dads after soccer matches? Mothers who struggle to be patient and kind under stress may worry as well. What happens when you focus on feelings of resentment or anger? Do you nag and complain and rage at your kids? Do you lose their affection and loyalty?

In truth, our research shows that people can be emotionally aware—and thus well equipped for Emotion Coaching—without being highly expressive, without feeling as if they are losing control. Emotional awareness simply means that you recognize when you are feeling an emotion, you can identify your feelings, and you are sensitive to the presence of emotions in other people.

### HOW GENDER AFFECTS EMOTIONAL AWARENESS

A person's comfort expressing emotion is partly influenced by cultural factors. Cross-cultural studies have demonstrated that Italian and Latino people, for example, are generally more outwardly passionate or expressive; that Japanese and Scandinavian people are more inhibited and stoic. Such cultural influences do not affect a person's ability to *feel*, however. Just because people are not overt in their expressions of affection, anger, or sadness does not mean that they do not experience such feelings internally. Nor does it mean they are incapable of recognizing and responding to such emotions in others. Certainly, people from all cultural backgrounds have the capacity to be sensitive to their children's feelings.

American men grow up in a culture that discourages them from showing emotion. Although popular mythology often casts men as unfeeling brutes, oblivious to the feelings of their partners and children, psychological research tells a different story. Studies conducted in our lab and at other institutions show that despite differences in the way men and women *express* emotion, the two sexes experience feelings in much the same way.

To find out if one gender is more empathetic than the other, my colleagues and I videotaped couples discussing an area of conflict in their marriage. We then asked each partner to review their tape and to tell us how they remembered feeling while the conversation was going on. To track their responses, we had them use a calibrated dial to rate emotional states from negative to positive. When they saw passages where they remembered feeling sad or angry, for example, they turned the dial to "negative"; when they saw passages that made them happy, they turned it to "positive." We then ran the tape again and asked them to rate the way they believed their spouse was feeling during the same conversation. By comparing the two ratings, we were able to determine how accurately each partner tracked the emotional experience of the other. Surprisingly, we found that husbands are just as skilled as wives at knowing what their spouses feel minute by minute. When we invited third parties to view the tapes and rate them, we found that male and female outsiders are equally adept at tracking people's emotional response. In addition, we discovered that people who can most accurately tune in to others' emotions have physiological responses that mimic the people they are observing. In other words, when the taped subjects' heart rates increased in response to anger, the most empathetic observers experienced a similar acceleration in heart rate. It didn't matter whether the observers were male or female; tuned-in participants of both genders had similarly empathetic physical responses.

If men are just as capable of empathizing and responding to emotion as women, why, then, do people so commonly believe that men are unfeeling? The answer is clear. While men and women have a similar internal experience of emotion, men tend to hide their emotions from the outside world. We found that women in our studies were much freer at expressing their feelings in words, facial expressions, and body language. Men were more likely to hold back, cover up, and discount their feelings.

One theory holds that men do this because they are socialized for toughness and wary of the consequences of "losing control." Indeed, some men take on such a distorted sense of masculine defensiveness that they shut themselves off completely from any awareness of emotional experience. I believe that such extreme cases represent a small percentage of the male population—perhaps less than 10 percent.

Although reluctance to face emotion has important implications for men's family relationships, it does *not* disqualify men from being good Emotion Coaches. Research shows that most men have what it takes on the inside: They are internally aware of their feelings; they have the ability to recognize and respond to their children's emotions; they are capable of empathy. For most men, becoming emotionally aware is not a matter of picking up new skills; it is a matter of granting themselves permission to experience what's already there.

## WHEN PARENTS FEEL OUT OF CONTROL

Permission to feel may also be an issue for parents who are afraid of losing control of negative emotions such as anger, sadness, and fear. Such parents avoid acknowledging their anger, in particular, for fear that things will only get out of hand. They may be afraid of alienating their children or that their children might copy their emotional style, spinning out of control themselves. Such parents may also fear hurting their children physically or psychologically.

In our studies, parents who felt out of control with an emotion generally showed one or more of the following characteristics:

- They have the emotion (anger, sadness, or fear) frequently.
- They believe they feel it too intensely.
- They have trouble calming down after experiencing intense feelings.
- They become disorganized and have trouble functioning when they have the emotion.
- They hate the way they behave when they are having the emotion.

- They are always on guard against the feeling.
- They find themselves acting neutral (calm, understanding, sympathetic), but it's only an act.
- They believe the feeling is destructive and even immoral.
- They feel they need help with the emotion.

Such moms and dads may try to compensate for their fear of losing control by being "super-parents," hiding their emotions from their children. (These same parents may display a great deal of anger toward their spouses, however—feelings that their children are likely to witness.) By trying to conceal their anger, such parents often ignore or dismiss emotional moments with their kids. The irony is that by hiding their emotions, these parents may be raising youngsters who are even less capable of handling negative emotions than they would have been if their parents had learned to let their feelings show in a nonabusive way. That's because the kids grow up emotionally distant from their parents. Also, the children have one less role model to teach them how to handle difficult emotions effectively.

One example is Sophie, a woman I met through our parenting groups. Raised by alcoholic parents, she suffered the low self-esteem common to people in that circumstance. Deeply religious, Sophie came to believe that the way to rise above her upbringing and become a good parent was through a kind of martyrdom and unbridled kindness. Constant self-denial often left her struggling against feelings of resentment and frustration, however. She tried to quash these emotions whenever they came up, chiding herself for being selfish. But she could never eradicate the "selfish" feelings completely. Under stress, she sometimes "flew off the handle," becoming uncharacteristically harsh toward her kids, meting out irrational punishments. "I knew my tantrums were bad for them," she says, "but I didn't know how to stop. It was like I had two speeds—nice and mean—and I didn't have any control over the switch."

It wasn't until Sophie's son got into trouble at school for his own tantrums that she went for counseling. That's when she began to see how her attitude toward emotion was actually harming her kids. By always denying her feelings, she had given her children no model for handling negative emotions that naturally surface in family life—feelings like anger, resentment, and jealousy. Still, chang-ing her ways has not been easy. She's had to learn to focus con-sciously on thoughts and feelings that she previously considered "self-centered" or "narcissistic"—even "sinful." But by doing so, she can now take care of her needs before she becomes overwhelmed and loses her temper. She's also beginning to see how getting in touch with her own negative feelings might help her to be a better guide for her children when they're feeling angry, sad, or fearful. "It's kind of like the safety instructions they give on airplanes," she explains. "You've got to get the oxygen in place for yourself first be-fore you can help your child."

What can parents who fear losing control do to feel more capable of engaging with their children concerning emotional issues? First, remember that it's okay to express anger if your child does some-thing that makes you mad. The key is to express your feelings in ways that are not destructive to your relationship. By doing so, you are demonstrating two things: (1) Strong feelings can be expressed and managed, and (2) Your child's behavior really matters to you. You can use your anger to demonstrate passion and sincerity, so long as you communicate respectfully. Our research shows it's best to avoid sarcasm, contempt, and derogatory comments toward your child, all of which are linked to low self-esteem in children. It's also better to focus on your child's actions rather than his character. Make your comments specific and tell your child how his actions af-fect you.

In addition, it also helps to be aware of your different levels of emotional arousal. If you find that you're mad, but you can continue to talk rationally to your child, leading to some degree of under-standing, stay engaged. Tell your child what's on your mind, listen to his response, and keep talking. If, on the other hand, you find that you're so intensely angry that you can't think clearly, take a break from the situation and return to it later when you feel less aroused. Parents should also retreat if they feel they're on the verge of doing or saying destructive things, such as hitting or insulting their kids. Spanking, sarcasm, threats, derogatory statements, or ex-pressions of contempt should definitely be avoided. (For more on spanking, see page 103.) Rather than hitting children or lobbing hurtful comments at them, parents should take a breather, promising they'll return to the discussion when they can be calmer.

If you feel you are at risk for seriously hurting your child physically or psychologically, you should seek professional counseling. Your health-care provider or a local crisis hotline can give you referrals.

Finally, parents who fear losing control might do well to remember the healing power of forgiveness. All parents make mistakes from time to time, losing their tempers with their children, saying or doing things they later regret. From about age four, children can understand the concept of "I'm sorry." So don't miss the chance to go back and repair an interaction when you feel remorse. Tell your child how you were feeling at the time of the incident and how you felt afterward. This can be a positive example to your child of how to handle feelings of regret and sorrow. Perhaps your child can even help you brainstorm solutions that will help both of you prevent future misunderstandings and conflicts.

Keep in mind also that kids generally crave intimacy and warmth with their parents. It's in their best interest to heal the relationship. They give their parents lots of second chances. Remember also that such forgiveness is a two-way street. It works best in families where children are allowed to be in crummy moods from time to time, where parents openly forgive their children as well.

While building emotional self-awareness can be a lifelong process, parents may see positive results from new insights right away. A mother who finally gives herself permission to get angry is in a much better position to allow her son to have the same feeling. Once a father can acknowledge his own sadness, he's far more capable of listening to his son's or daughter's sadness.

### EMOTIONAL AWARENESS SELF-TEST

The following test is designed to help you take a look at your own emotional life, how you permit yourself to experience anger and sadness, and how you feel about emotion in general. There are no right or wrong answers here, but the scoring key at the end will help you gauge your level of emotional awareness. Understanding this aspect of yourself can give you insights into why you react as you do to other people's emotions, and particularly to your child's emotions.

## ANGER

Start by taking a look at the most recent past, say, the last few weeks of your life. Think about the things you find stressful, and that cause you to feel frustrated, irritated, or angry. Also, think about people in your life who seem to be responding to you with impatience, frustration, anger, or irritation. Consider the thoughts, images, and basic feelings you have when faced with these angry, stressful emotions in others and in yourself. Read each of the following statements, which were all taken from statements made by people in our research studies. See how much you agree with them. Then circle the response that fits best.

**T = True      F = False      DK = Don't Know**

1. I feel many different kinds of anger.      T      F      DK

2. I am either calm or I blow up in anger, there's not much in between.      T      F      DK

3. People can tell when I am even a little irritated.
T      F      DK

4. I can tell way in advance of getting angry that I am on the nasty or grumpy side.      T      F      DK

5. In others I can detect even small signs that people are angry.      T      F      DK

6. Anger is toxic.      T      F      DK

7. When I get angry, I feel like I am chewing on something, clenching my jaw on it, biting it, and gnashing it.
T      F      DK

8. I can feel cues of my anger in my body.
T      F      DK

9. Feelings are private. I try not to express them.
T      F      DK

10. I experience anger as getting physically very hot.
T      F      DK

11. For me, feeling angry is like building up steam, increasing the pressure.    T    F    DK

12. For me, getting angry is like blowing off steam, letting go of the pressure.    T    F    DK

13. For me, getting angry is like the pressure building and building and not letting up.    T    F    DK

14. Getting angry makes me feel like I'm about to lose control.    T    F    DK

15. When I get angry it tells people that they can't push me around.    T    F    DK

16. Anger is my way of getting serious and stern.
T    F    DK

17. Anger gives me energy; it's a motivation to tackle things and not be defeated by them.    T    F    DK

18. I keep my anger suppressed and inside.
T    F    DK

19. My view is that if you suppress anger, you court disaster.
T    F    DK

20. In my view, anger is natural, like clearing your throat.
T    F    DK

21. For me, anger is like something's on fire, like something is going to explode.    T    F    DK

22. Anger, like fire, can consume you.    T    F    DK

23. I just ride out anger until it melts away.
T    F    DK

24. I see anger as destruction.    T    F    DK

25. I see anger as uncivilized.    T    F    DK

26. I see anger as drowning.    T    F    DK

27. To me there's not much difference between anger and aggression.    T    F    DK

**28.** I think that a child's anger is bad and ought to be punished.    T    F    DK

**29.** The energy from anger has to go somewhere. You might as well express it.    T    F    DK

**30.** Anger gives you drive, energy.    T    F    DK

**31.** For me, anger and hurt go together. When I am angry, it's because I have been hurt.    T    F    DK

**32.** For me, anger and fear go together. When I am angry, deep down there's an insecurity.    T    F    DK

**33.** When you get angry, you put yourself in a position where you feel like you've got power; you feel like you're standing up for yourself.    T    F    DK

**34.** Anger is mostly impatience.    T    F    DK

**35.** I cope with being angry just by letting time pass.
T    F    DK

**36.** For me anger means helplessness and frustration.
T    F    DK

**37.** I keep my anger bottled up.    T    F    DK

**38.** It is shameful for people to see you angry.
T    F    DK

**39.** Anger is okay if it is controlled.    T    F    DK

**40.** I would say that when people get angry, it's like they are dumping waste on others.    T    F    DK

**41.** Getting rid of anger is like expelling something very unpleasant from my body.    T    F    DK

**42.** I find the expression of emotions embarrassing.
T    F    DK

**43.** If a person were healthy there would be no anger.
T    F    DK

**44.** Anger implies engagement or contact.
T    F    DK

SADNESS

Now think about recent times when you felt sad, downhearted, or dejected. Think about people in your life who have expressed feelings of sadness, depression, or melancholia. What thoughts, images, and basic feelings come to mind when you think about the expression of these sad emotions by yourself and by others? Read each of the following statements about sadness and circle the answer that best describes your response.

**1.** Overall, I would have to say that sadness is toxic.
T    F    DK

**2.** Sadness is like illness and getting over sadness is like recovering from a disease.    T    F    DK

**3.** When I'm sad, I want to be alone.    T    F    DK

**4.** I feel lots of varieties of sadness.    T    F    DK

**5.** I can tell when I am even just a little bit sad.
T    F    DK

**6.** I can tell when other people are even just a small bit blue.
T    F    DK

**7.** My body gives me signals loud and clear that I am going to have a sad day.    T    F    DK

**8.** I view sadness as productive. It lets you know to slow down.    T    F    DK

**9.** I think sadness is good for you. It can tell you what's missing in your life.    T    F    DK

**10.** Sadness is a natural part of feeling loss and grief.
T    F    DK

**11.** Sadness is okay if it is over quickly.    T    F    DK

**12.** Attending to sadness is cleansing.    T    F    DK

13. Sadness is useless.     T     F     DK

14. There is no such thing as "a good cry."
T     F     DK

15. Sadness is not something that should be wasted on small things.     T     F     DK

16. Sadness is there for a reason.     T     F     DK

17. Sadness means weakness.     T     F     DK

18. Sadness means you can feel or empathize.
T     F     DK

19. Feeling sad is feeling helpless and/or hopeless.
T     F     DK

20. It is useless to talk to people if you're feeling sad.
T     F     DK

21. I sometimes have a good cry.     T     F     DK

22. Being sad makes me afraid.     T     F     DK

23. Showing people you are sad means a loss of control.
T     F     DK

24. If you can maintain control, sadness can be a pleasure.
T     F     DK

25. It is best not to show people your sadness.
T     F     DK

26. Sadness is like being violated.     T     F     DK

27. People should be alone when sad, like quarantined.
T     F     DK

28. Acting happy is an antidote to sadness.
T     F     DK

29. One emotion can be converted to another with enough thought.     T     F     DK

30. I try to get over sadness quickly.     T     F     DK

**31.** Sadness makes you reflect.     T     F     DK

**32.** A child's sadness reflects a negative trait.
T     F     DK

**33.** It's best not to react at all to a child's sadness.
T     F     DK

**34.** Sometimes when I'm sad, what I feel is self-loathing.
T     F     DK

**35.** In my view, emotions are always there; they're a part of life.     T     F     DK

**36.** To be in control means to be upbeat, positive, not sad.
T     F     DK

**37.** Feelings are private, not public.     T     F     DK

**38.** If you are emotional with children you might get out of control and become abusive.     T     F     DK

**39.** In life, it is best not to dwell too long with negative emotions; just accentuate the positive.     T     F     DK

**40.** To get over a negative emotion, just get on with life's routines.     T     F     DK

### SCORING

People who are aware of anger and sadness speak about these emotions in a differentiated manner. They can easily detect such emotions in themselves and in others. They experience a variety of nuances with these emotions, and they allow these feelings to be a part of their lives. Such people are likely to see and respond to smaller and less intense expressions of anger or sadness in their children than people lower in emotional awareness.

Can you be high in awareness for one emotion and low for another? This is quite possible. Awareness is not one-dimensional and it can change over time.

ANGER. To compute your score for anger, add up the number

of times you said "true" for the items in List No. 1 below, and then subtract the number of times you said "true" for the items in List No. 2 below. The higher your score, the greater your awareness.

**List No. 1**

1, 3, 4, 5, 7, 8, 10, 11, 12, 15, 16, 17, 19, 20, 29, 30, 31, 32, 33, 44.

**List No. 2**

2, 6, 9, 13, 14, 18, 21, 22, 23, 24, 25, 26, 27, 28, 34, 35, 36, 37, 38, 39, 40, 41, 42, 43.

If you responded "don't know" more than ten times, you may want to work at becoming more aware of anger in yourself and others.

SADNESS. To compute your score for sadness, add up the number of times you said "true" for the items in List No. 1 below, and then subtract the number of times you said "true" for the items in List No. 2 below. The higher your score, the greater your awareness.

**List No. 1**

4, 5, 6, 7, 8, 9, 10, 12, 16, 18, 21, 24, 31, 35.

**List No. 2**

1, 2, 3, 11, 13, 14, 15, 17, 19, 20, 22, 23, 25, 26, 27, 28, 29, 30, 32, 33, 34, 36, 37, 38, 39, 40.

If you responded "don't know" more than ten times, you may want to work at becoming more aware of sadness in yourself and others.

## TIPS FOR EMOTIONAL SELF-AWARENESS

After taking this test, you may find that you want to develop a deeper awareness of your own emotional life. Common ways to tap into your feelings include meditation, prayer, journal writing, and forms of artistic expression, such as playing a musical instrument or drawing. Keep in mind that building greater emotional awareness requires a bit of solitude, something that's often in short supply for today's busy parents. If you remind yourself, however, that time spent alone can help you to become a better parent, it doesn't seem so indulgent. Couples may want to take turns getting out alone for early morning walks or taking off for a weekend retreat from time to time. Single parents may want to trade child care with one another for the same purpose.

Keeping an "emotion log" is also an excellent way to become more aware of your feelings moment by moment. The chart on the next page is an example of a weekly checklist for keeping track of a variety of feelings as they come up. In addition to the checklist, you may want to keep a brief emotion diary for writing down thoughts about feelings as you are experiencing them. Such logs can help you to become more aware of incidents or thoughts that trigger your emotions and how you react to them. Do you remember, for example, the last time you cried or lost your temper? What was the catalyst? How did you feel about having the emotion? Did you feel relieved afterward or ashamed? Were others aware that you were having these feelings? Did you talk to anybody about the incident? These are the types of things you might note in an emotion log. You can also use the log to take note of your reactions to other people's emotions, particularly those of your children. Each time you see your child angry, sad, or fearful, you can jot down notes about your own reaction.

Emotion logs can also be helpful for people who feel scared or anxious about their own emotional responses. That's because the process of labeling an emotion and writing about it can help people define and contain the feeling. Emotions that once seemed mysterious and uncontrollable suddenly take on boundaries and limits. Our feelings become more manageable and they're not as frightening anymore.

As you work with the emotion log, notice the kinds of thoughts, images, and language your feelings elicit. Look for insights in the metaphors you choose to describe your feelings. For example, do you sometimes see your anger or your child's anger as destructive or explosive and therefore frightening? Or are you more likely to perceive it as powerful, cleansing, and energizing? What do such images tell you about your willingness to accept and work with negative emotions in your life? Do you notice attitudes or perceptions about emotion that you'd like to change?

*Week of:*

| EMOTION: | Monday | Tuesday | Wednesday | Thursday | Friday | Saturday | Sunday |
|---|---|---|---|---|---|---|---|
| HAPPINESS | | | | | | | |
| AFFECTION | | | | | | | |
| INTEREST | | | | | | | |
| EXCITEMENT | | | | | | | |
| PRIDE | | | | | | | |
| DESIRE | | | | | | | |
| LOVE | | | | | | | |
| LOVED | | | | | | | |
| THANKFULNESS | | | | | | | |
| STRESS | | | | | | | |
| HURT | | | | | | | |
| SADNESS | | | | | | | |
| IRRITATION | | | | | | | |
| ANGER | | | | | | | |
| PITY | | | | | | | |
| DISGUST | | | | | | | |
| GUILT | | | | | | | |
| ENVY | | | | | | | |
| REGRET | | | | | | | |
| SHAME | | | | | | | |

## BEING AWARE OF CHILDREN'S EMOTIONS

Parents who are aware of their own emotions can use their sensitivity to tune in to their children's feelings—no matter how subtle or intense. Being a sensitive, emotionally aware person, however, doesn't necessarily mean that you'll always find your child's feelings easy to understand. Kids often express their emotions indirectly and in ways that adults find puzzling. If we listen carefully with open hearts, however, we can often de-code messages children unconsciously hide in their interactions, their play, their everyday behavior.

David, a father in one of our parenting groups, told how an incident with his seven-year-old daughter helped him to understand the roots of her anger and showed him what she needed. Carly had been "in a dark mood" all day, he explained, picking fights with her four-year-old brother, taking offense at all sorts of imagined insults, including the classic: "Jimmy's looking at me again!" With every interaction, Carly cast Jimmy as the villain, although Jimmy seemed to be doing nothing wrong. When David asked Carly why she was so angry at her easygoing sibling, his questions elicited only silence and tears. The more he probed, the more defensive Carly became.

At the end of the day, David went to Carly's room to help her get ready for bed. There he found her pouting again. He opened her bureau to get her pajamas and found just one set clean—a tattered, outgrown pair with feet in the bottom. "Do you think these will fit?" he asked with a weak smile as he held them up for his lanky girl to see. David fetched a scissors, and together the two cut the feet off the pajamas so she could wear them. "I can't believe how quickly you're growing up," he told her. "You're getting to be such a big girl."

Five minutes later, Carly joined the family in the kitchen for a bedtime snack. "She was like a different kid," David remembers. She was chatty, upbeat. She even managed to crack a joke for Jimmy.

"Something happened during the business with the pajamas but I'm not sure what," David told the other parents. After tossing it around the group, however, the answer was clearer to him. A serious, sensitive kid, Carly had always been jealous of charming, sweet-natured Jimmy. And for some reason, on that day in particular, she may have been needing reassurance of her own special place in the family. Perhaps she wanted to know that David loved her in a way that's different from the way he loved Jimmy. Perhaps her father's sweet acknowledgment that she's growing up fast was just the ticket.

The point is, children—like all people—have reasons for their emotions, whether they can articulate those reasons or not. Whenever we find our children getting angry or upset over an issue that seems inconsequential, it may help to step back and look at the big picture of what's going on in their lives. A three-year-old can't tell you, "I'm sorry I've been so cranky lately, Mom; it's just that I've been under a lot stress since moving to the new daycare center." An eight-year-old probably won't tell you, "I feel so tense when I hear you and dad bickering over money," but that may be what he's feeling.

Among children about age seven and younger, clues to feelings are often revealed in fantasy play. Make-believe, using different characters, scenes, and props, allows children to safely try on various emotions. I remember my own daughter, Moriah, using her Barbie doll in this way at age four. Playing in the bathtub with the doll, she told me, "Barbie is really scared when you get mad." It was her way of opening up an important conversation between us regarding what makes me angry, how my voice gets louder when I'm angry, and how that makes her feel. Grateful for the chance to talk it over, I assured Barbie (and my daughter) that I didn't mean to scare her and that just because I get angry sometimes doesn't mean that I don't love her. Because Moriah was taking on the persona of Barbie, I talked directly to the doll and comforted her. This, I believe, made it easier for Moriah to continue talking about how she felt when I got angry.

Not all messages from children are this easy to decipher. Still, it's common for children to act out their fears through games with serious themes like abandonment, illness, injury, or death. (Is it any wonder that children like to pretend they have the strength and magic of a Mighty Morphin Power Ranger?) Alert parents can take cues from the fears they hear expressed in their children's play. Then, later on, they can address these fears and offer reassurances.

Hints of children's emotional distress may also show up in behaviors such as overeating, loss of appetite, nightmares, and complaints of headaches or stomachaches. Children who have been potty-trained for some time may suddenly start wetting the bed again.

If you suspect that your child is feeling sad, angry, or fearful, it's helpful to try to put yourself in their shoes, to see the world from their perspective. This can be more challenging than it sounds, especially when you consider how much more life experience you've had. When a pet dies, for example, *you* know that grief passes with time. But a child having this feeling for the first time may feel much more overwhelmed than you do by the intensity of the experience. While you can't eliminate the differences in your experience, you can try to remember that your child is facing life from a much fresher, less experienced, more vulnerable perspective.

When you feel your heart go out to your child, when you know you are feeling what your child is feeling, you are experiencing empathy, which is the foundation of Emotion Coaching. If you can stay with your child in this emotion—even though, at times, the feeling may be difficult or uncomfortable—you can take the next step, which is to recognize the emotional moment as a chance to build trust and offer guidance.

## STEP NO. 2: RECOGNIZING THE EMOTION AS AN OPPORTUNITY FOR INTIMACY AND TEACHING

IT IS SAID that in Chinese the ideogram representing "opportunity" is encompassed in the ideogram for "crisis." Nowhere is the linking of these two concepts more apt than in our role as parents. Whether the crisis is a broken balloon, a failing math grade, or the betrayal of a friend, such negative experiences can serve as superb opportunities to empathize, to build intimacy with our children, and to teach them ways to handle their feelings.

For many parents, recognizing children's negative emotions as opportunities for such bonding and teaching comes as a relief, a liberation, a great "ah-ha." We can look at our children's anger as something other than a challenge to our authority. Kids' fears are no longer evidence of our incompetence as parents. And their sadness doesn't have to represent just "one more blasted thing I'm going to have to fix today."

To reiterate an idea offered by one Emotion-Coaching father in our studies, a child needs his parents most when he is sad or angry or afraid. The ability to help soothe an upset child can be what makes us "feel most like parents." By acknowledging our children's emotions, we are helping them learn skills for soothing themselves, skills that will serve them well for a lifetime.

While some parents try to ignore children's negative feelings in the hope that they will go away, emotions rarely work that way. Instead, negative feelings dissipate when children can talk about their emotions, label them, and feel understood. It makes sense, therefore, to acknowledge low levels of emotion early on before they escalate into full-blown crises. If your five-year-old seems nervous about an upcoming trip to the dentist, it's better to explore that fear the day before than to wait until the child is in the dentist chair, throwing a full-blown tantrum. If your twelve-year-old feels envious because his best friend got the position he coveted on the baseball team, it's better to help him talk over those feelings with you than to let them boil over in a row between the two buddies next week.

Addressing feelings that are low in intensity before they escalate also gives families a chance to practice listening and problem-solving skills while the stakes are small. If you express interest and concern over your child's broken toy or a minor scrape, these experiences are building blocks. Your child learns that you are his ally and the two of you figure out how to collaborate. Then if a big crisis occurs, you are prepared to face it together.

## STEP NO. 3: LISTENING EMPATHETICALLY AND VALIDATING THE CHILD'S FEELINGS

ONCE YOU CAN see that a situation presents an opportunity to build intimacy and teach problem solving, you're ready for perhaps the most important step in the Emotion-Coaching process: empathetic listening.

In this context, listening means far more than collecting data with your ears. Empathetic listeners use their eyes to watch for physical evidence of their children's emotions. They use their imaginations to see the situation from the child's perspective. They use their words to reflect back, in a soothing, noncritical way, what they are hearing and to help their children label their emotions. But most importantly, they use their hearts to feel what their children are feeling.

Tuning in to your child's emotions requires that you pay attention to your child's body language, facial expressions, and gestures. Surely you've seen that furrowed brow, that tense jaw, or that tapping foot before. What does it tell you about the way he's feeling? Be aware that your child can read your body language as well. If your goal is to talk in a relaxed, attentive manner, adopt a posture that says so. Sit at his level, take a deep breath, relax, and focus. Your attentiveness will let your child know that you take his concerns seriously and that you're willing to spend some time on the matter.

As your child reveals his feelings, reflect back what you hear and notice. This will assure your child that you are listening carefully and that you think his feelings are valid. Here's an example:

When a birthday package arrives in the mail for Nicky, his four-year-old brother, Kyle, reacts with anger: "That's not fair!" Kyle protests. Typically, the boys' dad responds by explaining that, in time, it *will be* fair: "When your birthday comes, Grandma will probably send you a package, too," Dad says.

While this statement certainly explains the logic of the situation, it flatly denies how Kyle is feeling in the moment. Now, on top of feeling jealous about the package, Kyle probably feels angry that his dad doesn't understand his unenviable position.

Imagine how differently Kyle might feel if his dad were to respond to his outburst with a simple observation: "You wish Grandma had sent you a package, too. I bet that makes you feel kind of jealous." Yeah, that's right, Kyle might think. Even though it's Nicky's birthday and I'm supposed to be cool about this, I feel jealous. Dad understands. Now, Kyle's in a better spot to hear his dad's explanation that things will even out in time.

A mom in one of our parenting groups had a similar experience when her daughter came home from school complaining, "Nobody likes me."

"It was so hard not to argue the facts with her," the mother said, "I know she's popular at school. But when I listened and empathized instead of arguing, the crisis was over in a minute. I'm learning that when she's talking about her feelings, it doesn't really help to apply logic. It's better to just listen."

Here's another example of empathetic listening, taken from a conversation one of the moms in our parenting groups had with her nine-year-old daughter, Megan. Notice that the mom's first order of business is to acknowledge her daughter's feelings.

*Megan:* I don't want to go to school tomorrow.

*Mom:* You don't? That's strange. Usually you like to go to school. It makes me wonder if you're worried about something.

*Megan:* Yeah, kind of.

*Mom:* What are you worried about?

*Megan:* I don't know.

*Mom:* Something is sort of worrying you, but you're not sure what it is.

*Megan:* Yeah.

*Mom:* I can tell that you feel a little tense.

*Megan* (with tears): Yeah. Maybe it's because of Dawn and Patty.

*Mom:* Did something happen today at school with Dawn and Patty?

*Megan.* Yeah. Today at recess Dawn and Patty were just ignoring me.

*Mom:* Oh, that must have hurt your feelings.

*Megan:* It did.

*Mom:* It sounds like you don't want to go to school tomorrow because you're worried that Dawn and Patty might ignore you at recess again.

*Megan:* Yeah. Every time I went up to them, they just walked away and started doing something else.

*Mom:* Oh, gee. I'd feel terrible if my friends did that to me.

*Megan:* I did. I felt like I was going to cry.

*Mom:* Oh, honey (hugging her). I'm so sorry that happened to you. I can see that you feel very sad and angry about the way your friends were treating you.

*Megan:* I do. I don't know what to do tomorrow. I don't want to go to school.

*Mom:* Because you don't want your friends to hurt your feelings again.

*Megan:* Yeah, and that's who I always play with. Everybody else has their own friends.

And so the conversation continued with Megan giving the mother more details about her interaction with the girls. The mother reported that there were several times when she wanted to tell her daughter what to do. She wanted to say things like: "Don't worry. Dawn and Patty will change their tunes tomorrow," or, "To heck with those girls. Find some new friends."

The mother resisted doing this, however, because she wanted to convey her understanding and to allow Megan to come up with some answers on her own.

I think this was a good instinct. If the mother had told Megan not to worry, or if she had implied there was some simple solution, she would be saying that she finds her daughter's problem inconsequential, silly. Instead, in her mom, Megan found a confidante and felt comforted. After several more minutes of listening and reflecting back what her daughter was telling her, Megan's mother started exploring ideas of how to handle the situation. And because Megan knew that her mother understood her dilemma, she was receptive to her mom's advice. Here's how the rest of the conversation went:

*Megan:* I don't know what to do.

*Mother:* Do you want me to help you come up with some ideas of what you could do?

*Megan:* Yeah.

*Mother:* Maybe you could talk to Dawn and Patty about the way you feel when they ignore you.

*Megan:* I don't think I could. That would be too embarrassing.

*Mother:* Yeah, I can see why you might feel that way. That would take a lot of courage. Gee, I don't know. Let's think. (Time passes while the mother rubs her daughter's back.)

*Mother:* Maybe you could just wait and see what happens. You know Dawn; she can be really mean one day, but then the next day she'll be her old self again. Maybe she'll be a better friend tomorrow.

*Megan:* But what if she isn't?

*Mother:* I'm not sure. Do you have any ideas?

*Megan:* No.

*Mother:* Is there anybody else you'd like to play with?

*Megan:* No.

*Mother:* What else is happening on the playground?

*Megan:* Just kick ball.

*Mother:* Do you like to play kick ball?

*Megan:* I never played it.

*Mother:* Oh.

*Megan:* Krista always plays it.

*Mother:* You mean Krista, your friend from Camp Fire?

*Megan:* Yeah.

*Mother:* I've seen you with Krista at Camp Fire meetings and you're not shy around her at all. Maybe you could ask her to teach you how to play.

*Megan:* Maybe.

*Mother:* Good. Then you have another idea.

*Megan:* Yeah, maybe that would work. But what if it doesn't?

*Mother:* It seems like you're still worried. Like maybe you're afraid there just won't be anybody to play with and you won't know what to do with yourself.

*Megan:* Yeah.

*Mother:* Are there things that you can think of that are fun to play all by yourself?

*Megan:* You mean like jump rope?

*Mother:* Yeah, jump rope.

*Megan:* I could bring my jump rope just in case.

*Mother:* Yeah. Then if you don't play with Dawn and Patty, or the kick ball game doesn't work out, you could play jump rope.

*Megan:* Yeah I could do that.

*Mother:* Why don't you go put your jump rope in your backpack right now so you don't forget.

*Megan:* Okay. Then could I call Krista and see if she can come over after school tomorrow?

*Mother:* That's a great idea.

By empathizing, taking her time, and letting Megan come to her own conclusions, the mother was able to guide her daughter toward some workable options.

As you listen to your child in an emotional moment, be aware that sharing simple observations usually works better than probing questions to get a conversation rolling. You may ask your child "Why do you feel sad?" and she may not have a clue. As a child, she hasn't had the benefit (or detriment) of years of introspection, so she may not have an answer on the tip of her tongue. Maybe she's feeling sad about her parents' arguments, or because she feels over-tired, or she's worried about an upcoming piano recital. But she may or may not be able to articulate any of this. And even when she does come up with an answer, she might be worried that the answer is not good enough to justify the feeling. Under these circumstances, interrogation can just make a child clam up. It's better to simply reflect what you notice. You can say, "You seem a little tired today," or, "I noticed that you frowned when I mentioned the recital," and wait for her response.

Also, avoid questions to which you already know the answer. Queries like, "What time did you get in last night?" or, "Who broke the lamp?" set a tone of mistrust and entrapment—like you're just waiting for your child to lie. It's better to open such conversation with straightforward observations—something like, "I see you've broken the lamp and I'm disappointed" or, "You came in sometime after one last night and I don't think that's acceptable."

Sharing examples from your own life can also be an effective way to demonstrate your understanding. Take the case of Kyle, the little boy who was upset over his brother's birthday present. Imagine if Dad had said, "I used to feel jealous when I was a little boy and Aunt Mary got a gift." This would assure Kyle that emotions like his are so valid that even Dad experienced them. And now that he feels understood, he can accept Dad's comforting explanation that "Grandma will probably send you a present on your birthday, too."

## STEP NO. 4: HELPING THE CHILD VERBALLY LABEL EMOTIONS

ONE EASY AND extremely important step in Emotion Coaching is to help children label their emotions as they are having them. In the examples above, Kyle's dad helped him to identify his unpleasant feeling as jealousy. Megan's mom used lots of labels to help her daughter define her problem, including "tense," "worried," "hurt," "angry," "sad," and "afraid." Providing words in this way can help children transform an amorphous, scary, uncomfortable feeling into something definable, something that has boundaries and is a normal part of everyday life. Anger, sadness, and fear become experiences everybody has and everybody can handle.

Labeling emotions goes hand in hand with empathy. A parent

sees his child in tears and says, "You feel very sad, don't you?" Now, not only is the child understood, he has a word to describe this intense feeling.

Studies indicate that the act of labeling emotions can have a soothing effect on the nervous system, helping children to recover more quickly from upsetting incidents. While we're not certain how this soothing effect happens, it's my theory that talking about an emotion as you're experiencing it engages the left lobe of the brain, which is the center of language and logic. This, in turn, may help the child to focus and calm down. As we have discussed earlier, the implications of teaching a child to self-soothe are enormous. Kids who can calm themselves from an early age show several signs of emotional intelligence: They are more likely to concentrate better, have better peer relationships, higher academic achievement, and good health.

My advice to parents, then, is to help your kids find words to describe what they are feeling. This doesn't mean telling kids how they *ought* to feel. It simply means helping them develop a vocabulary with which to express their emotions.

The more precisely children can express their feelings in words the better, so see if you can help them hit the nail on the head. If he's angry, for example, he may also feel frustrated, enraged, confused, betrayed, or jealous. If she's sad, she might feel hurt, left-out, jealous, empty, gloomy.

Keep in mind that people often feel mixed emotions, which, to some children, can be troubling in itself. A child going off to camp, for example, may feel both proud of his independence and afraid that he'll be homesick. "Everybody else is happy to be going, but I feel anxious," the child may think. "So what's wrong with me?" Parents can help in such situations by guiding the child to explore his range of emotion, and by reassuring him that it's often normal to feel two ways at once.

## STEP NO. 5: SETTING LIMITS WHILE HELPING THE CHILD PROBLEM-SOLVE

ONCE YOU HAVE spent time listening to your child and helping her to label and understand her emotions, you will probably find yourself naturally drawn into a process of problem solving. This process can have as many as five steps, as well: (1) limit setting; (2) identifying goals; (3) thinking of possible solutions; (4) evaluating proposed solutions based on your family's values; and (5) helping your child choose a solution.

At first glance, this process may appear rather unwieldy, but with practice, it becomes automatic and can usually be accomplished quickly. That's the way you want problem solving to be with children: brief but often.

You can guide your child through the steps. But don't be surprised if, with experience, he starts to take the lead and begins solving difficult problems on his own.

## SET LIMITS

For small children especially, problem solving often starts with a parent setting limits on inappropriate behavior. A child gets frustrated, for example, and then expresses that negative feeling in an inappropriate way, such as hitting a playmate, breaking a toy, or name calling. After the parent acknowledges the emotion behind the misbehavior and helps him to label it, the parent can make sure the child understands that certain behaviors are inappropriate and can't be tolerated. Then the parent can guide the child into thinking of more appropriate ways to handle negative feelings.

"You're mad that Danny took that game away from you," the parent might say. "I would be, too. But it's not okay for you to hit him. What can you do instead?" Or, "It's okay for you to feel jealous because your sister jumped into the front seat of the car before you did, but it's not okay for you to call her nasty names. Can you think of a different way to deal with your feelings?"

As Ginott taught, it's important for children to understand that their *feelings* are not the problem, their *misbehavior* is. All feelings and all wishes are acceptable, but not all behaviors are. Therefore, it's the parent's job to set limits on acts, not on wishes.

This makes sense when you consider that it's not easy for children to change the way they feel about a situation. A child's emotions of sadness, fear, or rage don't just disappear because a parent says, "Stop that crying" or, "You shouldn't feel that way." If we tell a child how she *ought* to feel, it just makes her distrust what she *does* feel, a situation that leads to self-doubt and loss of self-esteem. On the other hand, if we tell a child she has a right to her feelings—but there may be better ways to *express* those feelings—the child is left with her character, her sense of self-esteem, intact. Also, she knows she has an understanding adult on her side who is going to help her go from feeling overwhelmed to finding a solution.

What kinds of behaviors should a parent limit? Ginott gives no hard-and-fast answers and that's as it should be; parents ought to set rules for children based on their own values. He did, however, offer some guidance regarding permissiveness, which he defined as "accepting the childishness of children." Parents should accept, for example, "that a clean shirt on a normal child will not stay clean for long, that running rather than walking is the child's normal means of locomotion, that a tree is for climbing, and a mirror is for making faces." Allowing such behaviors "brings confidence and increasing capacity to express feelings and thoughts." Overpermissiveness, on the other hand, is accepting undesirable acts, such as destructive behavior. Overpermissiveness is to be avoided because it "brings anxiety and increasing demands for privileges that cannot be granted."

Ginott also suggests that parents think about a system of rules based on three "zones" of behavior—the green zone, yellow zone, and red zone.

The green zone encompasses behavior that's sanctioned and desired. It's the way we want our children to act, so we grant them permission freely.

The yellow zone is misbehavior that's not sanctioned, but it's tolerated for either of two specific reasons. The first is "leeway for learners." Your four-year-old can't sit quietly through an entire church service, but you expect he'll get better with time. The second is "leeway for hard times." A five-year-old throws tantrums while suffering a cold. A teenager challenges her mom's authority during her parents' divorce. You may not approve of these types of behavior and you should let your child know this. But you may go ahead and tolerate it, telling your child you're doing so because of exceptional circumstances.

The red zone is behavior that cannot be tolerated no matter

what. This includes activities that are dangerous to the well-being of your child or others. It also includes behavior that's illegal, or behavior you consider immoral, unethical, or socially unacceptable.

When setting limits on inappropriate behavior, parents should let the child know what consequences he can expect for breaking or following rules. Consequences for good behavior can be positive attention, praise, privileges, or rewards. Consequences for misbehavior might be denial of attention, loss of privileges, or the absence of rewards. Children respond best if consequences are consistent, fair, and related to their misbehavior.

The time-out is a popular method used as a consequence for misbehavior among small children—say, ages three to eight. To use it correctly, children are briefly isolated from positive interactions with their peers and caregivers. When it's used correctly, it can be an effective way to help children stop their misbehavior, calm down, and start again on a more positive note. Unfortunately, too many parents and caregivers use time-outs incorrectly. They couple the isolation with harsh words and attitudes, making children feel rejected and humiliated. Little good is accomplished with this type of derogatory consequence. I urge parents who use time-outs to do so with sensitivity.

Another commonly used consequence of misbehavior among American parents is spanking. A 1990 survey of college students, for example, revealed that 93 percent were spanked as children, with 10.6 percent reporting physical punishment severe enough to cause welts or bruises. While spanking may be popular in the United States, it is not standard among parents worldwide. Only about 11 percent of parents in Sweden, for example, report spanking their kids—a statistic many believe may be connected to the lower incidence of violence in general in that country.

Many parents who spank say they do so because it makes their children obey. Indeed, many kids will do what they're told to avoid physical pain. The problem is, a threat of spanking works *too well* in the short term: It stops misbehavior immediately, often without discussion, cutting off chances to teach the child self-control and problem solving. And in the long term, spanking may not work at all. In fact, spanking often backfires because it makes kids feel powerless, unfairly treated, and angry with their parents. After a spanking, children are more likely to think about revenge than self-improvement. A sense of humiliation may cause them to deny wrongdoing, or they may plot ways to keep from getting caught the next time they misbehave.

Spanking also teaches, by example, that aggression is an appropriate way to get what you want. Studies show that children who are hit are more likely to hit their playmates, especially those playmates who are smaller and weaker. The effects of spanking may have a long-term impact as well. Research indicates that, in relation to the severity of physical punishment received, spanked children become more aggressive. As teenagers, they are more likely to hit their parents. As adults, they are more likely to be violent and tolerate violence in their relationships. And finally, people who were physically punished as children are less likely to care for their aging parents.

Although a vast majority of American parents use spanking, I believe most want a better way to respond to their children's misbehavior. Interestingly, studies of parents who have trained in other methods of child discipline show that once they find effective alternatives, they drop the spanking.

Families do better with methods of limit setting that allow children to keep their sense of dignity, self-esteem, and power. When children are given rules they understand, and a sense of control over their own lives, they are less likely to misbehave in the first place. When they learn to regulate their own negative emotions, parental limit setting and discipline are less frequently needed. And with fair, reliable allies in Mom and Dad, children are more open to mutual problem solving.

## IDENTIFY GOALS

Once a parent has listened empathetically to a child, labeled feelings, and set limits on any inappropriate behavior, the next step is usually to identify goals around problem solving. If this doesn't feel like a logical next step, chances are you're rushing; your child may still need more time to express her feelings. Should you find yourself in this position, try not to get discouraged. Simply continue encouraging your child to talk. Reflect on what you're hearing and observing. Empathize and label. It may help to ask open-ended questions like, "What do you think is making you sad (or angry or anxious)?" "Is it something that happened today?" You can offer your own tentative ideas to help your child name the causes. Eventually your child is likely to reach the point where he says, "Now I know why I'm feeling badly and I know what problem brought about these feelings. What am I going to do about this problem?"

To identify a goal around problem solving, ask your child what he would like to accomplish related to the problem at hand. Often, the answer is simple: He wants to fix a lopsided kite; he wants to answer a confounding math problem. Other situations may require clarification. Following a fight with his sister, for example, he may need to determine whether the best goal is to get revenge, or to find a way to prevent future tussles. And sometimes, it may seem like there's no solution in sight. Your child's pet has died. His best friend is moving to another state. He didn't get the part he really wanted in the school play. In cases like these, your child's goal may simply be to accept loss or find comfort.

## THINK OF POSSIBLE SOLUTIONS

Work with your child to come up with options for solving the problem. Parents' ideas can be a boon—especially for younger kids who often have a hard time generating alternative solutions. It's important to refrain from taking over, however. If you really want your child to own the outcome, you should encourage her to generate her own ideas.

How best to handle this brainstorming process depends, in large part, on your child's age. Most kids under age ten are not great abstract thinkers. Consequently, they may have a hard time holding more than one option in mind at a time. Therefore, as soon as the two of you come up with one idea, a child this age is likely to want to try it right away, before considering other alternatives. I remember talking to my daughter, Moriah, when she was four about strategies for handling her fear of "a monster" she encountered in a nightmare. "You could draw a picture of your feelings," I suggested, and in a flash she was off looking for her crayons. Because you don't want to squelch such enthusiasm, you may have to try one solution after another and then ask the child to decide, after the fact, which solution worked best.

Role playing or fantasy play can also be a concrete and handy way to demonstrate alternative solutions to young children. You can use puppets, dolls, or yourself to act out various solutions to a problem. Since young children are often black-and-white thinkers, it may be helpful to pretend two different versions of a situation— one representing the "right" solution, and one representing the "wrong" solution. Two puppets, for example, might be involved in a dispute over a toy. In the first scenario, one puppet grabs the toy from the other without asking. In the second version, one puppet proposes taking turns with the toy.

With older children, you can use a more traditional brainstorming process, where you and your child try to come up with every possible option you can think of. To help creative ideas flow, tell your child from the start that no idea is too silly to consider, and that you won't start weeding out the list of options until all possibilities are on the table. You can show your child that you take the process seriously by actually writing down all the options the two of you generate.

One technique for encouraging a child's growth as you generate solutions is to draw relationships between past and future triumphs. You can remind them of a past achievement and then encourage them to visualize themselves trying something new with similar success.

I recently had the opportunity to try this out with Moriah when she was having trouble managing her friendships at preschool. She was so troubled by the problem that she didn't want to go to school that day. I decided that rather than telling her what to do, I'd ask her for her ideas, while offering information to help her think about the situation in new ways. The conversation went something like this:

*Moriah:* I don't want to go to school because when we have to get partners for swimming class, Margaret always wants to be my partner and I'd rather be partners with Polly.
*Me:* I can see that this problem really makes you feel frustrated.
*Moriah:* Yeah, it's a bummer.
*Me:* What can you do about it?

*Moriah:* I don't know. I like Margaret but I'm just tired of always being her partner. Maybe I could grab Polly's hand before Margaret asks me to be her partner.

*Me:* Good. That's one idea. You'd have to be really fast, but you could probably do it.

At this point, I felt quite tempted to start jumping in with my own suggestions, but I realized it would be much better for Moriah's development to hold back and to just keep coaching her, letting her explore the situation from her own perspective and experience. Here's how the conversation continued:

*Me:* Can you think of anything else?

*Moriah:* No.

*Me:* Okay, well let's talk about it some more. You have this feeling where you feel bugged and frustrated at school. Can you ever remember feeling that way before?

*Moriah:* Yeah. Sort of. Like when Daniel was always pulling my hair.

*Me:* I remember that. What did you do about that problem?

*Moriah:* I told him I wanted him to stop it. That I was going to tell the teacher if he didn't.

*Me:* Did it work?

*Moriah:* Yeah. He stopped doing it.

*Me:* Does that remind you of anything you could do in this situation?

*Moriah:* Well, maybe I could talk to Margaret and tell her I don't want to be her partner for a while. I could tell her I still want to be her friend, but I just want to be Polly's partner sometimes.

*Me:* Good. Now you've got two solutions. I knew you could come up with some good ideas!

## EVALUATE PROPOSED SOLUTIONS BASED ON YOUR FAMILY'S VALUES

This is the time to go over each idea you've generated, deciding which to try and which to eliminate. Encourage your child to consider each solution separately, asking the following questions:

"Is this solution fair?"

"Will this solution work?"

"Is it safe?"

"How am I likely to feel? How are other people likely to feel?"

This exercise provides another opportunity to explore with your child the necessity of limits on certain behaviors. Say, for example, that Moriah had suggested staying home from school the day she was having problems with her swimming partner. I could have pointed out that this solution wouldn't work because Moriah would just have to face the problem the next day. Such conversations also give parents a chance to reinforce the family's values. I might have said to her: "We believe that it's better to face your problems rather than trying to hide from them by staying home." I could also have used this situation to reinforce Moriah's ethic of kindness: "I'm glad you thought about telling Margaret that you still want to be her friend. I think it's important to be sensitive to your friend's feelings."

## HELP YOUR CHILD CHOOSE A SOLUTION

Once you and your child have explored the ramifications of various choices, encourage her to select one or more options and try it.

While you want to encourage kids to think for themselves, this is also a good time to offer your opinions and guidance. Don't be afraid at this point to tell your child how you handled similar problems when you were young. What did you learn from your experience? What mistakes did you make? What decisions made you feel proud? Teaching your child your values within the context of helping her solve a difficult problem is much more effective than simply laying out abstract concepts that are unrelated to your child's everyday life.

While you want to help your children make good decisions, keep in mind that children also learn from their mistakes. If your child seems to be veering toward an idea that you know is unworkable but harmless, you may want to let her try it anyway. Then if it fails, encourage her to move on to the next possibility.

Once your child chooses a solution, help her come up with a concrete plan for following through. Say two siblings who have been squabbling over kitchen chores devise a plan for sharing duty. Encourage them to come up with specific ground rules, designating responsibilities and agreeing on time lines. (Jason does dinner dishes, Joshua does lunch dishes. Then after a week, the two switch.) It's also a good idea to have a plan for evaluating how the solution is working. The pair can agree, for example, to try out one solution for a month, then to talk about how it's going and to make changes if needed. In this way, children come to understand that solutions can be works-in-progress, open to refinement.

When children choose a solution to a problem that doesn't work out, help them analyze why it's failing. Then you can start problem solving anew. This teaches kids that scrapping one idea does not mean the effort is a total failure. Point out that it's all part of a learning process and that each adjustment moves them closer to a successful outcome.

## Chapter 4

## EMOTION-COACHING

## STRATEGIES

AS YOU AND YOUR CHILD USE THE FIVE STEPS OF EMOTION Coaching regularly, both of you probably will become increasingly proficient. You and your child will likely become more aware of feelings and more willing to express them. Your child also may learn to appreciate the benefits of working with an Emotion Coach to solve problems.

This does not mean that Emotion Coaching guarantees smooth sailing, however. Your family is bound to encounter at least a few obstacles. There may be times when you want to be in touch with your child's emotions, but for any number of reasons, you can't get a clear signal. There also may be times when, no matter what you say or do, you can't seem to get your message across to your child. You may feel he's lost in his own world and you might as well be talking to the wall.

In this chapter, you will find a list of strategies that may prove helpful if such blocks occur in the Emotion-Coaching process. They are based on what my colleagues and I have learned through parent groups, clinical work, and observational studies. I've also included a description of common family situations where Emotion Coaching is rarely effective. In these situations, it's usually best to try other techniques and to postpone Emotion Coaching for another time. And finally, at the end of this chapter, you'll find a test to help you evaluate and build your Emotion-Coaching skills.

## Additional Strategies

### AVOID EXCESSIVE CRITICISM, HUMILIATING COMMENTS, OR MOCKING YOUR CHILD

Our research clearly shows that such derogation is destructive to parent-child communication and to children's self-esteem.

In the lab experiments we conducted with families, we saw parents express such behavior in a variety of ways, such as repeating their children's comments verbatim in a contemptuous tone. ("I don't remember the story," the child would say. "You don't *remember?*" came the parent's mocking response.) During the video game exercise, some were overalert to their kids' mistakes, calling attention to each error, overwhelming their children with a barrage of criticism. Others would push their child's hands aside and take over the game, demonstrating their belief in their child's incompetence. In interviews about their children's emotions, many parents told us they responded to their preschoolers' tantrums by laughing at them or mocking them.

When we checked in with these same families three years later, we found that the children who experienced such disrespectful, contemptuous behavior from their parents were the same kids who were having more trouble with schoolwork and getting along with friends. These were the kids who had higher levels of stress-related hormones in their bodies. Their teachers reported they were having more behavior problems, and their moms reported they had more illnesses.

This kind of negative, derogatory parenting can be observed in the real world as well as in labs. Minute by minute, well-intentioned parents chip away at their kids' self-confidence by constantly correcting their manners, deriding their mistakes, and unnecessarily intruding as kids try to perform the simplest tasks. They absent-mindedly describe their children with labels that stick like glue to the child's self-concept. (Bobby is "hyperactive." Karie is "the quiet one." Bill is "lazy." Angie is "our little Puddin' Head.") It's also common to hear parents make jokes for other adults at a child's expense; or to see parents mock their children's sadness, using words like, "Don't be such a baby."

Obviously, parents who are truly in touch with their kids' feelings are not as likely to put them down in this way. Still, our studies show that even parents we identified as Emotion Coaches were sometimes derogatory toward their kids without really meaning to be. That's why I urge all parents to be vigilant against the insidious habits of criticism, sarcasm, and derogation. Be careful that you don't make fun of your kids. Give them space as they try to learn new skills, even if it means letting them make a few mistakes. Avoid trait labels by talking in terms of specific behaviors, not broad-brush character sketches. Say, "We don't climb on the furniture at Grandma's," rather than, "Quit being such a terror!"

Although some kids can be thick-skinned, none are made of Teflon. Children look to their parents for identity and they tend to believe whatever their parents say about them. If parents degrade or humiliate their kids with jokes, hypercriticism, and intrusiveness, their children will not trust them. And without trust, intimacy is lost, listening is moot, and joint problem solving becomes impossible.

## USE "SCAFFOLDING" AND PRAISE TO COACH YOUR CHILD

"Scaffolding" is a technique we observed Emotion-Coaching families using with success to teach their children during the video game lab experiment. Their behavior serves as a stark contrast to that of the overly critical parents described above. First, the Emotion-Coaching families would talk in a slow, calm manner, giving their children just enough information to get started. Then they would wait for the child to do something right and offer her specific—not global—praise for their action. (For example, a father might say, "Good! You're pushing the button at the just the right time." This type of focused compliment is much more effective in a teaching situation than broad compliments, such as, "Good! You've really got the hang of it now!") Next, following such praise, the parents would typically add just a little bit more instruction. And finally, the family would repeat the steps, with their children learning the game in increments. We call this teaching technique scaffolding because parents use each small success to boost the child's confidence, helping her to reach the next level of competence.

In contrast to the overly critical parents described in the section above, the Emotion-Coaching parents rarely used criticism or humiliation to teach their children. Nor did they intrude by taking over the game and playing it themselves.

The slow, calm manner Emotion-Coaching parents typically used while scaffolding can be compared to the way public television's Mister Rogers talks to children. Contrast this style with another popular TV show for kids, *Sesame Street*. While *Sesame Street* uses witty, flashy characters and a quick pace to grab and maintain children's attention, Mister Rogers speaks directly to the camera in a measured, gentle pace that's easy for young children to follow. *Sesame Street*'s rote repetition works to teach children numbers, the alphabet, and such. But Mister Rogers's quiet manner and soothing tone is more appropriate for teaching young children complex concepts having to do with feelings and behavior.

## IGNORE YOUR "PARENTAL AGENDA"

Although emotional moments can be a marvelous opportunity for empathy, bonding, and coaching, they also can present a real challenge for parents who have what I call a "parental agenda"—that is, a goal based on a particular problem the parent has identified as interfering with the child's best interests. Such agendas often are linked to promoting admirable values such as courage, thriftiness, kindness, and discipline. They can vary from one child to another. Parents may worry that one of their kids is too assertive and the other is too timid. While some children are seen as lazy and undisciplined, others are called too serious, lacking in spontaneity and humor. Regardless of the specific problem, such agendas cause parents to keep a watchful eye on behavior, constantly trying to adjust their children's course. When conflicts arise over agenda issues, vigilant parents see it as their responsibility—indeed, their moral obligation—to drive home their own points of view: "Because of your forgetfulness, you failed to feed the cat again and that's cruel." "Because of your impulsiveness, you spent part of your college savings on concert tickets and that's foolish."

I applaud parents who share their values with their children; I believe such teaching is an extremely important part of parenting.

Parents need to be aware, however, that unless parental agendas are communicated sensitively, they can get in the way of a close parent-child relationship. For one, the parental agenda often prevents mothers and fathers from listening empathetically to their kids. When this happens, the agenda can backfire, actually eroding the parent's ability to influence the child's decisions. Let me give you an example: Jean, a sensitive and concerned mom in one of our parenting groups, has long been worried about her son, Andrew's, "gloomy attitude." She is concerned that the nine-year-old tends to "play the victim" and she worries about how that affects his relationships with others. Consequently, in a short exchange with Andrew about an argument he had with his older sister, Jean's agenda was to get Andrew to take more personal responsibility for getting along with his sibling.

"What's the matter, sweetheart?" she began. "You look kind of sad."

"I just wish I had a nicer sister," Andrew replied.

"Well, are you nice to her?" Jean responded.

Imagine now how Andrew must have felt about this question. Here was Mom, appearing to be interested in how he was feeling. But as soon as he opens up, she responds with criticism. Granted, it's well-intentioned, mild criticism, but it's criticism nonetheless.

Now imagine how Andrew might have felt if Jean had responded instead with something like, "I can see why you might feel that way some days." Such a statement would have made it clear to Andrew that Mom was focused on his sadness, that she was there to help him sort through his feelings about his sister and to come up with solutions. Instead, Jean put the blame on Andrew's shoulders, a move guaranteed to make Andrew more defensive and less willing to own up to his role in the rift.

Parental agendas can get in the way even in situations where a parent knows a child has misbehaved, says Alice Ginott-Cohen, a parent educator and therapist who worked with her late husband, Haim Ginott. She advises parents to postpone talking about a child's misdeed until after the feelings underlying the misbehavior have been addressed.

To get at the emotion underlying misbehavior, it's best to avoid asking questions like, "Why did you do that?" This question sounds like an accusation or a criticism. The child will be more likely to respond defensively than to offer useful information. Instead, try asking the child in a concerned way how he was feeling when the misbehavior occurred.

Granted, it's not easy to ignore your parental agenda in the face of misbehavior—especially when you can feel the sermon on the tip of your tongue. But moralizing about a misdeed without addressing the feelings behind it is usually ineffective. It's like putting a cold compress on your child's fevered brow without treating the infection that's causing the fever in the first place.

Let me give you an example: A mother arrives at the child-care center an hour later than usual to pick up her three-year-old son. The child, whom the mother often refers to as "stubborn," starts acting sulky. He refuses to cooperate in putting on his jacket and heading for the door. The mother can either scold her son for noncompliance, or she can stop, think about the preceding events, and try to understand what the boy is experiencing emotionally. Choosing the latter, she might say this: "I was later than usual today, wasn't I? Most of your friends have already gone home. Did that make you feel kind of worried?" The child, with his feelings of anxiety and tension validated, might feel suddenly relieved and offer his mom a hug. The struggle over the jacket might then dissolve and the two would be on their way.

To successfully connect with her son, the mother had to ignore her long-term agenda for making the boy less "stubborn," more cooperative. Too often, parents react to a child's misbehavior in just the opposite way. They cling tighter to the parental agenda, expressing concern over a child's problem as if it were part of an enduring, negative character flaw. They may blame the child for having the trait. Andrew is oversensitive. Janet is too aggressive. Bobby is too shy. Sarah is too scatterbrained. Such labeling gets in the way of empathy. The labels are destructive because young children will, unfortunately, believe their parents and then try to fulfill their parents' views as if they were divine prophecy.

In his memoir, *Father to the Man*, writer Christopher Hallowell remembers his father's attempts to teach him to build a wooden box. "If you can't build a box square," his father said, "you can't build anything." After much work, Hallowell had a box, albeit a wobbly one. Reflecting on the incident, he wrote, "every time my father examined it, he scowled and said, 'You didn't get something square. You will never be a good builder unless you can get everything square.' At last he gave up scowling and never said anything more about the box. I kept odds and ends in it for years, feeling a certain affection for it each time I lifted the top, although never far away was a picture of my father's disapproving look."

For Hallowell, a successful writer, this sad interaction became a lasting memory of his relationship with his father. For us, it can serve as a poignant reminder that parental criticism has a powerful impact on children.

As parents, none of us wants our children to be satisfied building wobbly boxes. Nor do we want them to grow up lazy, withdrawn, aggressive, stupid, cowardly, deceitful. But we don't want such weaknesses to become the characteristics by which our children define themselves, either. How can this type of negative labeling be avoided? The answer is to steer clear of global, enduring critiques of children's personality traits. When correcting kids, focus instead on a specific event that happened here and now in their lives. Rather than, "You are so careless and messy," say to your child, "There are toys scattered all over your room." Instead of, "You're such a slow reader," say, "Reading every night for thirty minutes will make you faster." Instead of, "Don't be such a wallflower," say, "If you speak louder, the waitress can hear you."

## CREATE A MENTAL MAP OF YOUR CHILD'S DAILY LIFE

Children are not always highly skilled at expressing their emotions. Your child may appear upset one day, but not be able to tell you what she is feeling and why. When this happens, it is useful to know a lot about the people, places, and events in your child's life. This way, you will be better equipped to explore the possible source of your child's feelings and help your child label them. You'll also demonstrate to her that you think her world is important and this may help her to feel closer to you.

I like to think of this base of knowledge as a kind of map—one that parents make a conscious effort to carry in their minds. Considering such a map, a parent might say, "This is my child's world and these are the people who populate it. I know their names, their faces, and their personalities. I know how my child feels about each one. Here are my child's closest friends and this one is his foe. My child thinks this teacher is nice, this coach is funny, but that teacher intimidates him. This is the layout of his school. I know where he feels most comfortable, and I know what dangers he feels he has to face here. This is his daily schedule. These subjects interest him most and these cause him trouble."

Creating such a map of your child's emotional world takes a lot of work and attention to detail. Parents need to spend time at their children's daycare centers, schools, and after-school activities. They need to talk to their kids and get to know their kids' friends and teachers. And like the map of any living community, this one needs to be updated regularly. Parents who keep such a map as a resource, however, find that it provides lots of common ground for meaningful discussion.

## AVOID "SIDING WITH THE ENEMY"

When kids feel mistreated, they may turn to their parents for loyalty, compassion, and support. These are good opportunities for Emotion Coaching, as long as parents don't make the mistake of "siding with the enemy." It's a challenge of course, especially when parents feel naturally aligned with the very authority figures their kids are likely to cross—such people as teachers, coaches, bosses, or other kids' parents.

Imagine, for example, that an overweight girl comes home upset because her dance teacher made an insensitive comment about her size. If the mother's been trying unsuccessfully to get her daughter to diet, she might be tempted to tell the girl the teacher is right. This would probably make the girl feel as though the whole world is against her. But what if the mother empathized with the girl, saying something like, "I'm so sorry that happened to you. You must have felt embarrassed and hurt." This might draw the girl closer to her mom. And if the mother maintains her empathetic, supportive stance over time, her daughter eventually might allow her mother to help.

What do you do, however, if *you're* the enemy, the target of your child's anger? I believe empathy can work in these situations as well, particularly if you're honest about your position, which allows you to be nondefensive. Say, for example, that your child is angry because you have declared the television off-limits until she brings up her grades. Without changing your mind, you can say, "I understand why you're mad. I'd feel the same way if I was in your position."

Honesty and open-mindedness in the face of conflict may encourage your child to express *her* feelings as well, particularly if you can invite debate with comments like, "I may be wrong about this; I'm not always right. I'd like to hear your side." While many parents find this unarmed position difficult, it pays off if it helps your kids see you as fair and willing to listen.

Remember that the goal of your conversations isn't necessarily to seek agreement, but to communicate understanding. If your child suddenly announces "multiplication tables are stupid," or "nose rings are neat," you may be tempted to launch into a long-winded tirade to prove him wrong. You'll probably have more impact, however, by responding in a way that leads to dialogue. You can start by saying something like, "I had a hard time learning multiplication tables, too." Or, "I don't care for nose rings myself, but why do you like them?"

## THINK ABOUT YOUR CHILD'S EXPERIENCES IN TERMS OF SIMILAR ADULT SITUATIONS

This technique is helpful in situations where you're having trouble feeling empathy for your child. Perhaps he is distressed about something you consider trivial or childish. Somebody made a crack about his glasses when he got up in class to give a report, or he feels anxious about his first day at summer camp. Knowing he'll survive these trials (and many more), you may feel tempted to trivialize his concerns or ignore them. While this response may make *you* feel more comfortable, it's not going to help your child much. In fact, he may feel worse, knowing that his mom or dad thinks he's being silly.

One way to form a more sympathetic frame of mind is to translate your child's situation to adult terms. Think how you'd feel if you overheard a co-worker whispering something about your appearance just as you stood up to give a sales report. Remember how nervous you felt that first day on a new job.

In *Siblings Without Rivalry*, authors Adele Faber and Elaine Mazlish offer the following tip to help parents understand the jealousy a small child feels at the arrival of a new sibling: Imagine your spouse bringing home a new lover and announcing that all of you will now live happily together under one roof.

## DON'T TRY TO IMPOSE YOUR SOLUTIONS ON YOUR CHILD'S PROBLEMS

One of the quickest ways to short-circuit Emotion Coaching is to tell a child who's sad or angry how you would solve the problem at hand. To understand why, think about the way this ill-fated dynamic commonly occurs in marriage. A typical scenario goes something like this: The wife arrives home from the office, distraught over a disagreement she's had with a co-worker. Her husband analyzes the problem and, within minutes, outlines a plan for resolving it. But instead of feeling grateful for the advice, the wife feels worse. That's because he has given her no indication that he understands how sad and angry and frustrated she feels. He has only demonstrated how simply the problem can be solved. To her, this may imply that she's not too bright, or she would have come up with such a solution herself.

Imagine how much better the wife would feel if, instead of instant advice, her husband offers her a back rub. And as he massages her back, he simply listens while she describes the problem—and her feelings about the problem—in detail. With that done, she starts formulating her own solutions. Then, because she is trusting her spouse by now (and feeling great after the back rub) she might ask him for his opinion. In the end, the husband has a chance to offer his advice, and the wife has a solution she can hear. Instead of feeling put down, she feels empowered and supported by her partner.

This is how it works with parents and children as well. Parents may feel frustrated with kids' unwillingness to take unsolicited advice—especially considering the relative amount of wisdom and life experience parents have to share with their kids. But that's not the way children typically learn. To propose solutions before you empathize with children is like trying to build the frame of a house before you lay a firm foundation.

## EMPOWER YOUR CHILD BY GIVING CHOICES, RESPECTING WISHES

As adults, it's easy to forget how powerless children can feel. But if you look at the world through their eyes, you can see how much emphasis society puts on getting children to comply and cooperate. Most small children have very little control over their daily lives. Sleepy babies get whisked out of their cribs and carted off to daycare. Older children bolt at the sound of the schoolyard bell and form straight lines for attendance. Parents set rules like, "No dessert until you clean your plate." Or, "You're not leaving the house in *that* outfit." Then there's the classic: "Because I said so." Can you imagine making such controlling statements to a spouse or a friend?

I'm not saying that it's bad to require children to obey and cooperate. For the safety and health of children—and the sanity of parents—children should not be allowed to domineer the household. But I have observed how commonly parents dramatize their children's powerlessness by ignoring fairly trivial preferences and requests. This usually is not done in a mean way; rather, it's the result of parents being overly stressed and hurried. ("No, you can't play with your paints. We just cleaned up and there's no time to do it!")

Unfortunately for many kids, this heavy emphasis on cooperation means wishes and preferences are habitually ignored. Some children don't get the chance to make even the smallest choices—such as what to wear, what to eat, how to spend their time. Many such grow up without a strong sense of their own likes and dislikes. Some never learn how to make choices at all. All of this hinders a child's ability to act responsibly.

Children need practice weighing their options, finding solutions. They need to see what happens when they make choices based on their family's value system; what happens when they choose to ignore family standards. Such lessons are sometimes painful, but with Emotion Coaching, they can also be powerful opportunities for parents to offer guidance.

Parents can be assured that the earlier a child learns to express preferences and make wise choices, the better. Once a child reaches adolescence, with its increased freedom and accompanying risks, irresponsible decision making can be far more dangerous.

In addition to a sense of responsibility, giving children choices helps them to build self-esteem. A child whose parents constantly limit choice gets the message, "You're not only small; your desires don't matter very much." If this works, she may grow to be obedient and cooperative, but she will have very little sense of herself.

True, giving children choices and honoring their wishes takes time and patience. Recall that one researcher found preschoolers make an average of three demands per minute. Not all these requests require a response, but many requests come at a fairly trivial cost for parents. Your daughter wants you to fix her plate so the peas and potatoes don't touch. Your son wants to see Big Bird one more time before you turn the channel. Your daughter doesn't want you to buy the ice cream with nuts. Your son wants you to leave the hall light on. Amazing as it may seem, hearing and granting such wishes can have important long-term consequences. That's because children's preferences help them form their identities. When their wishes are granted, children get the message, "What I want matters after all; how I feel makes a difference." Your daughter can say to herself, "Yes, that's the way I like it. I'm the kind of child who doesn't like foods mixing on my plate. I have power to make this food yummy."

In time, such statements can be building blocks for assertions like "I'm the kind of kid who likes hard challenges on the monkey bars." Or, "I'm the kind of person who enjoys math."

So the next time your child makes a small request—no matter how silly or trivial it may seem to you at the time—try not to perceive it as a battle of wills. Instead, ask yourself whether it's really such a big deal that you can't honor it. The results may benefit your child, who uses such interactions to develop a sense of self.

## SHARE IN YOUR CHILD'S DREAMS AND FANTASIES

This technique is a great way to get on your child's wavelength, making empathy easier. It's particularly helpful when children express desires that are beyond the realm of possibility. Say, for example, that your teenager tells you he wants a new mountain bike, but you're not sure you can afford it. If you're like many parents, your first impulse may be to feel irritated. "After all," you want to tell him, "I just got you a new racing bike last year. Do you think I'm made of money?"

But imagine what might happen if you simply thought about his wish for a few moments and indulged in his fantasy. Then you might respond by saying, "Yeah, I can understand why you'd like to get a mountain bike. You like getting out on trails, don't you?" You could even take the fantasy further, adding: "Wouldn't it be great if all your friends had mountain bikes, too? Imagine if I could take a bunch of you camping for a week. We'd bring our tents and fishing gear and . . ."

From here you might explore the merits of camping trips with or without mountain bikes. You can still make the point that you're not going to spend money on the bike yourself, but you might also start brainstorming ways for your son to earn his own money to buy it. The important thing is that your son knows you have heard him and that you think he and his desires are okay.

## BE HONEST WITH YOUR CHILD

Most children seem to have a sixth sense about when their parents—particularly their fathers—are telling the truth. Therefore, Emotion Coaching must be more than the rote mouthing of phrases like, "I understand," or, "That would make me mad, too." You can *say* the right thing, but if your heart isn't in it, it won't draw you any closer to your child. In fact, fudging may cause you to lose credibility with your child, which can drive a wedge in your relationship. Be sure, therefore, that you truly understand your child before you say you do. If you're not sure whether you understand, simply reflect back what you see and hear. Ask a few questions. Try to keep the line of communication open. But by all means, don't fake it.

## READ CHILDREN'S LITERATURE TOGETHER

From infancy through adolescence, high-quality children's books can be a great way for parents and kids to learn about emotions. Stories can help children build a vocabulary for talking about feelings, and illustrate the different ways people handle their anger, fear, and sadness.

Well-chosen, age-appropriate books can even provide a way for parents to talk about subjects they may find difficult to address—subjects like "where babies come from" and "what happened to Grandpa when he died."

Television programs and movies can also be fuel for such family conversations. But I think books work better because the reader and listener can stop at any point and discuss what's happening in the story. Reading aloud also gives children a better sense that the family is participating in the storytelling, and so they may feel a greater investment in the narrative and its characters.

Well-written children's literature can also help adults get in touch with the emotional world of youngsters. One mother in our groups told of reading a story with her ten-year-old about a group of preteen girls who were sad when one member had to move away. Although it was just a simple story about a common situation, it touched the mother deeply as she remembered her own sense of loss moving cross-country when she was her daughter's age. Reminded of how passionate children's friendships can be in middle childhood, the mother better understood the significance of her daughter's own blossoming relationships.

Many parents, unfortunately, quit reading aloud to their children once the youngsters learn to read on their own. But others continue into the teen years, taking turns at reading increasingly sophisticated books. Like regular family meals, such habits provide assurance that parent and child will connect on a consistent basis to share something enjoyable.

The Appendix lists titles of good children's books that deal with emotions. Your child's teacher or librarian may also offer suggestions.

## BE PATIENT WITH THE PROCESS

To be effective as an Emotion Coach, you must allow your child time to express feelings without becoming impatient. If your child is sad, he may cry. If she is angry, she may stomp her feet. It may be uncomfortable for you to spend time with your child in this state. You may feel as though Trouble has become your middle name.

It helps, however, to remember that the goal of Emotion Coaching is to explore and understand emotions, not to suppress them. It may be easier in the short run to dismiss your child's negativity, ignore it, and hope that it will take care of itself. You can form the deluded philosophy that the mere passage of time will make things better. What you get for this attitude is less trouble in the short run, but more trouble in the long run. Problems are much harder to cope with after they have been neglected and your child has become emotionally distant.

In contrast, the rewards of parenting come from being attentive to our children's feelings. It is impossible to accept and validate a child's emotion at the same time you wish it would just go away. Acceptance and validation come instead from empathy—that is, feeling what your child is feeling in the moment.

As you empathize, see if you can experience your shared emotions as a physical sensation. I compare this to the way you might allow a rousing piece of music to stir up your emotions, making you feel excited, sad, passionate, inspired. You can choose to be with your child's feelings in the same way, allowing them to resonate within you. If you can do this, you'll be able to say from your heart, "It *is* sad that Daddy had to leave without you." "Being hit by a friend would make *me* angry, too." "I can see that you *hate* it when I correct you."

Remember also that you don't always need words to communicate understanding. Your willingness to sit quietly with a child as the two of you grapple with feelings speaks volumes. For one, it can indicate to your child that you take the matter seriously. It can also say that you agree that this is not an insignificant problem; it requires thought and attention.

As you sit together with an emotion, know that a hug or a back rub often says more than words—especially if the child is grappling with sadness or fear.

Sometimes a child may say she's not ready to talk about an issue and that should be respected, for the most part. Try to make a date to talk with her about the matter soon, however. Then make a note and pursue the issue as promised.

Once you dedicate yourself to being present with your child's emotions, you will find opportunities to connect with her in meaningful ways on a day-to-day basis. From a series of seemingly mundane incidents, you'll form an important, lasting bond. You'll become what my friend and developmental psychologist Ross Parke refers to as "a collector of moments." You'll recognize your interactions as precious opportunities and value aspects that others might miss. And when you look back, you'll see your relationship with your child as you would a treasured string of pearls.

## UNDERSTAND YOUR BASE OF POWER AS A PARENT

By "base of power" I mean the element in the parent-child relationship that makes it possible for parents to set limits on children's misbehavior—something all kids want and need. For some parents, the base of power is threats, humiliation, or spanking. Others, who are overly permissive, may feel they have no base of power at all. For Emotion-Coaching parents, the base of power is the emotional bond between parent and child.

When you are emotionally connected to your child, limit setting comes out of the your genuine reactions to your child's misbehavior. Your child responds to your anger, disappointment, and worries, so you don't have to resort to negative consequences such as spanking and time-outs to amplify your feelings. The respect and affection you and your child have for each other become your primary vehicle for limit setting.

Because respect and affection are so important to this equation, it's easy to see why it's crucial to avoid derogatory comments and humiliation when you correct your child's behavior. A child who has just been spanked or called sloppy, mean, or stupid is likely to be more interested in retaliating against his parents than in pleasing them.

If you have resorted to methods like humiliation and spanking in the past, you may wonder whether it's possible to shift your base of parental power to one that's rooted in shared positive feelings. I believe such change *is* possible, but it will take a lot of work. You will need to correct old patterns of disciplinary behavior, integrating Emotion Coaching into your interactions with your child. You will have to work hard at building a relationship that's based on trust rather than intimidation.

As you work to make this shift, it will help to keep these two of Haim Ginott's principles in mind: (1) All feelings are permissible; not all behavior is permissible. And, (2) The parent-child relationship is not a democracy; it is the parent who determines what behavior is permissible.

If your child is a teen or preteen, you can discuss such base-of-power issues directly, especially as they relate to rules. Try to arrive at rules (and consequences for breaking rules) through compromise and respectful discussion. Don't be afraid to be firm—especially when it comes to your child's safety and well-being. As a mature adult, you know better what behaviors are potentially dangerous. Keep in mind also that research shows children whose parents monitor their friends, activities, and whereabouts are less prone to risky behavior. They are less likely to fall into a deviant peer group, get in trouble with the police, abuse drugs, commit pranks and crimes, become promiscuous, and run away.

Some parents have more difficulty than others shifting to a more positive base of power. This is particularly true when trust, respect, and affection have faded from the parent-child relationship. Family therapy is often effective in such cases and I would encourage parents to consider this option. Don't be surprised if the therapist you choose wants to have individual sessions with your child. And be aware that the therapist may serve as your child's advocate in your "family court." It's hard to say how long it takes for family therapy to be effective. Like going to the dentist, much depends on how long problems have been ignored. But research shows that family therapists are developing reasonably effective methods of helping families to reestablish trust and communication. So there is a lot of reason for hope.

## BELIEVE IN THE POSITIVE NATURE OF HUMAN DEVELOPMENT

The more I learn about children, the more I believe that the natural course of human development is an incredibly positive force. By this, I mean that children's brains are naturally wired to seek security and love, knowledge, and understanding. Your child wants to be affectionate and altruistic. She wants to explore the environment, find out what causes lightning, what's inside a dog. He wants to know what is right and good, what is bad and evil. She wants to know about dangers in the world and how to avoid them. He wants very much to do the right thing, to become increasingly strong and capable. Your child wants to be the kind of person you will admire and love.

With all these natural forces are on your side as a parent, you can trust in your child's feelings and know that you are not alone.

## WHEN EMOTION COACHING IS NOT APPROPRIATE

IT'S HARD TO say with certainty how frequently a parent can use Emotion Coaching to build intimacy and teach coping skills. As children move through their days, learning to get along with others and to weather common crises, it seems their lives are rife with opportunity.

Still, Emotion Coaching should not be perceived as a panacea for every negative feeling that arises. For one, it requires some degree of patience and creativity, so parents need to be in a reasonably undistracted (if not calm) frame of mind to do it well. It also helps if children are in a relatively teachable state. Thinking strategically, you want to seize opportunities when your child is most likely to be receptive.

Clearly, there are situations when Emotion Coaching should be postponed. These include:

## WHEN YOU'RE PRESSED FOR TIME

Today's families spend much of their time together watching the clock, trying to get themselves off to daycare, school, and work on schedule. Although kids' emotions often surface during such stressful transitions, these are usually not ideal times for Emotion Coaching, which is a process. Kids are not robots and we can't expect them to move through emotional experiences according to an arbitrary timetable.

A businesswoman in one of our groups perfectly described the folly of trying to rush a child through Emotion Coaching. She was dropping her daughter off at daycare one morning on her way to an important client meeting. Arriving at the door to the daycare center, the four-year-old suddenly bolted. "My teacher Katie's not here," the girl told her mother. "I don't want to stay."

The woman looked at her watch and knew that she could spend only five minutes on the matter without being late. Mentally reviewing the steps to Emotion Coaching, she sat her daughter down and started working the problem. "You seem upset . . . Tell me what's going on . . . You feel uncomfortable because your favorite teacher is not here . . . I know how you're feeling . . . You feel sad about starting the day without her . . . I have to go soon . . . What can we do to help you feel more comfortable?"

Meanwhile, her daughter sat there, sputtering answers and fighting back tears. The minutes ticked by without a resolution. The girl seemed to sense her mother's urgency and the pressure only made matters worse. The more the mother probed, the more upset the daughter became. After twenty minutes of frustration, the woman finally gave up and pushed her sobbing daughter into the arms of the substitute teacher. Driving like a madwoman, she dashed to her appointment. "When I got there, my client was gone," the woman lamented.

Reflecting back, the mother saw her mistake. "I gave her a mixed message. I told her I was concerned and willing to help, but I was watching the clock and she knew it. That made her feel more abandoned than ever." In retrospect, the mother believes she should have simply told her daughter that her attendance at daycare that morning was nonnegotiable; that they would talk later about her "uncomfortable feelings." Then, leaving her daughter to her own emerging social skills and the able hands of the substitute teacher, she should have left for her appointment.

In an ideal world, we'd always have time to sit and talk with our kids as feelings come up. But for most parents, that's not always an option. It's important, therefore, to designate a time—preferably at the same period each day—when you can talk to your child without time pressures or interruptions. Families of small children often do this before bedtime or during a bath. With school-age kids and teenagers, heart-to-heart chats often happen as you share chores, such as washing dishes or folding laundry. Regularly scheduled drives to music lessons or other outings provide more opportunities. By designating such times for talking, you can be assured that issues won't be tabled indefinitely because of time constraints.

## WHEN YOU HAVE AN AUDIENCE

It's difficult to build intimacy and trust unless you have time alone with your child. That's why I recommend doing Emotion Coaching one on one, rather than in front of other family members, friends, or strangers. This way, you'll avoid embarrassing your child. Also, you'll both be freer to respond honestly without worrying about how the scene plays for others.

This advice is particularly important for families who are dealing with problems of sibling rivalry. One mom from our parenting groups described trying to intervene in one of her children's arguments using Emotion-Coaching techniques. "Whenever I started empathizing with one kid, the other one went ballistic," she said.

Under the best circumstances, an objective parent might be able to serve as a facilitator while two or more siblings work out their conflicts together. But Emotion Coaching involves a deeper level of empathy and listening. It's hard to empathize openly with two people in conflict without appearing to take sides. Therefore, Emotion Coaching usually works better if neither the parent nor the child has to worry about a sibling's perceptions, interruptions, or objections to what's being said. Given time alone with a sympathetic parent, a child might be more willing to let down his defenses and to share genuine feelings.

The key, of course, is to give each kid equal time. Again, designating a special time alone with each child on a regular basis can ensure that this will happen.

Parents should also be aware of how the presence of their own peers and adult relatives (especially grandparents) may affect their ability to empathize and listen to their children. It may be hard to accept your kids' feelings when you're listening to your own mother's (spoken or unspoken) judgment that "all that child needs is a good paddling."

If you're in a situation that calls for Emotion Coaching, but the presence of others makes it impossible, make a mental note to do it later. You may want to tell your child (without embarrassing her) that you plan to discuss this at another time. Then be sure to follow up.

## WHEN YOU ARE TOO UPSET OR TOO TIRED FOR COACHING TO BE PRODUCTIVE

Emotion Coaching takes a certain level of creative thought and energy. Intense anger or exhaustion can interfere with your ability to think clearly and communicate effectively. You may find you simply can't muster enough patience and willingness to empathize and listen well. In addition, there may be times when you're just too tired to deal effectively with your child's emotions. If this happens, postpone Emotion Coaching until you can get the rest or comfort you need to revitalize yourself. This may simply mean taking a walk, a nap, a hot bath, or getting out to a movie. If you find that exhaustion, stress, or anger is continually interfering with your ability to engage with your child, you may want to consider lifestyle changes. A mental health counselor or other health-care provider may help you sort through possible solutions.

## WHEN YOU NEED TO ADDRESS SERIOUS MISBEHAVIOR

Sometimes you have to engage in a kind of discipline that goes beyond the realm of simple limit setting addressed in Step No. 5 (page 100). When your child behaves in a way that upsets you and clearly goes against your moral code, you need to voice your disapproval. While you may understand the emotions underlying your child's misbehavior, this is not the time for empathy. Emotion Coaching to address the child's feelings that may have led to the misbehavior can be postponed. Right now it's a time to state unequivocally that you think your child's actions were wrong and why you feel that way. Expressing your feelings of anger and disappointment (in a nonderogatory manner) is appropriate. It is also appropriate to talk about your values.

This can be a difficult lesson for parents who are sensitive to (and feel responsible for) the reasons their kids may be acting out. If a couple embroiled in divorce proceedings, for example, finds out that their thirteen-year-old daughter has been skipping school, they may feel uncertain about how to react. Understanding the girl's confusion and sadness, they may be tempted to skip the reprimand and go straight to dealing with their daughter's feelings about the divorce. Making excuses for the child's misbehavior, however, only hurts her in the long run. The best approach is to deal with her truancy as one issue and her feelings about the divorce as another.

Let me give you another example, which happened under less extreme circumstances. When my daughter, Moriah, was three, we had a houseguest who stayed for several days. One evening after dinner, I found Moriah standing alone in the living room with a red marking pen in hand. Before her, on the side panel of our new, peach-colored sofa was a shocking red hieroglyphic.

"What happened here?" I asked, clearly incensed.

Moriah looked up at me, wide-eyed, still gripping the pen. "I have no idea," she sputtered.

Great, I thought. Now we had two problems: vandalism and lying. At the same time, I was aware that Moriah had not been a happy girl for the past twenty-four hours. I figured she was tired of her daily routines being disrupted by our guest's visit. My intuition told me she felt jealous because my wife and I had spent so much time talking with him instead of playing with her. That might explain why she had acted out with the red pen—behavior she knew was wrong. And the lie was easy to understand; she was trying to avoid my anger.

I knew I could respond empathetically, saying something like,

"Moriah, did you write on the sofa because you feel angry?" Then, I could add, "I understand that you feel angry, but writing on the couch is not okay."

But all of this would skirt the much larger moral issue at hand: Moriah's lie. So instead, I decided to postpone talking about Moriah's anger and jealousy. Tonight we would talk about the importance of telling the truth. I told her I was angry and upset about the marks on the couch, and I told her I was even more upset that she had lied about making the marks.

Eventually, after we got the stains off the couch, Moriah, her mom, and I did talk about the emotions that led to the incident. My wife and I listened and tried to understand Moriah's anger, loneliness, and frustration. We talked with our daughter about other ways she could have expressed her emotions, such as talking to us about them and asking for attention.

Even though I did not engage Moriah in Emotion Coaching immediately after the incident happened, I knew the emotional connection I had with my daughter as a result of previous coaching was at work in this situation. When a child has that strong emotional connection with a parent, the parent's upset, disappointment, or anger creates enough pain in the child to become a disciplinary event in itself. Your child's goal then becomes repairing the relationship, returning to a state where she feels emotionally close to you. She then learns that she must follow a certain code in order to experience that level of emotional comfort.

## WHEN YOUR CHILD IS "FAKING" AN EMOTION TO MANIPULATE YOU

I'm not talking about ordinary whining and tantrums here; I'm talking about the kind of simulated, inauthentic whining and tantrums that all children try to use at some time to get their way.

Let me give you an example: The five-year-old son of one of the couples in our parenting groups got angry when he found out they were leaving him with a baby-sitter the next night to celebrate their anniversary. After talking at length to Shawn about his feelings, they could reach no resolution. The boy kept insisting that the only way he would feel comfortable with the situation was to be included in the night out. Finally the couple gave up talking, leaving the boy wailing alone in his room. The crying continued for thirty minutes, with the parents periodically peeking in to check on him. At one point, the father said, he looked in to see Shawn peacefully building a tower of blocks while continuing his very genuine-sounding cry. "He looked at me and turned up the volume," the father described. "Then I saw him crack a smile. He knew the ruse was up."

Shawn had hoped that his crying would make his parents change their minds. That's not to say he wasn't still angry about being left with a baby-sitter. But for the parents to try to engage in empathetic listening and Emotion Coaching while the child was attempting to manipulate them with his emotions would have been fruitless. They had to make it clear to the boy that he wasn't going to control them with his crying. That's what the father did. He gently and firmly told the boy, "I know you are angry about this, but your crying is not going to make Mom and me change our minds. We are going to go out to dinner and you are going to stay with the baby-sitter." At that point, the boy finally understood that the situation was not negotiable and he stopped wailing. After a while, the father asked Shawn if he would like to try to think of ways to make the evening with the baby-sitter more enjoyable, such as planning games, preparing snacks, and so forth, and the boy agreed.

WHEN YOU DECIDE to postpone Emotion Coaching, make a commitment to yourself and to your child that you will get back to the issue soon. This is much different from the tactics used by the Dismissing or Disapproving parents described in Chapter 2. For them, ignoring emotion is their overriding style of parenting. They feel uncomfortable with strong emotions, and so they sidestep them entirely. I am simply proposing that you postpone your discussion until it's more likely to be productive.

If you do postpone talking about an issue, telling your child that you'll get back to it later, make sure you follow through. Failing to keep a promise made to a child is probably not as catastrophic as it's been made out to be in the media. Kids are very fair, very understanding, and they have lots of second chances to give. Still, keeping promises is a form of respect—one your child will reciprocate if you show a good example.

I also want to encourage parents to postpone Emotion Coaching only when they feel it's necessary. In general, you should give as much time to Emotion Coaching as you can. For some, this will mean relinquishing the belief that talking about feelings somehow "indulges" or "spoils" a child. As our studies show, Emotion-Coached kids become better behaved as they learn to regulate their emotions. Nor will focusing on negative emotions "make matters worse." If a child has a difficult problem, his parents should support him in learning to cope with it. If the problem at hand is insignificant, then talking about it certainly won't hurt.

Finally, I want to reiterate that Emotion Coaching should not be seen as some kind of magic formula that eliminates family conflict and the need for setting limits.

Emotion Coaching, however, can help you grow closer to your kids. It lays the groundwork for a collaborative relationship where you solve problems together. Your children will learn that they can trust you with their feelings. They'll know you're not going to criticize them or tear them down "for their own good." Nor will your kids carry that feeling familiar to many adults—that "I loved my dad a lot, but I could never really talk to him." When your children have a problem, they'll come to you because they know you offer more than platitudes and lectures. You really listen.

But the true beauty of Emotion Coaching is that its effects will last into your child's adolescent years. By then, your kids will have internalized your values and they'll reap the benefits that come with emotional intelligence. They'll know how to concentrate, how to get along with peers, and how to handle strong emotions. They'll also avoid the risks that fall to kids who don't have these skills.

## TEST YOUR EMOTION-COACHING SKILLS

Here's an exercise to test your ability to recognize children's feelings and parents' agendas in a variety of intense emotional situations. It will also give you a chance to practice Emotion-Coaching responses to children's negative feelings. Following each item, a "wrong" parental response is given. Then you are asked to guess what the parent's agenda and the child's feelings might be in this situation. And finally, you are asked to provide a new response that validates the child's feelings.

**Sample:** A child disappears in a large department store and the parents are very worried about the child. After a while, a clearly upset child is found by a store employee, who helps the child find the parent.

Wrong response: "You stupid child! I am so mad at you, I am never taking you shopping again."

Parent's agenda: The parent was scared and wants to keep the child safe and prevent this from happening again.

Child's feeling: Fear.

Right response: "You must have been so scared. I was scared, too. Come here and let me hold you for a while. Then let's talk over what happened."

1. A child comes home from school and says, "I'm never going back to that school again! The teacher yelled at me in front of my friends!"

Wrong response: "What did you do to make the teacher yell at you?"

Parent's agenda:

Child's feeling:

Right response:

2. In the bathtub, your child says, "I hate my brother. I wish he would be dead."

Wrong response: "That's a terrible thing to say. We don't talk that way in this house. You don't hate your brother. You love your brother. I never want to hear you say that again!"

Parent's agenda:

Child's feeling:

Right response:

3. At dinner your child says, "Yuk! I hate this food. I won't eat it."

Wrong response: "You will eat what we have and like it!"

Parent's agenda:

Child's feeling:

Right response:

4. Your child comes in from outside and says, "I hate those kids. They won't play with me. They are so mean to me!"

Wrong response: "If you weren't such a wimp they would want to play with you. Don't make such a big deal out of every little thing. You have to roll with the punches."

Parent's agenda:
Child's feeling:
Right response:


5. Your child says, "I wish you weren't taking care of me tonight. I wish that (fill in the blank) were taking care of me."

Wrong response: "What an awful thing to say! You're a thoughtless child."

Parent's agenda:
Child's feeling:
Right response:


6. Your child's friend is visiting. Your child says to the friend, "I don't want to share this toy with you. You can't play with it!"

Wrong response: "You're a selfish child. You have to learn to share!"

Parent's agenda:
Child's feeling:
Right response:


## ANSWERS

Although there are no single correct answers to this exercise, the following responses are typical of the Emotion-Coaching style of parenting. Notice how both "wrong" and "right" parental responses address the parent's agenda. But the "right" response provides the child with empathy and guidance.

1. Parent's agenda: The parent wants the child to succeed at school and be liked by the teacher. The parent is worried that the child is doing something wrong at school that will result in the teacher's disapproval.

Child's feeling: Embarrassment.

Right response: "That must have been so embarrassing for you."

2. Parent's agenda: The parent wants the two siblings to get along.

Child's feeling: Anger.

Right response: "I know your brother can really make you mad and upset sometimes. What happened?"

3. Parent's agenda: The parent wants the child to like the food that was prepared and the parent wants to avoid more cooking.

Child's feeling: Disgust.

Right response: "Today this food doesn't seem appetizing to you. What do you feel like eating?"

4. Parent's agenda: The parent wants the child to be able to get along with other children easily and not have his or her feelings hurt so easily.

Child's feeling: Sadness.

Right response: "That must have hurt your feelings. Tell me what happened."

5. Parent's agenda: The parent wants the child to be appreciative that he or she is spending time and effort to be with the child tonight.

Child's feeling: Sadness.

Right response: "You really miss (fill in the blank). I can understand that. I miss (fill in the blank) too."

6. Parent's agenda: The parent wants the child to share and to be more generous with guests.

Child's feeling: Anger.

Right response: "Sometimes it's hard to share a favorite toy. Let's put that toy away and take out some toys that you feel more comfortable sharing."

*Chapter 5*

---

# MARRIAGE, DIVORCE, AND
# YOUR CHILD'S EMOTIONAL
# HEALTH

---

ASK ADULTS WHOSE PARENTS WERE UNHAPPILY MARRIED to describe their childhood memories, and chances are you'll hear tales of sadness, confusion, false hope, and bitterness. They may remember how disorienting and painful it was to see their parents divorce. Or their folks may have been among those stalwart couples who were miserable in marriage, but determined to stick it out "for the sake of the kids." If so, you might learn about the pain of watching the two most important people in that young person's life hurt each other day in and day out.

It hardly matters whether a couple is married, separated, or divorced; when a mother and father display hostility and contempt for each other, their children suffer. That's because the tenor of a marriage—or divorce—creates a kind of "emotional ecology" for children. Just as a tree is affected by the quality of air, water, and soil in its environment, the emotional health of children is determined by the quality of intimate relationships that surround them. As a parent, your interactions with your child's other parent influence your child's attitudes and achievements, her ability to regulate her emotions, and her capacity for getting along with others. In general, when parents nurture and support each other, their children's emotional intelligence flourishes. But children who are constantly exposed to their parents' hostility toward each other may encounter serious risks.

While this can be disturbing news for parents who are experiencing marital conflict, there is hope—especially for parenting couples (married or divorced) who are motivated to improve their relationship. We now know that it's not interparental conflict itself that's so harmful to children, but the way in which parents handle their disputes.

We have also found that Emotion Coaching can have a buffering effect. That is, when parents can be present for their children emotionally, helping them to cope with negative feelings, and guiding them through periods of family stress, their children are shielded from many of the damaging effects of family turmoil, including divorce. To date, Emotion Coaching is the only proven buffer against these deleterious effects.

And finally, we have found that the road map for being a good parent is the same road map for improving a marriage. The same interpersonal style that Emotion-Coaching parents practice with their children—emotionally aware, empathetic, and open to joint problem solving—is a good style for their marriage. In addition to becoming better parents, they improve the relationship with their spouses.

Before we explore how the protective effect of Emotion Coaching works, it helps to understand the ways in which marital conflict and divorce affect kids.

## HOW MARITAL CONFLICT AND DIVORCE CAN HARM CHILDREN

THROUGH OUR OBSERVATION and laboratory work with families of small children, my research colleagues and I discovered that certain kinds of marital discord had profound effects on the children's physical and emotional health, as well as their ability to get along with peers. Our data show that children raised by parents whose marriages are characterized by criticism, defensiveness, and contempt are much more likely to show antisocial behavior and aggression toward their playmates. They have more difficulty regulating their emotions, focusing their attention, and soothing themselves when they become upset. In addition, the mothers of these children reported that the kids had an increased number of health problems such as coughs and colds. These children also seemed to be under more chronic stress, as shown by higher levels of catecholamines, which are stress-related hormones, in their urine.

To gauge how well the children related to their peers, we watched them during thirty-minute unsupervised play sessions in the children's homes. Each family had invited their child's best friend to participate as part of the experiment. To evaluate the sessions, we looked at how involved the children behaved with each other as they played. Did they, for example, spend a lot of time engaged in fantasy games that take a high degree of cooperation? Or were they more likely to spend their time in parallel play—that is, playing independently alongside each other with few attempts to collaborate?

We also watched for overtly negative behavior from the children we were studying—interactions such as arguing, threats, name calling, tattling, and physical aggression. When squabbles broke out, did the children try to find ways to resolve them, or did their conflicts cause their play to disintegrate? Previous research tells us such behavior can make an important difference in children's lives over the long term; negative and antisocial behavior is a major reason children are rejected by their peers in early childhood. We also know that a child's failure to form friendships is a leading indicator of a child's risk for psychiatric problems.

When we compared the data from these play sessions to the information we had gathered from the families in interviews and lab experiments described in Chapter 1, we found a strong connection between the marital relationships and the children's behavior with their friends. Children whose parents were distressed in their marriages played less collaboratively and had more negative interactions with their playmates than children whose parents were happily married.

Many other social scientists have made similar discoveries about behavior problems among children from troubled marriages. Taken together, the research shows that marital conflict and divorce can put children on a trajectory that leads to serious problems later on. Trouble may begin in early childhood with poor interpersonal skills and aggressive behavior, which leads to peer rejection. Parents, distracted by their own problems, have less time and attention for their children, so the kids drift, unsupervised, toward a more deviant peer group. By early adolescence, many children from disrupted families have stumbled into a whole hornet's nest of teenage woes, including failing grades, precocious sexual behavior, substance abuse, and delinquency. There's also some evidence, although it's not as strong, that children from families with a high degree of conflict and divorce experience more depression, anxiety, and withdrawal. One study, conducted by the University of Virginia's E. Mavis Hetherington, found that the rate of clinically significant mental health problems was nearly three times higher in teens from divorced homes than among teens in the general population.

Social scientists propose various theories for why young children from conflict-ridden families have more behavior problems and more difficulty with peer relationships. Some suggest that parents who are embroiled in disputes with their spouses or ex-spouses have less time and energy to spend with their children. Divorce and the conflicts leading up to divorce leave parents too exhausted, distracted, or depressed to be effective disciplinarians.

E. Mavis Hetherington describes the period during the parents' separation and divorce, as well as the first two years following the split, as a time of serious disruption of parent-child relationships. During this period, "a preoccupied and/or emotionally disturbed parent and a distressed, demanding child are likely to have difficulty supporting or consoling each other and may even exacerbate each other's problems," Hetherington writes. Divorced mothers with custody of their children "frequently become temporarily erratic, uncommunicating, nonsupporting, and inconsistently punitive in dealing with their children." And the problems don't necessarily evaporate with time: "Difficulty controlling and monitoring children's behavior is the most sustaining parenting problem faced by divorced mothers."

Such findings echo the parenting problems we observed among participants in our own study who were experiencing stress in their marriages. These parents were more likely to be cold and unresponsive toward their children. They were also less likely to set limits on their children's behavior.

Besides providing poor parenting, many experts believe that parents in stressed marriages provide poor examples to their children of how to get along with others. They believe children who see their moms and dads being aggressive, belligerent, or contemptuous toward each other are more likely to exhibit such behavior in their relationships with their friends. With no role models to teach them how to listen empathetically and solve problems cooperatively, the children follow the script their parents have handed them—one that says hostility and defensiveness are appropriate responses to conflict; that aggressive people get what they want.

While it certainly makes sense that children who live with the negative influence of parental conflict learn by example, I believe marital discord may also have a deeper, more profound impact on kids—especially for those who are exposed to severe family problems from the time they are very small. I think the stress of living with parental conflict can affect the development of an infant's autonomic nervous system, which, in turn, determines a child's ability to cope.

There's no arguing that children get distressed when they witness their parents fighting. Studies have shown that even small children react to adult arguments with physiological changes such as increases in heart rate and blood pressure. Research psychologist E. Mark Cummings, who has studied children's reactions to adult arguments, notes that kids typically respond by crying, standing motionless with tension, covering their ears, grimacing, or requesting to leave. Others have observed nonverbal stress reactions to anger in children as young as six months. While babies may not understand the content of their parents' disagreements, they know when something is amiss and react with agitation and tears.

My colleagues and I have observed this type of reaction among families in our own labs. One couple participating in our study of recently married parents, for example, brought their three-month-old daughter in for observation. Earlier interviews had revealed that the parents' relationship was extremely competitive and contentious—characteristics that became even more evident in this experiment. Instructed to play together with their baby, the father caught his child's gaze by jiggling her foot, while the mother started making cooing noises to steal the baby's attention away from dad. It appeared that this conflict confused and agitated the baby, who looked away and began to cry. At the same time, her heart started beating much faster. Then, despite her parents efforts to soothe her, it took an uncommonly long time for the baby's heart rate to return to normal.

Although our study of infants is not yet complete, such observations strengthen my belief that parental conflict can begin to take its toll in infancy—a time when the very pathways of a child's autonomic nervous system are developing. Whatever happens to that child emotionally during those first few months may have a significant and lifelong effect on a child's vagal tone—that is, the child's ability to regulate her nervous system. Whether an infant's cries are answered, whether she is frequently soothed or irritated by the sensations around her, whether the people who feed her, bathe her, and play with her are calm and engaging or anxious and depressed—all of this may make a difference in a baby's long-term ability to respond to stimuli, to calm herself, and recover from stress.

Such abilities become increasingly important as kids grow and begin to interact more with others. Children need to regulate their emotions in order to focus attention, to concentrate and learn, to read other people's body language, facial expressions, and social cues. Without these components of emotional intelligence, children enter social and academic settings at a disadvantage.

Our studies and many others have shown that children of divorced and high-conflict couples get lower grades. Teachers typically rate children from disrupted homes lower on scales of aptitude and intelligence. Writing in the *Atlantic Monthly*, social critic Barbara Dafoe Whitehead described the situation this way: "The great education tragedy of our time is that many American children are failing in school, not because they are intellectually or physically impaired, but because they are emotionally incapacitated. . . . Teachers find many children emotionally distracted, so upset and preoccupied by the explosive drama of their own family lives that they are unable to concentrate on such mundane matters as multiplication tables."

Children carry such problems into their adult years, as indicated by an analysis of the National Survey of Children by Nicholas Zill. Researchers interviewed a nationally representative sample of people in middle childhood, adolescence, and early adulthood. Zill looked at data from 240 young people whose parents had separated or divorced before they were age sixteen. Even after controlling for variations in parent education, race, and other factors, Zill found that eighteen- to twenty-two-year-olds from disrupted families were

twice as likely as other youths to show high levels of emotional distress or problem behavior. They were also nearly twice as likely as
those in nondivorced families to drop out of high school. And
among children who did drop out, those from disrupted families
were less likely eventually to earn a diploma or a GED.

But perhaps the most heartbreaking result of Zill's analysis has to
do with the connection between divorce and the parent-child relationship itself. His research shows that 65 percent of those young
people whose parents divorced reported poor relationships with
their fathers, compared to 9 percent of those whose parents did not
divorce. Zill comments that this result is "hardly surprising," given
the fact that a majority of separated or divorced fathers in this group
neither provided financial support nor maintained regular contact
with their children. At the same time, many children's bonds with
their mothers appeared to suffer from divorce as well. Some 30 percent from the divorced families reported poor relationships with the
mothers, compared with 16 percent in the nondivorced group.

"The fact that most grown children of divorce are alienated from
at least one parent and a substantial minority are alienated from
both is, we believe, a legitimate cause for societal concern," writes
Zill. "It means that many of these young people are especially vulnerable to influences outside the family, such as from boyfriends or
girlfriends, other peers, adult authority figures, and the media. Although not necessarily negative, these influences are unlikely to be
an adequate substitute for a stable and positive relationship with a
parent."

Other studies reveal how parental divorce affects people across
the life span. In a variety of studies, adults whose parents have divorced report having more stress, less satisfaction with family and
friends, greater anxiety, and a diminished ability to cope with life's
problems in general.

And now we find, according to results of a recent long-term investigation, that parental divorce may even cut a person's life short.
Begun in 1921 by psychologist Lewis Terman to test his theories of
heritability of intelligence, this study followed the psychosocial and
intellectual development of some 1,500 gifted California children,
checking on them every five to ten years. To find out how social
stresses affect longevity, Howard Friedman of the University of Cal-

ifornia at Riverside recently checked the death certificates of Terman's participants, half of whom had died. In 1995, Friedman reported that those participants whose parents divorced before they were age twenty-one died four years earlier than participants whose parents remained together. (By contrast, he found that a parent's death during a participant's childhood had little impact on life span. This is consistent, he notes, with other research that shows that parental divorce and separation has a bigger influence on psychological problems later on than does the death of a parent.) Friedman also found that children of divorced parents were more likely to become divorced themselves, although the participants' own divorces did not necessarily account for their shorter life span. Friedman concludes that parental divorce is a key event in the social fabric of young people's lives for predicting their premature deaths.

With so much evidence pointing to the harmful effects of divorce on children, unhappily married parents may wonder whether it's best to stay in a truly miserable and undeniably hopeless marriage for their children's welfare. Our research, and that of others, answers this question with a definite and resounding no. That's because certain kinds of marital conflict can have the same deleterious effects on children as divorce. In other words, it's not necessarily the divorce that hurts kids, but the intense hostility and bad communication that can develop between unhappily married mothers and fathers and may continue after the divorce. Some marital problems, including those where the husband withdraws emotionally from his family, are associated with children developing what psychologists call "internalizing" problems—the kids become anxious, depressed, introverted, and withdrawn. Hostility and contempt between spouses, on the other hand, is linked to kids becoming aggressive with their peers.

Given that staying together in an ailing marriage and divorcing can have equally harmful effects on children, is there any proven way for unhappily married couples to protect their kids? Our data shows there is. The way to buffer children is through Emotion Coaching.

## PROTECTING YOUR CHILD FROM THE NEGATIVE EFFECTS OF MARITAL CONFLICT

WITH SO MUCH evidence that children can be harmed by strife between their mothers and fathers, some parents may wonder whether their goal should be to ban all forms of marital conflict, or at least to keep disagreements hidden from the kids. Not only would this be a bad idea; it would be impossible. Conflict and anger are normal components of everyday married life. Couples who can openly express their inevitable differences and work through them have happier relationships in the long run. And, as we have learned, parents who acknowledge negative emotions are in a better position to help their children cope with their own feelings of anger, sadness, and fear.

In addition, studies show that children may benefit from witnessing certain kinds of family conflict, particularly when their parents disagree in a respectful way and when it's clear that the parents are working constructively toward a resolution. If children never see the adults in their lives get angry with one another, disagree, and then settle their differences, they are missing crucial lessons that can contribute to emotional intelligence.

The key is to manage conflict with your child's other parent so that it can become a positive example rather than a harmful experience for the child. Obviously, this is easier said than done—especially considering the way only spouses (and ex-spouses) can ignite each other's emotions. Still, recent research provides some clues for how parents can relate to each other in a way that protects and benefits their children.

### PRACTICE EMOTION COACHING IN YOUR MARRIAGE

Our research into the emotional needs of children makes it clear that kids are happiest and most successful when they are listened to, understood, and taken seriously by their parents. But what effects do such habits have on the parents themselves and on their marriages?

To find the answer to that question, my colleagues and I looked at the marriages of the parents in our study we had identified as

Emotion Coaches. (These are the men and women who are aware of their emotions as well as those of their children. They are inclined to use their kids' negative emotional moments as opportunities to listen. They display empathy with their kids, set limits, and offer them guidance on how to cope with negative emotions and how to solve problems.)

In addition to learning about the Emotion Coaches' lives as parents, we gathered in-depth information about their married lives. In lengthy interviews, we learned about the history of their marital relationships and their philosophies of marriage. In lab experiments, we observed them working out areas of conflict. And by checking in with them over an eleven-year period, we learned how many had divorced, how many had considered divorce, and how many were still happily married.

What we found is, Emotion Coaching not only protects these couples' children, it protects their marriages as well. Compared to the other parents in our study, Emotion Coaches were more satisfied and stable in their marriages. They showed more affection, fondness, and admiration for each other. When these couples talked about their philosophies of marriage, they were more likely to emphasize the value of companionship. They talked more in terms of "we-ness," viewing their lives together as a joint undertaking. They were more validating, less belligerent, and less contemptuous toward each other. The husbands were less apt to stonewall, or shut down during heated exchanges. They were more likely to express the belief that couples need to discuss their negative feelings, get problems out in the open, and deal with conflict rather than avoid it. These couples were less prone to see their lives together as chaotic. They were more likely to say they felt that the pain and struggle of making a marriage work is worth it.

Considering these findings, one might wonder which comes first: a happy marriage or the social skills needed to be a good Emotion Coach to your children. At this point in our research, it's hard to say. On one hand, it's probably easier for parents to devote their attention, time, and emotional energy to their children when their marriages are happy and stable. On the other hand, adults who are adept at listening, empathizing, and problem solving may use these skills equally well with their spouses and their kids—all to a good outcome. Until more research is done we can't say with certainty which factor drives the other, but I'm inclined to believe the latter is the primary force. That is, those who are emotionally attendant to their children are also there for their spouses and this behavior is good for the marriage.

I base this hypothesis on work we've done that shows what kind of marital interactions predict the stability of a marriage. This research is described in depth in my book *Why Marriages Succeed or Fail*. Suffice it to say here that if you take the elements of Emotion Coaching we explored in Chapter 3 (emotional awareness, empathetic listening, problem solving, and so forth) and use them with your spouse, you're likely to see some happy results.

We saw this demonstrated to some degree among mothers and fathers who participated in our parenting sessions. Ann, for example, reported that helping her two-year-old son to recognize his emotions has made her more aware of her own feelings. This, in turn, has encouraged her and her husband to practice more empathy and validation in their own relationship.

"It's crazy-making not to use validation," says Ann, who works as an artist. "If I say, 'I got a rejection letter today and I'm disappointed,' I don't want to hear my husband respond, 'Well, what did you expect? They are all too busy to deal with your work right now.' It's better to hear, 'I can see that you are disappointed about getting a negative response.' " Now aware that their son is not the only family member who needs this kind of nurturing and understanding, Ann and her husband are becoming Emotion Coaches for each other as well.

## AVOID THE FOUR HORSEMEN OF THE APOCALYPSE

As part of our long-term research into families and emotion, we discovered that couples who are unhappily married or headed for divorce typically go through a certain downward spiral of interactions, emotions, and attitudes that leads to the disintegration of their marriages. This cascade usually happens in four predictable steps, which I refer to as "The Four Horsemen of the Apocalypse." Like harbingers of disaster, each horseman paves the way for the next, eroding communication and causing partners to focus increasingly on the failure of their spouses and their marriages. Listed in order of their relative danger to the relationship, the four horsemen are: criticism, contempt, defensiveness, and stonewalling.

Not surprisingly, we found these same four elements to be harmful to the couples' children. In other words, when a child's environment is contaminated by her parents' critical, contemptuous, defensive, and stonewalling behavior toward each other, the child is more likely to suffer the damaging effects of marital conflict.

The good news is that we can now use these findings to recommend ways for parents to improve their relationship with each other, and thereby protect their children from harmful outcomes. Below you'll find advice for dodging the horsemen—even as you and your spouse are trying to sort through contentious issues. While this advice is directed at married couples, it may also be useful for couples who are separated or divorced but need to come together over issues involving their children.

HORSEMAN NO. 1: Criticism. By criticism, I mean making negative remarks about your partner's personality, usually in a way that assigns blame. On the surface, criticism may seem a lot like complaining, and complaining can be healthy for a relationship, especially when one spouse feels his or her needs aren't being met. But there's a crucial difference between complaints and criticism. Complaints are aimed at a specific behavior, while criticism attacks a person's character. Here are some examples of each.

COMPLAINT: "When you spend so much on clothes, I worry about our finances."

CRITICISM: "How could you spend so much on clothes when you know we have bills to pay? You act so vain and selfish."

COMPLAINT: "I feel lonely when you go out with friends on Friday nights instead of coming home."

CRITICISM: "You are so irresponsible, going out every weekend and leaving me home with the kids. You obviously don't care about your family."

COMPLAINT: "I wish you wouldn't drop your clothes on the floor. It makes the bedroom look so messy."

CRITICISM: "I'm so tired of picking up after you. You are inconsiderate and sloppy."

WHILE A COMPLAINT simply states the facts, criticism is often judgmental, suggesting the word "should." It implies that one's partner is hopelessly flawed. For example, instead of saying, "I wish you'd buy strawberry ice cream sometimes," a spouse might say: "Why do you always buy chocolate mint? You should know by now that I hate that flavor."

Betrayal is another common theme. Instead of, "I wish you hadn't arrived late with the kids to my mother's party; she was disappointed," a spouse might say: "I trusted you to get the kids to my mother's house in time for the party, but you were late again. I should have known you'd ruin another family celebration."

And criticism is often expressed in global terms: "You *never* help with housework." "You *always* run up the phone bill."

Criticism is often an expression of pent-up frustration and unresolved anger. One spouse "suffers in silence" while the other remains oblivious to the escalating irritation. When the silent one can't repress negative feelings any longer, he or she "blows up" with a slew of grievances. The result may be a technique I call "kitchen sinking." That is, the critic strings together a whole batch of unrelated complaints, like this: "You're always late picking me up from work. You never spend enough time with the kids. You don't even care about your appearance anymore. And when was the last time we went out together?" The barrage is so universal and overwhelming, the recipient can only interpret it as a personal affront. He or she may feel stunned, ambushed, hurt, and victimized—all of which opens the path for the arrival of the second and more dangerous horseman: contempt.

How do you avoid this harmful type of criticism? Address conflicts and problems as they arise. Don't wait until you're so angry or hurt you can't take it anymore. Express your anger or displeasure in specific ways and keep it directed at your partner's actions rather than his or her personality or character. Try not to place blame. Focus on the present and refrain from making global claims. Avoid these words when stating a complaint: "You should have . . ." "You always . . ." "You never . . ."

Our studies show wives criticize more than husbands do. This is partly because women seem to see it as their job to bring problems to the couple's attention. Husbands, on the other hand, are more likely to deal with conflict only when they have to. This can be an unfortunate combination because the wife's criticism often results from the husband's lack of response to her anger and irritability. When a wife complains but can't get a decent response from her husband, her anger will inevitably escalate to criticism. Husbands can help prevent this by seeing their wives' anger as a resource for improving the marriage. When she gets angry, she is simply putting her complaint "in italics." The secret is for husbands to accept and respond to their wives' anger before it escalates to criticism.

HORSEMAN NO. 2: Contempt. Contempt is much like criticism, but it's taken to a further extreme. A spouse who has contempt for his or her partner actually *intends* to insult or psychologically wound that person. Contempt often comes from feeling disgusted or fed up with your spouse, disapproving of his or her behavior, and wanting to get even. When you are feeling contemptuous, you fill your mind with demeaning thoughts—my spouse is ignorant, repulsive, inadequate, an idiot. In marriage, the longer you hold on to such thoughts, the harder it becomes to remember what attributes you found attractive in your spouse in the first place. With time, compliments, loving thoughts, and tender gestures go out the window. Kind acts and positive feelings are overrun by negative emotions and nasty exchanges.

Common signs that contempt has infected a marriage include insults, name calling, and hostile forms of humor, such as mockery and ridicule. One spouse might respond to another's expression of anger in dismissive, demeaning ways, such as correcting the angry partner's grammar. Body language can reveal that partners don't find each other worthy of respect or trust. A wife might roll her eyes when her husband is talking. A husband might sneer with disgust.

Once the horseman of contempt has made himself comfortable in your marriage, it takes real vigilance to drive him away. It can be done, however, if partners are willing to change their thoughts, words, and actions toward each other. This begins by listening to the internal script each of us carries in our minds. When you hear your-self rehearsing insulting or vengeful thoughts about your partner, imagine erasing or deleting such thoughts. Replace them with more soothing ideas such as, "This is a bad moment, but things aren't al-ways like this." Or, "Although I may feel upset (disappointed, angry, sad, hurt), my partner has good qualities worth remembering."

Keep in mind that you choose whether to assign negative or posi-tive motives to your spouse's behavior. If your partner fails to take out the garbage, for example, your beliefs can go one of two ways. You can tell yourself: "She thinks handling trash is below her. She's such a prima donna that she waits for me and everybody else in her life to clean up her messes." But you can also say: "She didn't take out the trash because she didn't notice it was full. She probably had her mind on something else. Maybe she'll take care of it after a while." Notice that the positive response is focused on the current, specific issue of the wife's behavior regarding today's trash. It doesn't use the incident as evidence with which to seal a life sentence.

Although it may be difficult, try letting go of the idea that you need to win arguments with your spouse in order to prove an upper moral hand. Consider whether it might be better to simply forfeit fights from time to time.

Because contempt can erode admiration and affectionate feel-ings, the antidote is to generate more positive, loving thoughts about your spouse. Some couples find it helpful to reflect on the rea-sons they fell in love in the first place. Perhaps you thought she was funny, smart, sexy. Maybe he struck you as a kind, strong, fun-loving man. Spend some time with your memories. Look at old photos to-gether if that's helpful. Take time alone together to nurture and re-store your relationship. Doing so could help you turn the tide before the next horseman arrives.

HORSEMAN NO. 3: Defensiveness. When a spouse feels attacked by contemptuous insults, it's only natural for him or her to become defensive. Still, defensiveness spells big trouble in a marriage because spouses don't listen to each other when they be-lieve they're under siege. Instead, they often react by denying re-sponsibility ("It's not my fault Jason's in trouble at school. You're the one who babies him.") Or, they make excuses for their prob-lems. ("I would have been at Katie's recital, but I had to work late.")

Cross-complaining is another common form of defensiveness. (He protests her spending, so she comes back by complaining that he ought to earn more.) So is the "yes, but . . ." response, where agreements are transformed into resistance with the turn of a phrase. ("Yes, we need counseling, but it won't do any good.")

Sometimes people try to defend themselves by simply repeating the same point over and over again. It doesn't matter what logic or additional information their spouses offer; the speaker simply keeps hammering away with the same point.

Defensiveness can also be expressed with tone of voice or body language. Whining is classic, implying that the speaker feels he is an innocent victim and not responsible for solving the problem at hand. Arms folded across the chest signify when someone has his guard up. A woman may touch her neck, as if fiddling with a necklace.

While feeling defensive is certainly understandable once a relationship has become contemptuous, it is also counterproductive to saving the marriage. That's because these and other types of defensiveness shut down lines of communication.

The key to letting go of defensive communication is to hear your partner's words not as an attack but as useful information that is being expressed in very strong terms. Obviously, this is easier said than done. But imagine what's possible once disarmament begins. Your partner lobs an insult your way, and instead of denying what's being said and hurling another insult in his or her direction, you find some kernel of truth in the statement and simply reflect on it for a moment. You might respond, "I never realized you felt so strongly about this. Let's talk about it some more." Your spouse is likely to be shocked at first, perhaps even distrustful of your reaction, and this may cause tensions to escalate. But over time, as you lay down weapons and armor, your partner is likely to see that you really mean for things to be different. You care about the relationship and you want your life together to be more peaceful.

HORSEMAN NO. 4: Stonewalling. If partners can't reach a truce—and if they continue to allow criticism, contempt, and defensiveness to rule their relationship—they are likely to meet the fourth horseman: stonewalling. This happens when one partner simply shuts down because the conversation has become too intense. In essence, one partner becomes like a stone wall, offering no indication that he hears and understands what the other partner is saying.

In our studies, 85 percent of the stonewallers were men—not surprising, since men seem to have a more extreme physiological response to marital stress and thus are more inclined to want to flee from it. This effect could be due to basic sex differences in physiology, or it could be due to the fact that men are more likely than women to dwell on thoughts that maintain distress when they are not with their spouses. When interviewed about their behavior, many of the stonewalling men saw their silence as "neutral," and not as something that could harm their marriages. The men didn't understand that their wives were often upset by their quiet, unresponsive attitudes, that they saw their husbands' behavior as smugness, lack of interest, or disapproval. The men felt it was better not to speak, because speaking might risk escalating tensions. Regardless of the stonewallers' positive intentions, studies show that habitual silence in the face of marital distress causes problems. Unless both partners are willing to talk, problems go unresolved and isolation worsens. Men withdraw when things become emotionally heated. Women tend more than men to take their emotional cues from the social environment rather than from what they feel physically. This may be one reason why women are more likely than men to stay in a failing marriage even when it is detrimental to their health.

For partners who are aware they are stonewalling and want to change, I recommend making a conscious effort to give your spouse more feedback during discussions. Even the simple act of nodding or murmuring "um-hm" during a conversation lets the speaker know he or she is being heard. Such validation can help improve the relationship. From here, the stonewaller can graduate to higher levels of effective listening, such as reflecting back to your partner what you are hearing.

Because physiological responses to stress may play a key role, spouses who want to stop stonewalling and start communicating may wish to explore new ways to stay calm while discussing hot topics with their partners. Some couples we've worked with have actually kept track of their pulse during arguments, which proved to be useful. When these couples found their heart rates had climbed to more than twenty points over their normal resting rates, they would take a break from the discussion. Then they would return to the issue later on when they were feeling more relaxed. For couples who would like to try this method, I recommend that you get back to the discussion within a half hour or so, which usually gives you enough time to recover from overarousal, without running the risk of dropping the issue altogether and impeding progress toward a better relationship. What you do with your tension and thoughts during this interim period is important. Deep breathing, relaxation, or aerobic exercise may be calming. Let go of vengeful or distressing thoughts about your partner during this time, if possible. Concentrate instead on positive, soothing, optimistic messages.

More information about staving off the four horsemen and improving your marital relationship can be found in my book *Why Marriages Succeed or Fail*. The crucial message for parents is that children suffer from the very same elements that are most likely to bring a marriage down. But if parents—even divorcing parents—can work together to improve their communication, their children will benefit.

## MANAGE YOUR MARITAL CONFLICT

In addition to practicing Emotion Coaching with your spouse, there is some very practical advice parents can follow to further protect their kids from the negative impact of marital disputes. The idea is to manage marital conflict so that your children don't become enmeshed in your problems or feel that they are somehow responsible for them. Protecting kids also requires having the kind of open communication with them that's inherent in Emotion Coaching. In addition, it's important to have trustworthy sources of social support for your children beyond your immediate family.

**Don't use your children as weapons in marital conflict.** Perhaps it's because parents recognize the precious value of their relationships with their children that angry spouses sometimes feel tempted to use those relationships to hurt each other. Divorced couples may try to restrict each other's ability to see the kids. This technique is particularly common among mothers who feel betrayed and powerless, who feel as though access to the children is the only leverage they have left in the marital relationship. The problem is exacerbated when the noncustodial fathers fail to help support their children, which makes mothers feel even more justified in keeping the children away.

Angry parents may also attempt to hurt their spouses or exspouses by turning their children's affections against the other. This can be done by saying damaging things (true or false) about the other parent or asking the child to choose sides in a marital dispute.

I believe that such attempts at purposely alienating a child from his or her other parent are among the most harmful things couples in conflict can do to their kids. Such acts can create a chronic source of agonizing conflict for the child who loves both parents, wants to be loyal to both, and feels obliged to protect each from the other's attacks. Continually involving children in marital disputes can make them feel as though they are somehow responsible for the family rift and therefore responsible for repairing it. Obviously, there is little a child can or should do to keep his parents' marriage together. This leaves the child feeling powerless, confused, and discouraged.

Most children need the love and support of both parents, particularly when they are trying to cope with the turmoil of their parents' conflicts. When one parent uses a child as a political football to hurt the other, it's the child who loses.

My advice to parents who find themselves in long-term battles with their spouses is to perform a "marriage-ectomy" on their family life. By this I mean that they should separate in their minds the two roles of parent and embattled spouse. Then, as parents, they should do everything within their power to help their children feel secure and well loved by both mother and father, even if that means giving up some power and authority to the spouse.

Parents in conflict should refrain from talking about the spouse in a critical or blaming way, since this may damage the child's relationship with that other parent or cause her to feel disloyal, guilty, and further stressed. If you can do so honestly, focus instead on the constructive aspects of your conflicts. When possible, tell your child that your disagreements are helping Mom and Dad sort through their differences and that the two of you are working on solutions.

**Don't allow your kids to get in the middle.** It's not unusual for children in high-conflict marriages to try to act as a mediator between Mom and Dad. Some researchers theorize that this is all part of the child's attempt to regulate his or her emotions. The children feel frightened by the turmoil in the family and are desperate to do something about it, so they take on the role of amateur marriage counselor and referee. But holding together a family is far too strenuous for any child and will only lead to additional problems.

If you sense that your child is trying to be a mediator between you and your spouse, take it as a sign that the level of conflict in your home is much too high. For the well-being of your child, you must de-escalate the battle. Here's where the techniques of Emotion Coaching can be of great benefit. Use them to find out what your child is feeling and to empathize. If you have a younger child, let her know that it's not her responsibility to take care of her parents. Tell her this is something grown-ups need to work out by themselves and that all of you will be okay. With an older child, your talk can be more sophisticated, but try conveying the same message— that conflicts between Mom and Dad are not her responsibility to resolve.

You can acknowledge that it's upsetting to hear Mom and Dad arguing, but that sometimes it's necessary for parents to disagree in order to work through problems. Again, assure your child, if you can, that Mom and Dad are trying to find a way to make things better.

By the same token, let your child know that he or she is not the source of problems between you and your spouse. Research shows that a child old enough to understand the content of his parents' fights will experience more stress when witnessing an argument that's about the child himself. When this happens, he is likely to experience feelings of shame, self-blame, and fear of being drawn into the dispute. Under such circumstances, you might say, "Mom and Dad have different ideas about what to do in this situation. But it's not your fault that we don't agree."

To further prevent children from becoming entangled in marital conflict, don't ask them to serve as a go-between regarding issues of conflict. Imagine the stress a child must feel if asked to carry messages so loaded that his own parent doesn't want to deliver them in person. ("You tell your father that I don't want him picking you up from school without asking me first.")

Nor should a child be asked by one parent to withhold sensitive information from the other. Such practices serve as a model for deception in family relationships and only prove to your child that you and other family members can't be trusted. Also, children need to feel that they can talk to their parents about anything that's bothering them without fear that doing so would betray one parent's confidence. And finally, children need to feel that despite Mom and Dad's disagreements, the two adults are working together in the child's best interest. Asking a child to keep secrets undermines all of this.

*Let your kids know when conflicts are resolved.* Just as children are distressed by seeing their parents argue, so, too, are they soothed by knowing Mom and Dad have reached a resolution. Studies conducted by University of West Virginia professor E. Mark Cummings showed that children often displayed aggression and distress in reaction to seeing adults argue. But their reactions were much calmer if they understood that the adults had solved their differences. In addition, Cummings found that the degree of resolution mattered to the children. For example, the kids responded more positively when they actually witnessed adults apologizing to each other, or working out a compromise. The children did not have as positive a reaction to more subtle resolutions such as adults' simply changing the subject, or one adult's submission to the other. Silence between the adults or continued, open fighting produced the highest negative response from the children.

In addition, Cummings found that the emotional content of the resolution is important to children. In other words, they can tell if an adult is expressing an apology in an angry way or agreeing to a compromise without enthusiasm. Very young children, of course, may have trouble understanding abstract ideas about resolution and forgiveness. For them, it may be beneficial for their parents to give some physical cues that a resolution has been reached. A warm hug between Mom and Dad, for example, lets kids know that their parents are getting back on an even keel.

*Establish networks of emotional support for your children.* When parents experience a high degree of marital stress, it's not unusual for older children—especially teenagers—to disengage from their families and seek emotional support in other places. They may start spending more time with peers or on hobbies. They may attach themselves to the families of friends or relatives who do not have so many problems. While a child's withdrawal from his or her own family may be distressing, it can also be a positive coping mechanism for the child, provided that the people and activities they choose are positive influences in their lives.

Unfortunately, that's not the case for many children. Some kids don't have responsible adults in their lives to whom they can turn. Nor do they have good access to constructive outlets such as sports, academic activities, or the arts. When this is the case, kids often fall prey to unwholesome influences. As research shows, children from unstable homes are at a particularly high risk for being drawn into deviant peer groups and delinquent behavior.

It's important, therefore, to pay more, not less attention to your child's friends and activities during periods of family strife. Find out how he is spending his time and with whom. Stay in touch with the parents of his friends and do what you can to monitor and supervise the kids' activities. Talk to your child's teachers and counselors to let them know that your family is experiencing some stress. Tell them you would appreciate their support and a watchful eye over your child. Do what you can to ensure that your child has other trustworthy adults around him—coaches, teachers, aunts and uncles, neighbors, grandparents, and friends' parents—whom he can turn to for nurturing and support.

Although younger children don't have the mobility and independence to seek emotional support outside the home during times of family crisis, that doesn't mean they don't need such refuge as well. Again, talk with your child's teachers and child-care providers. Let them know when the family is going through a particularly tough time and ask them to provide your child with a little extra patience and nurturing given the circumstances. Visit often with other families, perhaps within your own extended family, so that your children can experience a sense of belonging and emotional support.

*Use Emotion Coaching to talk about marital conflicts.* If ever there is a time to talk to your children about their feelings, it is when marital conflict erupts at home. Although it may be difficult for parents who are feeling sad or angry over conflicts with their spouses to find the emotional energy to talk to their children about it, chances are the kids are also feeling bad and need some guidance in handling those emotions.

Set aside some time when you are feeling relatively calm and can talk to your child about his or her reactions to stress in the household. You might begin by saying something like, "I noticed you got really quiet and went in your room when Daddy and I were arguing. It makes me wonder if you found our argument upsetting." Encourage your child to talk about the sadness, fear, or anger he may feel. Listen empathetically as he talks and help him to label his emotions. You may be able to uncover fears in your child that you weren't previously aware of. Perhaps he's afraid that if you and your spouse separate, he'll never see one of you again. Maybe he wonders where he would live, how just one parent would be able to provide for him. Maybe he's afraid that he somehow caused the problems and so he's feeling guilty or distressed about that. Or, maybe he's not certain what he's afraid of; he just feels that something bad is happening and he's anxious not knowing what's going to happen next. Whatever fears he expresses, you can let him know that even though Mom and Dad aren't getting along, the two of you will always love him and care for him. Perhaps you're in the position to reassure him that even though you and your spouse are having problems, separation or divorce is not a consideration. On the other hand, you may indeed be planning to separate and this can be a time to tell him about those plans. Either way, you can assure him that the problems aren't his fault and that it's not his responsibility to fix them. Tell him that Mom and Dad are working on finding the best solution for everybody and that you'll continue talking to him about what's going on.

After explaining the situation and helping your child to express his feelings about it, you can use this time to help him find ways of coping with the sadness and anger he may feel. Options may include seeing a professional counselor who helps kids deal with family problems, or joining a support group for children whose parents are divorcing. Children may also find solace in keeping a journal, drawing, or other forms of artistic expression. Ask him for his ideas about how he might feel soothed. Don't expect miracles, however. Our research showed that even though Emotion-Coached kids from ailing marriages fared better than other children through their parents' divorces, they experienced just as much sadness as children who were not coached. Under such circumstances, the best a parent can do may be to assure a child that his sadness is normal, warranted, and understood.

Just as Emotion Coaching can serve a family well through marital conflict and divorce if it happens, Emotion Coaching may continue to be of benefit later on, should you need to deal with other resulting issues such as the introduction of stepparents or conflicts over custody matters. A divorced mother who suspects her daughter feels anxious about plans for remarriage, for example, can use techniques of Emotion Coaching to talk about this sensitive issue. She might say, for example, "You seem kind of distracted lately. Are you worried about what it's going to be like after the wedding?" Or, "Lots of times kids feel uneasy about stepdads moving into their houses. They're afraid they won't like their stepdad. Or they're afraid that if they do like their stepdad, their real dad is going to be mad. Do you ever have feelings like that?"

Talking with children about their feelings regarding marital conflict is rarely easy. You may wonder how to begin the conversation or you may worry about how the child will respond. Perhaps it will help to keep in mind that by bringing up the subject, you are demonstrating your desire and willingness to stay close. Remember Nicholas Zill's heartbreaking findings on the long-term aftermath of divorce—that adult children who saw their parents' marriages dissolve report far more alienation from their parents years later than those whose parents' marriages were stable. Although we don't have data yet from our studies to tell us how Emotion-Coaching families who divorce are weathering the passage of adolescence, perhaps we'll find that this style of communication makes a difference in their relationships with their children long-term. Perhaps Emotion Coaching will allow parents and children to form and maintain a lasting bond—one that can be sustained into adulthood despite all the turmoil and changes brought about by marital conflict and divorce.

**Stay engaged in the details of your children's everyday lives.** The secret to buffering kids from the negative effects of marital conflict is to stay emotionally available to them. This requires paying attention to the everyday, mundane incidents that give rise to their emotions. Such issues may have very little to do with your marital problems. Life goes on for kids even when their parents are distracted by adult issues. Small children, for example, might be feeling anxious about a new baby-sitter, or fearful of sleeping in a "big-boy bed" for the first time. For an older child, issues could range from frustration over math lessons to worries about a classroom crush. If parents can muster the energy and focus to practice Emotion Coaching with their children over such matters—despite the stresses of marital crisis—they are doing their children a great service. Kids need their parents to be emotionally close, and they especially need them close during times of family upheaval.

*Chapter 6*

# THE FATHER'S CRUCIAL ROLE

IMAGINE THREE DIFFERENT MEN, EACH COMING HOME AT THE end of the day. Each is in his late thirties and each has two kids, a boy, eight, and a girl, ten. Each man carries home the evening paper and slips the key in the door. But once the doors open, the similarities vanish.

The first man comes home to a dark apartment. Listening to messages on his answering machine, he hears the terse, familiar voice of his ex-wife, reminding him that it's his daughter's birthday.

"I knew that," he mumbles and dials a long-distance number. He's relieved when the girl, and not her mother, answers the phone.

"Happy Birthday, sweetheart!"

"Hi, Daddy," she says quietly.

"So, did you get my package?" he asks after an awkward silence.

"Yeah. Thanks."

"So what do you think? They said at the store it was the newest kind."

"Yeah. It's great, only . . ."

"Only what?"

"Well, I'm not really into Barbie dolls so much anymore."

"Oh. Okay. Well, we can take it back. Hang on to it and we'll get something different when you visit me at Christmas, okay?"

"Okay."

"So, how's it going?"

"Okay."

"How's school?"

"Fine."

"How's your little brother?"

"He's all right."

And so the conversation continues, with Dad the interrogator, his daughter the reluctant witness. Winding up with a monologue about the great time they'll have when the kids come to visit in December, the man hangs up, feeling empty, defeated.

MAN NUMBER TWO opens the door to a brightly lit home, which is filled with the smell of supper cooking. Something Italian, he suspects.

"Hey, there," he says to his kids, who are busy with a video game. He swats each child playfully with the newspaper, then makes his way to the kitchen to help his wife with dinner.

"So how was school?" he asks when the kids take their places at the table.

"Fine," they answer in unison.

"Learn anything?"

"Not really," mumbles his daughter.

"We're doing times tables," his son offers.

"Good," Dad replies and then he turns to his wife. "Say, did that guy ever call about the mortgage?"

"You wanna hear me do the four-times table?" the boy interrupts.

"Not right now, son," Dad replies wearily. "I'm trying to talk to your mother."

The boy falls silent while his parents discuss the pros and cons of refinancing. But as soon as there's a break in the conversation, he tries again. "Hey, Dad, you wanna hear me do the four-times table?"

"Not with your mouth full of garlic bread," Dad answers sarcastically. Undaunted, the boy takes a swig of milk and begins, "Four times one is four; four times two is eight; four times three . . ."

When the boy finally hits forty-eight, Dad says flatly, "Very good."

"Want to hear me do five-times?" his son asks.

"Later on," the man answers. "Now, why don't you go finish that game with your sister so your mom and I can talk."

THE THIRD MAN opens the door to a similar scene as the second man. His wife is cooking, his kids are busily engaged in a video game. But at the supper table, the conversation unfolds differently.

"So what happened at school today?" he asks.

"Nothing," his kids reply in unison.

"Did you play with your new mitt at recess?" he asks his son.

"Yeah."

"And did you play first base like you wanted to?"

"Yeah."

"No flak from Peter about it, then?"

"Nah. He was cool. He played second. We made a double play."

"That's great! How was your batting?

"Terrible! I struck out twice."

"Oh, man, what a bummer. Maybe you just need some practice."

"Yeah, prob'ly."

"How 'bout if I toss you some pitches after supper."

"Okay!"

"And what about you?" he says to his daughter

"What?" she replies, a little defensive.

"Did you have a good day?"

"It was all right," she says, clearly sad about something.

"What did Mrs. Brown think of your duet?"

"We didn't do it. Cassie was sick."

"Not again. Was it her asthma?"

"Yeah, I guess so."

"That's too bad. Well, at least that will give you more time to work on the piece."

"But I'm sick of it, Daddy."

"Yeah, rehearsing the same piece of music over and over again gets boring sometimes, doesn't it?"

"I don't want to play the flute anymore," she announces.

And so the conversation continues as Dad listens to his daughter complain, helping her decide how to cope with her frustration.

EXAMINED SHOULDER TO shoulder like this, it's clear that fathers can vary widely in levels of involvement with their children. The last dad seemed to be aware of countless details in his kids' lives—including their friends' names, their daily activities, their challenges on the playground. Such awareness allows him to lend his kids emotional support and guidance. By contrast, the dad before him seemed uninterested, preoccupied, almost contemptuous when his son tried to get his attention. And the long-distance father knew so little about his daughter's life that he could barely engage her in a conversation.

Psychologists have long believed that a father's involvement in child-rearing is important. Mounting scientific evidence now suggests that involved fathers—and especially those who are emotionally available to their kids—make a unique contribution to their children's well-being. Fathers may influence children in ways that mothers don't, particularly in areas such as the child's peer relationships and achievement at school. Research indicates, for example, that boys with absent fathers have a harder time finding a balance between masculine assertiveness and self-restraint. Consequently, it's tougher for them to learn self-control and to delay gratification, skills that become increasingly important as boys grow and reach out for friendship, academic success, and career goals. A father's positive presence can be a significant factor in a girl's academic and career achievement as well, although the evidence here is more ambiguous. It's clear, however, that girls whose fathers are present and involved in their lives are less likely to become sexually promiscuous at a young age, and more likely to forge healthy relationships with men when they become adults.

Research also shows that a father's influence has staying power. One long-term study begun in the 1950s, for example, shows that kids whose dads were present and involved in their care when they were age five grew up to be more empathetic, compassionate adults than those whose dads were absent. By age forty-one, study participants who experienced more warmth from their fathers as children were more likely to have better social relationships. The evidence of this included longer, happier marriages, having their own kids, and engaging in recreational activities with nonfamily members.

Such findings about the importance of fathers come at a critical time in the history of the American family. You only need to turn on the nightly news to hear the cacophony of concern over the changing role of dads in our society. From fire-in-the-belly followers of spiritualist poet Robert Bly to fundamentalist Christians involved in groups like the Promise Keepers, men are awakening to the profound significance of the father-child bond. Whether it's conservative politicians like Dan Quayle decrying the media's glorification of TV's single mom Murphy Brown, or throngs of African-American men demonstrating in the 1995 Million Man March on Washington, D.C., there is a common theme: Too many men have been absent from their families for too long. Linking soaring rates of divorce and out-of-wedlock births to the rising tide of youth violence and other social problems, government officials, religious leaders, and social activists of all persuasions are calling on men to take more personal responsibility for raising their children. They are saying that it's time for dads to come home.

The research my colleagues and I have done lends support to the conviction that children do indeed need fathers. But our work also offers this important distinction: *Not just any dad will do*. Children's lives are greatly enhanced by fathers who are emotionally present, validating, able to offer comfort in times of distress. By the same token, children can be deeply harmed by fathers who are abusive, highly critical, humiliating, or emotionally cold.

## FATHERHOOD IN TRANSITION

To FURTHER UNDERSTAND the significance of having an involved, emotionally present father, it helps to look at how families have changed over time. In the past several generations, fathers have gone from being the primary source of their children's welfare to being, in many cases, superfluous. With high rates of divorce and births to unmarried women, too many children today live without their dads. Many kids know their fathers only as the guy who was here but left, or the man who is supposed to pay child support, but doesn't.

Historians trace the beginning of this shift back two hundred years to the Industrial Revolution when men started spending their days apart from women and children. Still, it wasn't until the 1960s that economic forces and the modern wave of feminism converged to deal the father-dominated family system a crippling blow. Since then, women have entered the workforce in record numbers. In 1960, only 19 percent of married women with children under age six worked at jobs outside the home. By 1990, that number had climbed to 59 percent. Over the same period, the average worker's purchasing power declined so that many families felt they could no longer get by on a single income. In 1960, 42 percent of all American families had a sole male breadwinner; by 1988, this figure had dropped to 15 percent.

"Such change has rendered traditional assumptions about fatherhood and breadwinning obsolete," writes historian Robert L. Griswold, author of *Fatherhood in America*. "Women's work, in short, has destroyed old assumptions about fatherhood and required new negotiations of gender relations."

At the same time, the institution of marriage has seriously eroded. Between 1960 and 1987, divorce rates more than doubled. Today, more than half of all first marriages end in divorce. One study from the University of Michigan predicts that among first-time marriages, the rate of divorce may be as high as 67 percent. Birth to single mothers has also become increasingly common, now accounting for nearly a third of all children born in the United States.

Without the bonds of marriage, many of today's fathers relinquish their responsibility for their children altogether. Unless the relationship between mother and father is stable, the father often withdraws all forms of support from his children—emotional and financial.

Ironically, this shift away from paternal responsibility is happening at the same time men have many new opportunities for intimate involvement in the lives of their children. Some men are taking advantage of such opportunities. Studies show that fathers—especially those in dual-career households—are providing more child care than men did in past generations. Today's fathers are also more likely than their predecessors to participate in their children's births, to request paternity leave and flexible work schedules, to cut back on hours and pass up promotions in order to spend time with their kids.

As hopeful as these trends appear, however, evidence suggests that progress toward involving fathers more in their children's lives is extremely slow. Some blame employers, claiming that today's male workers still don't get the flexibility that successful parenthood requires. A recent survey of medium to large U.S. businesses, for example, showed that just 18 percent of full-time male employees were offered unpaid paternity leave. Only 1 percent got paid leave. Good part-time jobs with substantial benefits are hard to find, and workers' careers are often stalled when they refuse to work overtime or uproot their families for cross-country job transfers.

Others blame the courts, claiming that the number of children with absent dads will continue to grow until divorced fathers are treated more fairly; in about 90 percent of divorces, custody is awarded to moms.

And finally, many say the problem lies with dads themselves for not taking more initiative to get involved in the mundane details of their children's lives. One researcher estimates that in two-career families, fathers are engaged with their kids about a third as much as their mothers are, and actually provide child care only about 10 percent of the time. In addition, when men pitch in with child-care responsibilities, they typically take on the role of "baby-sitter"; that is, they tend to rely on their wives to assign tasks and give them direction, rather than taking initiative themselves.

As a result of such problems, many men remain detached from their kids' lives. I am reminded of how this detachment played out in the custody battle between film director Woody Allen and his former partner Mia Farrow. To get a sense of Allen's relationship with his children, the judge asked him to name his kids' friends and doctors, but Allen could not do so. Like the first two fathers described at the beginning of this chapter, Allen lived in a world apart from his children. Such fathers are outsiders looking in, missing countless opportunities to connect with their kids in meaningful and helpful ways.

## THE DIFFERENCE A DAD MAKES

WHAT DO CHILDREN miss when their fathers are absent, distant, or preoccupied? Research in child development tells us they are losing far more than an "assistant mom." Fathers typically relate to children differently than mothers do, which means their involvement leads to the development of different competencies, particularly in the area of social relationships.

A father's influence begins at a very early age. One investigation, for example, found that five-month-old baby boys who have lots of contact with their fathers are more comfortable around adult strangers. The babies vocalized more for the strangers and showed more readiness to be picked up by them than babies who had less involved fathers. Another study showed that one-year-old babies cried less when left alone with a stranger if they had more contact with their dads.

Many researchers believe that fathers influence their children primarily through play. Not only do dads typically spend a greater percentage of their time with children in playful activities, but they also engage in styles of play that are more physical and exciting than the way mothers interact. Observing parents with their newborns, Michael Yogman and T. Berry Brazelton found that fathers talked less, but touched their babies more. The dads were more likely to make rhythmic, tapping noises to get the babies' attention. Their play was also more likely to take their children on an emotional roller coaster, going from activities that commanded minimal interest to those that got the babies quite excited. Mothers, in contrast, kept their play and their babies' emotions on a more even keel.

Such differences continue well into childhood, with fathers engaging their kids in more rough-and-tumble activities including lifting, bouncing, and tickling. Dads often make up idiosyncratic or unusual games, while moms are more likely to stick with the tried-and-true pursuits like peek-a-boo, pat-a-cake, reading a book, or manipulating toys and puzzles.

Many psychologists believe that dad's raucous style of "horseplay" provides an important avenue for helping children learn about emotions. Imagine dad as a "scary bear," chasing a delighted toddler across the yard, or lifting and twirling the child over his head for an "airplane ride." Such games allow the child to experience the thrill of being just a little bit scared, but amused and aroused at the same time. The child learns to watch and react to Dad's cues for a positive experience. He finds out, for instance, that squealing and giggling makes Dad laugh and so it prolongs the game. He also watches Dad for indications that play is winding down ("Okay, that's enough for now") and he learns how to recover from excitement and to be calm again.

Such skills serve a child well as he ventures out into the wide world of playmates. Having roughhoused with Dad, he knows how to read other people's signals when feelings run high. He knows how to generate his own exciting play and react to others in ways that are neither too sedate nor spinning out of control. He knows how to keep his emotions at a level that's optimal for fun-filled play.

Studies of three- and four-year-old children conducted by Ross Parke and Kevin MacDonald provide evidence of this link between fathers' physical play and how children get along with peers. Observing children in twenty-minute play sessions with their dads, the researchers found that kids whose fathers showed high levels of physical play were most popular among their peers. An interesting and significant qualifier emerged in this study, however: Kids with highly physical dads were only rated as popular if their dads played with them in ways that were *nondirective, noncoercive.* The children whose dads were highly physical but also highly bossy received the lowest popularity scores.

Other studies have provided similar evidence. Across the board, researchers have found that children seem to develop the best social skills when their dads keep the tone of their interactions positive and allow kids to take part in directing the course of play.

Such discoveries fit hand in glove with my own findings, which highlighted the importance of dads avoiding criticism, humiliation, derogation, and intrusiveness with their kids. The children in our studies who did best in terms of peer relationships and academic achievement were those whose dads validated their feelings and praised their accomplishments. These fathers were the Emotion Coaches, who neither dismissed nor disapproved of their kids' negative emotions, but showed empathy and provided guidance to help their kids deal with negative feelings.

During the exercise where parents taught their child to play a video game, for example, Emotion-Coaching dads cheered their children on, providing just the right amount of guidance without being intrusive. They often practiced the teaching technique of scaffolding that we discussed earlier. That is, they used each of the child's successes as incremental evidence of his or her competence. With simple words like, "atta boy," or, "I knew you could do it," these dads turned each small victory into a foundation for a better self-concept. Their praise gave their children the confidence to keep going, keep learning.

Conversely, the children in our studies who had the hardest time with grades and social relationships were those whose dads were cold and authoritarian, derogatory and intrusive. During the video game exercise, such dads might make humiliating remarks to their kids, mocking and criticizing them for their mistakes. They might also take over when the game was not going well, providing the child with evidence of his or her incompetence.

Three years later, when we checked in with these families and with the children's teachers, we found that kids with the humiliating, nonsupportive dads were the ones most likely to be headed for trouble. They were kids displaying aggressive behavior toward their friends. They were the ones who were having the most trouble in school. They were the ones with problems often linked to delinquency and youth violence.

While our studies showed that mother-child interactions were also important, we found that, compared with the fathers' responses, the quality of contact with the mother was not as strong a predictor of the child's later success or failure with school and friends. This discovery is undoubtedly surprising, especially since mothers typically spend more time with children than fathers do. We believe the reason fathers have this extreme influence on their children is because the father-child relationship evokes such powerful emotions in kids.

## BEING THERE FOR YOUR KIDS, PHYSICALLY AND EMOTIONALLY

BEING CLOSE TO your children doesn't have to be *that* hard for men. And yet, as psychologist Ronald Levant explains in his book *Masculinity Reconstructed*, many of today's fathers are struggling for a definition of dad that feels right. "Just as men of the Baby Boom generation are becoming fathers themselves, they're being told that everything they learned about fathering from their own dads—that a father is someone who works hard, who isn't around much, who criticizes more than he compliments, who doesn't show affection or any other emotion except anger—no longer applies," Levant writes. "Instead men are supposed to be sensitive, caring, enlightened dads who are really there for and involved with their kids. . . . The only problem is many men don't know how to be that kind of father, for the simple reason that their own dads weren't that kind of father to them."

In ancient times a father guarded his offspring by being a warrior and a hunter. Over the centuries, his role shifted to that of bread-winner. Through hard work and self-sacrifice, he earned money to pay for his children's safety and security in the form of house pay-ments, grocery bills, and college tuition. Today, we feel the father's role shifting again as dads are called upon to provide yet another level of protection for their kids—one that might buffer children from destructive forces like gangs, drug abuse, and sexual promiscu-ity. Science tells us that a man's conventional psychological de-fenses cannot produce a shield against such dangers. Today, children's safety comes from their fathers' hearts. It is based on men being present with their children emotionally as well as physically.

As we discussed in Chapter 3, men have the capacity to recog-nize and respond constructively to their kids' emotions. This has been demonstrated in projects like Levant's Fatherhood Project, aimed at improving the ways dads communicate with their kids around emotions. After eight weeks of training in sensitivity and listening skills, fathers in this course improved their communica-tion with their kids and showed more acceptance of their children's emotional expression.

But men don't have to take a course to become more sensitive to their children; they can practice Emotion-Coaching skills, which begin with emotional awareness. Men must allow themselves to be aware of their feelings so they can empathize with their children. Then they must take whatever steps necessary to make themselves available to their kids. They must structure their lives so they can give more time and attention to their children—a step that sounds simple, but is by no means easy. Making time for kids can be espe-cially challenging for fathers living apart from their children and those highly focused on their work. Unless men do this, however, they can lose touch with their children as they grow and change, and they may find it increasingly harder to have meaningful relationships with them.

I am reminded of how changes in my own schedule over the years made a difference in my relationship with my daughter, Moriah. When she was a toddler and I was responsible for dropping her off at daycare before rushing off to the university, our mornings together were often hectic. I found myself being more abrupt and less playful with her than either of us liked. Then I decided not to schedule any classes or appointments before ten A.M. and this made all the difference. Although I still got to work by nine most mornings, my daily interactions with Moriah improved because I knew that I wouldn't be breaking any job commitments if she required extra time. If she wanted to stop on the way out to the car to stare at a spiderweb, I had time to share that with her. If she suddenly decided she wanted to change from wearing red shoes to blue shoes, it was no big deal.

Granted, some occupations allow dads more flexibility in this way than others. But fathers make conscious choices each day that influence the quality and quantity of time and attention they can give their kids. Which parent is going to bathe the baby each day? Who's going to read the kids a bedtime story? Who's going to help them find matching socks? Although such matters may seem mundane, these are important considerations because it is from within the structure of our ordinary lives that emotional bonds between father and child emerge. In the next few pages, we'll explore ideas to help fathers strengthen that tie.

## GET INVOLVED IN YOUR CHILD'S CARE FROM PREGNANCY ON

Studies show that a dad's involvement in his partner's pregnancy can help set the stage for a whole series of positive family interactions that benefit the marriage, benefit the child, and strengthen the father-child bond.

When a father takes an active part in childbirth preparation classes, for example, he learns to be an effective labor coach, lending encouragement to his partner throughout the birthing process. This, in turn, can have a positive outcome for both mother and child. One study found that women whose husbands participated in labor and delivery reported less pain, received less medication, and felt more positive about the birth experience than women whose husbands were not present. Similar correlations between the father's presence and the mother's perception of the birth have been observed when babies are delivered by cesarean section. In addition, another study revealed that a dad who shows a high interest in his partner's pregnancy spends more time holding the baby once it arrives and is more likely to respond to the baby when it cries.

Acquiring such hands-on experience during an infant's early days is important. One researcher found that fathers who begin diapering, bathing, rocking, and otherwise caring for their babies in the hospital shortly after birth are more likely to be doing such activities months down the road—all of which provides babies and dads with face-to-face opportunities to learn each other's cues, getting their relationship off to a positive start.

In addition, the habits a father forms during his child's infancy often stick. If a dad is involved in caring for the baby at an early age, he's more likely to continue his involvement into middle childhood and adolescence.

In light of such findings, fathers who want a solid relationship with their children should lay the groundwork during pregnancy and the baby's first months. First-time dads should be aware, however, that caring for an infant is mostly a hands-on learning experience, full of trial and error. The beauty of being involved from day one is that father and mother can learn about their unique baby together. And because communication between parent and infant is a two-way street, the newborn has a chance to begin learning from father early on as well. As she becomes familiar with Dad's face, his voice, the rhythm of his walk, the way he smells, and the way he holds her, she learns to associate his presence, as well as her mother's, with comfort and security. She also learns important lessons in social control from his responsiveness; she learns that she can affect the way her father treats her, that she can influence other people through her own behavior.

While it's normal for dads to feel a bit left out of the caregiving equation when moms breastfeed, there are dozens of other ways for fathers to provide essential nurturing. These include bottle-feeding the baby water, supplemental formula, or expressed breast milk.

They can bathe their babies, diaper them, rock them, and walk the floor with them. And of course, dads should never forget their gender's special aptitude for play. Even among newborns, psychologist Andrew Meltzoff has observed subtle indications that babies imitate their caregivers' facial expressions. This means the time a father spends face-to-face in conversation with even the tiniest children can mark the beginning of a rewarding relationship.

Of course, all of this presupposes that fathers will have time to spend with their newborn infants, which is why I am a strong proponent of paternity leave. If a father's employment situation makes that impossible, I urge him at least to take as much vacation time as he can during those important, irreplaceable, early weeks of his child's life.

Extended-family members can also help to ensure that dads are not inadvertently shuffled off to the sidelines when the baby arrives. Concerned grandmothers, for example, may do well to step back and let dad play the supporting role, caring for the newborn while mother gets her rest. When this happens, father gets the time he needs as a primary caretaker to learn the baby's signals.

Of course, mothers themselves play the most powerful gatekeeper role, supporting or discouraging fathers' involvement in the care of their children. In studying mothers' attitudes toward fathers' participation in infant care, researchers Ross Parke and Ashley Beitel learned that dads are less likely to be involved if the mother is critical of the quality of her husband's caregiving and if the mother believes that women are innately more capable of nurturing infants.

Many women, however, see great value in a father's involvement, and want to know how to encourage it. For them, the answer is clear: Allow your partner to have his own style of caring for the baby. Offer the wisdom of your experience, but avoid being highly critical of the way he pins the diaper, shakes the bottle, swaddles the baby, and whatnot. Keep in mind that babies can benefit from a variety of caregiving styles, including a typically masculine one that's more playful, more physical, less limit setting. If couples find they have conflict over the way care is given, they may want to designate certain responsibilities as the purview of one parent or the other. In other words, you take care of the baby's feeding, and I'll do bath time each morning. Also, if it seems that dad is having a hard time learning how to soothe the baby, it may be that he and the child simply need more time without mom's intervention to learn each other's cues. Sending mom out for a few afternoons with friends, leaving dad and baby to fend for themselves, might do the trick.

Relinquishing control over an area that has long been the sole purview of women may be a challenge for some new mothers. But if mom can step back and let dad and baby have their time together, hopefully she'll see how their child benefits from a healthy, well-developed, nurturing relationship with dad.

## STAY TUNED IN TO YOUR CHILD'S EVERYDAY NEEDS AS HE OR SHE GROWS

Ideally, dads who get in the habit of providing daily care and nurturing for their children as infants will continue to do their part as the children grow. The challenge is to maintain such commitment over time as schedules and priorities shift at work and at home. Unless fathers make a conscious effort to be part of their kids' daily lives, many may find themselves drifting further away, losing track of the intimate details—the stuff that gives dads and children their common ground.

Much has been written over the years about the importance of mothers spending "quality time" with their kids. The idea, which has grown in popularity as more moms enter the workforce, is that simply clocking hours with your kids is less important than how you relate to them when you are together. And indeed, studies of working moms have shown that the quality of mother-child interactions has more effect on kids than how much time the two spend in each other's company. It only makes sense that the same is true for fathers. It doesn't matter how many evenings and weekends dad spends with his child if that time is spent avoiding interaction, buried in work, or sitting dumbstruck with his child in front of a television set.

The importance of fathers' accessibility to their children was driven home in a study by Robert Blanchard and Henry Biller, who compared groups of third-grade boys, some whose fathers were absent, some whose fathers were present and available, and some whose fathers were present and unavailable. Looking at the academic achievement in all groups, the study found that the boys with absent fathers did the worst and the boys whose fathers were present and available did best. The boys whose fathers were present but not available fell somewhere in between. "Having a competent father will not facilitate a boy's intellectual development if the father is not consistently accessible to the boy or if the father/son relationship is negative in quality," Biller wrote. (Few studies of this type have been done on girls and fathers, although high involvement by fathers seems to be linked to girls' career and academic achievement as well.)

While it's hard to say how much involvement or accessibility children need from their fathers, it takes more than occasional outings to the baseball game, the amusement park, and the zoo to make a real difference to kids. Indeed, the best way for dads to be part of their children's lives is to participate in what psychologist Ronald Levant calls "family work," the day-to-day feeding, bathing, dressing, and nurturing of children. "It's by performing these traditionally feminine tasks that men become truly integrated and indispensable members of their families," Levant writes. Family life is "not only about providing for their families' material needs. It's about being there on a daily basis providing for the never-ending, ever-changing, day-to-day physical and emotional needs as well."

As during their children's infancy, mothers of older children can encourage their partners to take more responsibility for daily care by suspending judgment when men approach tasks in their own style. There's more than one way to wipe a runny nose or make a peanut butter sandwich.

For many men, being present and accessible in the world of children requires a real shift in perceptions about time and the importance of meeting concrete, task-oriented goals. Many men have been socialized all their lives to believe in moving through the day efficiently, accomplishing one goal after another, without dawdling, backtracking, and leaving work unfinished. Men's lives are less concerned with taking care of the way people feel and more concerned with simply solving problems, getting things done. Men who are home caring for a preschooler may have the expectation that they can do other things, too—mow the lawn, watch the game, pay taxes. When that doesn't work out because child care takes so much time, men may become frustrated. They may discover they feel less patient and empathetic than they would like to be.

Successful fathering is not about getting things done despite our children. It's about accepting our role in this twenty-year work-in-progress called the growth of a human being. It's about slowing down, taking time to be with our children one on one, relating to them on a level their age requires.

I learned much of this the hard way, trying futilely, for example, to write on days when I stayed home with my daughter, Moriah. I've finally decided that until she's old enough to meet more of her own needs (a bittersweet thought), our time together is better spent playing, reading aloud, doing chores.

Consequently, I've also learned the high value of actually getting involved in her world, of joining her in activities like coloring, games, and pretend play. With both Moriah and the kids in my studies, I've seen the way small children open their hearts to adults in play situations, willingly discussing topics they might never broach while simply being questioned. Some of my best talks with Moriah at age four or five happened while we colored together or played Barbies. Out of the blue, she'd ask questions like, "Why did my friend Helena have to move to Michigan?" or, "Was Mommy mad at you?" Such intimate conversations about kids' deepest thoughts and feelings—their worries, fears, and dreams—are most likely to happen when families have relaxed time together, doing things they enjoy. (And, by the way, I found coloring very relaxing. Now I can even stay within the lines.)

As children grow and become involved in more activities away from home, it may get harder for fathers to find such time alone with them. Yet, one-on-one exchanges with dad when a child is any age can be quite valuable. That's why I urge fathers to structure their schedules in ways that allow them to regularly spend time alone with each child. The opportunity may simply be a thirty-minute car ride across town each Saturday for music lessons. Or perhaps there's a hobby or sport dad can share with his kid. Sometimes the best conversations happen while families share chores like making dinner, washing the car, or weeding the garden.

Conversations come easier if you know about the events and people in your child's life, including their daily activities, the names of their friends, teachers, and coaches. Spend time, if you can, in your child's school, attending open houses and curriculum nights. Offer to work in the classroom or go on field trips. Volunteer to be a coach (or assistant coach) for your child's athletic activities.

Learn what you can about your child's friends and social life as well. Get to know their friends' parents. Open your house to the slumber party. Volunteer to drive the kids to parties, the bowling alley, the skating rink. Tune in to their conversations. Listen to their concerns.

And finally, recognize that family time is full of a million opportunities either to connect with your children or to distance yourself from them. You decide in many mundane moments whether to turn toward or away from your kids. Say, for instance, that you're trying to read when you find yourself distracted by music blaring from your teenager's room. As you ask him to turn down the volume, you can start the conversation by saying, "I can't believe you call that stuff music." Or you can say, "I've never heard that group before. Who is it?" While the first is an affront, the second is an invitation, a chance to bridge your differences and stay involved.

## STRIKE A BALANCE BETWEEN WORK LIFE AND HOME LIFE

For many men, finding enough time and energy for their children means giving over less of themselves to their jobs. That's because it's difficult, if not impossible, to be present for your kids physically and emotionally if you work sixty hours a week, or if you're so distracted by work stresses that you can't focus on your children's concerns.

Resolving this conflict is not easy for a man whose primary identity is that of family breadwinner. He has been socialized to believe that hard work, long hours, and self-sacrifice demonstrate his commitment to his family. But now, many men fear that unless they change, they risk losing touch with their wives and children—the very people who give their work meaning in the first place.

As our society becomes more conscious of this irony, I hope we'll see more progress toward family-friendly working conditions. For years, working women have lobbied for flextime jobs, more part-time jobs (with substantive benefits), employer-based child care, and adequate family leave. Such changes, when they come, will benefit male employees, too, especially those who want to be more involved with their children. A British study of scientific workers, for example, showed that the introduction of flextime made a difference in the amount of time fathers in dual-career families spent caring for their children. Another study showed that workers on flextime didn't necessarily spend more time with their kids, but they reported less conflict between home and work responsibilities, presumably leading to less stress in the family and a happier environment for children.

Still, men are often required to sacrifice financial gains and career development in order to strike a better balance between their work and family lives. As sociologist Pepper Schwartz found in her research on egalitarian marriages, men who play an equal and active role in household work and child care have less developed careers than men who take the more traditional role of primary breadwinner. The corporate manager who refuses to uproot his family for a cross-country job transfer is still passed over for promotions and raises. And the salesman who skips a marketing retreat in favor of a Cub Scout camp-out may miss out on a bonus or promotion.

Whether or not a man is willing to choose the "daddy track," working fewer hours for lower pay, he may want at least to consider ways to reduce job stress. One bad day at the office after another can be a detriment to a father's relationship with his kids. This was demonstrated in a study of fathers working as air-traffic controllers. Following distressing social experiences at work, the fathers in this study were more likely to express anger toward their children when they got home. High job satisfaction, on the other hand, can actually enhance parenting skills, studies show, even though it also results in dads spending less time with their kids.

Whether a dad feels some sense of autonomy in his job seems to make a big difference. One group of researchers found that when dads have more independence in their work, they are more likely to give their kids autonomy as well. But if they work in jobs that are highly supervised, they seem to expect more conformity and obedience from their children, and they are more likely to use physical forms of discipline.

Making a career change, or at least finding ways to make your current job less stressful, can be a significant move.

## STAY INVOLVED IN YOUR CHILD'S LIFE DESPITE YOUR MARITAL STATUS

Whether parents stay together or not, children generally do best with both a father and a mother involved in their lives. And although cooperative parenting can be tricky when couples separate, children usually benefit if their mothers and fathers view raising children as a joint venture.

As we explored in Chapter 5, marital separation and divorce can be harmful to children. But some problems may be avoided if children are able to maintain regular contact with both parents. And as our own studies suggest, children of troubled couples generally do better when their parents stay emotionally available to them, adopting the parenting style of the Emotion Coach. Effective Emotion Coaching requires time, intimacy, and detailed knowledge of a child's life. That's why I encourage fathers (90 percent of whom live apart from their kids following divorce) to maintain close contact with their kids despite separation from their children's mother.

Divorced and single fathers often have difficulty staying involved with their children for a variety of reasons, including geographical distance, remarriage, issues related to child support payments, and ongoing conflict with the children's mother. Several studies have shown that a divorced father's contact with his kids diminishes over time, despite the quality of the father's relationship with the child at the time of the divorce. And, as a father's contact with his children declines, so does his influence. Without the emotional bond that forms when fathers interact daily with their children over a million matters—both trivial and significant—dads certainly can't hope to have much influence in the big issues that typically surface around adolescence.

What can divorced dads do to prevent their children from gradually fading away from their lives? For one thing, they can treat their relationships with their children's mother as a partnership. Parents should not let conflicts between them get in the way of making good decisions together on behalf of their children. And, as we dis-cussed in Chapter 5, parents should never use their relationships with the kids against each other. Ex-spouses should try to support each other in upholding collaborative agreements around issues like limit setting and discipline.

Dads should work out an arrangement for child support payments that seems fair and stick with it. Studies show that dads who keep up their payments are more likely to spend time with their kids on a regular basis. Conversely, fathers often fail to see their children due to financial problems or conflicts over payment. Mothers often use the child support issue as a justification for blocking a father's access to his kids. And fathers, who often feel guilty or fearful about failing to pay, avoid contacting their kids as well. Meanwhile, time slips away, with children believing that their father's absence signals his indifference.

When fathers do spend time with their kids, whether as a visita-tion or as part of a joint-custody arrangement, they should make that time as normal as possible. Kids adjust better to divorce when time with the noncustodial parent is spent doing everyday activi-ties, such as schoolwork, lessons, and chores. In other words, fathers should avoid the "Disneyland Dad" syndrome of constantly making time with their children a party. Children may benefit more from their relationship with dad by helping him cook dinner and do the dishes than by watching him pick up the tab at Burger King.

Although a father may not have as much time with his child as he'd like, it helps to keep in touch with frequent phone calls, say as many as two or three a week. Conversations will get easier with practice, especially if dads make an effort to keep up with the every-day details of their children's lives. Getting to know a kid's friends and teachers, and attending school functions, performances, and athletic events will help.

Staying close to kids can be even more challenging for a divorced dad if he or his ex remarries. Such a challenge is likely, given that 75 percent of all women and 80 percent of all men marry again fol-lowing a divorce. While studies show that a mother's remarriage can be a great help to kids economically, afterward, children typically see their biological fathers less. A parent's remarriage can also cause kids (especially teenagers) some degree of anxiety as they struggle to adapt to a new stepparent and wonder what this person's presence means for their relationship with their "real" dad or mom.

Psychologists have learned that it's a big mistake to tell kids they have to choose between one dad and the other. Also, it's usually best for stepfathers to refrain from taking over the role of disciplinarian. Children adjust much better if the stepfather simply stands by and supports the mother in her parenting decisions. Children also do best following remarriage when they can continue to have regular contact with both biological parents.

Perhaps the strongest advice to dads who live apart from the children is to be patient with their children as they adjust to changes. Parents can expect the first two years following a divorce to be the roughest. In addition to the pain and anger dads are likely to feel in their relationship with their former spouse, the children may be expressing a great deal of negativity as well. Small children, who typically have difficulty with transitions under any circumstances, may resist going with dad when he comes to pick them up. Older children may act mean or despondent, expressing lots of anger at their fathers for not working things out so the family can stay together. Because men typically withdraw from relationships when emotions get hot, many fathers may feel tempted simply to stop seeing their kids at all. For the benefit of their children over the long term, dads must not do this. It's important to concentrate on helping kids work through their negative feelings. The techniques of Emotion Coaching discussed in Chapter 3 may be helpful. Remember that by listening empathetically, helping children to label their feelings, and guiding them on ways to handle their anger and sadness, dads can grow closer to their kids in times of emotional crisis.

# Chapter 7

# Emotion Coaching as Your

# Child Grows

Have you ever heard this lament from new parents? "Just when I think I've got the baby figured out—how much to feed him, how much he'll sleep, how to soothe his crying—everything changes!"

The comment rings true because raising children brings about steady change. As our kids grow, we continually adjust our lives to accommodate their latest needs, fears, interests, and competencies. And yet, despite all the changes, there is one constant: each child's desire for an emotional connection with loving, caring adults.

In this chapter, I'll explore five different periods of childhood: infancy, the toddler years, early childhood, middle childhood, and adolescence. I'll explain some of the major developmental milestones children typically achieve during each of these periods and offer advice to help you enhance your child's emotional intelligence during these phases. Understanding what's "normal" and anticipating what issues are likely to be important to your child at different ages can help you understand his or her feelings better. This, in turn, can make you more effective as an Emotion Coach.

## INFANCY

### Three Months or So

Who can say when a baby's emotional relationship with its parents begins? Some speculate that it starts in utero as the baby responds to its mother's relative states of stress or serenity. Others say it begins immediately after birth as parents feed, rock, and soothe their baby. And still others point to that magic moment a few weeks after birth when the baby beams its first genuine smile at mother or dad, making all their hard work and sleepless nights finally seem worthwhile.

Most parents would agree, however, that the real fun begins at about three months when babies typically become interested in face-to-face social interaction. Developmental psychologists speak of the infant's eyes "brightening" at this age, meaning that babies seem for the first time really to look at their parents and hold their gaze. As little as a three-month-old baby is, she is learning an enormous amount through observation and imitation about how to read and express emotions. This means that parents, through their responsiveness and attention, can begin an active process of Emotion-Coaching their infants—even at this very early age.

Research shows that parents typically go to great lengths to get and hold their babies' attention during early exchanges of emotional information. For example, parents often use a speech pattern described as "motherese" (although dads can be fluent in this language as well). It involves using a high-pitched voice and talking slowly and repetitively, while exaggerating facial expressions. Although such "baby talk" may seem comical and extreme, parents use it for good reason—it works! Infants usually perk up and pay closer attention when they hear and see their parents talking this way.

Most parents also engage in face-to-face, nonverbal "conversations" with their babies, taking turns making expressions. The mother raises her eyebrows, for example, so the baby raises his. The baby sticks out his tongue and the mother does the same. One partner coos or gurgles and the other returns the sound, using the same pitch or rhythm. Babies typically find such imitation games riveting, particularly if the parent mimics the baby in a different mode. For example, if the baby bangs her rattle on the floor three times, the mother might repeat the rhythm with her voice—something that fascinates her child.

These imitative conversations are important because they tell the baby that the parent is paying close attention to her and responding to her feelings. This is the infant's first experience of being understood by another person; it's the beginning of emotional communication.

Experiments conducted with mothers and their three-month-old infants have highlighted the babies' resourcefulness and competence at emotional communication. In one experiment called "The Still Face Game," researcher Edward Tronick asked mothers to look at their infants, but to resist the urge to move their faces in the playful way moms and dads typically do with their babies. Faced with this uncharacteristic lack of response from their moms, the babies tried repeatedly to initiate the "conversation" themselves, futilely making one interesting facial expression after another. Researchers observed that the babies attempted an average of four different strategies with their mothers before they finally gave up. In an experiment to study the effects of parents' depression on three-month-olds, Tronick asked the mothers to pretend to be a little sad or depressed in front of their three-month-old babies. Even this slight change in the mother's mood had huge effects on the infants. They became more negative emotionally, more withdrawn, and less responsive. Such research shows that even at three months, babies have an expectation that their parents will be emotionally engaged and responsive.

Such research dramatizes that infants are not passive characters in parent-child relationships. Instead, they take a very active role in social play. They seek to be stimulated, have fun, and connect emotionally with their parents.

What happens to infants over time when their parents aren't responsive, or respond only in negative ways? Researcher Tiffany Field, who has studied depressed mothers and their babies, found some troubling answers: Babies with depressed moms tend to mirror their mothers' sadness, low energy, low involvement, anger, and irritability. And if a mother's depression continues for a year a more, her baby will begin to show lasting delays in growth and development.

The period between ages three months and six months appears to be crucial in terms of the way a mother's depression can affect the development of her baby's nervous system, according to Field's studies. When she and her colleagues compared two groups of three-month-old babies (one with depressed moms and one with nondepressed moms), the researchers discovered little difference. But when they looked at six-month-old babies, they found that those with depressed mothers were less expressive vocally and had lower scores on tests of nervous-system functioning.

A mother's depressed state may even influence whether her

baby's brain processes an emotional event as a negative experience or a positive experience. Scientists can make such determinations by looking at electroencephalographic data (i.e., brain waves) as people have different types of emotional reactions. Negative responses are processed in one part of the brain while positive ones are processed in another. Using this technology, University of Washington researcher Geraldine Dawson monitored infants' responses to watching soap bubbles rise from behind a curtain. Surprisingly, the babies of depressed mothers processed this rather neutral event as emotionally negative.

While such research points to disturbing consequences for babies of nonresponsive, depressed moms, there is reason for hope. Further studies in Field's labs revealed that the babies of depressed moms showed considerable improvement when interacting with their nursery school teachers and nondepressed dads. This opposite effect provides yet more evidence that adult caregivers can have a powerful impact on the emotional development of young children.

At the same time infants are learning to read and imitate emotional cues from their parents, they are working on another important developmental milestone: the ability to regulate the physiological arousal that results from their social and emotional interactions. Many developmental psychologists believe babies do this by cycling in and out of active engagement with others. One minute they are paying close attention to other people, and are responsive to play. The next minute they look away, ignoring adults' attempts to engage them with toys and baby talk. While parents are sometimes bewildered by their infants' apparent fickleness, there is some evidence that the baby disengages because he needs to do so. He may be experiencing heart rate increases and a physiological state that's too overwhelming. He's like a K-mart shopper after the third blue-light special is announced; he's overstimulated and eager for some rest. Therefore, he averts his eyes and turns his head, doing all he can to avoid further contact. The baby is trying to learn to calm down.

People who are inexperienced with babies may not realize that they need periods of "downtime." They may keep trying to stimulate the infant with toys, baby talk, and jostling. The infant, of course, is captive. He can't ask his overbearing playmate to stop. He can't go to another room. He may not even have the physical coordination and strength to bury his head in a blanket. Hence, he must rely on the most persistent and effective defense he has—he begins to cry.

Such instances of "miscoordination" between babies and parents are fairly common. Some researchers estimate that parents fail to read their infants' cues 70 percent of the time! Not to worry, however. Infancy is a time of extraordinary trial and error on the part of parents and their babies. As long as parents are sensitive to their infants, emotional communication will gradually improve and miscues will be less frequent.

My advice to Emotion-Coaching parents, then, is to pay attention to your baby's moods and to respond to them. If your baby seems suddenly uninterested in play following a period of interaction, give her some quiet time. If your baby gets cranky in situations where she's being held and talked to a great deal (a family gathering, for instance), take her away to a quiet room from time to time, where she can calm down from all the excitement.

If it seems that the baby has become so wound up that she can't calm down on her own, do what you can to quiet her. Again, this is a trial-and-error process as parents and babies search for strategies that work best for the individual baby's temperament. Common techniques, however, include dimming the lights; rocking the baby, talking softly, or walking with her so that she can feel the two of you moving together in soft, rhythmic patterns. Parents also report success with soft music and lullabies, gentle massage, or soft patting. Some babies even seem to be soothed by white noise from a running dishwasher or soft static from an untuned radio.

Research tells us that parents who are more sensitive to their babies' moods—those, for example, who recognize when babies need to switch gears from highly stimulating activities to more quiet ones—do a better job of enhancing their children's emotional intelligence. This Emotion-Coaching style gives children more opportunities to experience going from a highly aroused state to a calmer one. In other words, they are helping the babies learn to soothe themselves and regulate their own physiological states.

Parents who respond in soothing ways to their babies' distress are teaching them important lessons as well. Number one, their babies are learning that their strong negative emotions have an effect on the world—they cry and their parents respond. Number two, they are learning it is possible to be soothed after experiencing strong emotions. At this age, most of the soothing comes from the parent. But as the baby grows, she will internalize her parents' efforts and will learn ways to soothe herself, which is an important part of emotional well-being.

By the same token, babies need to have plenty of stimulation in their lives so that they can experience the process of getting thoroughly excited and then calming down again. As we explored in Chapter 6, the highly physical games fathers typically play with their babies provide children with this crucial experience.

I also encourage parents to invent and play games that give their babies practice at reading and expressing various emotions. Research shows this can begin by simply imitating something your infant does. The baby sticks out his tongue or coughs and the parent does the same. The baby will then do it again and the game has been created.

Be animated and emotional when you play with your baby, repeating silly phrases and gentle, rhythmic actions. Playing in this way, the baby becomes aware of game routines and learns to anticipate what you are going to do. It's as if the baby is saying to himself, "Oh boy, here comes that grab-the-toes-and-twirl-the-feet-in-opposite-circles game," or, "Whoopee, here comes the 'I'm-gonna-get-you' tickle game." When he enjoys the game, he learns to communicate his glee with smiles, giggles, excited kicks, and squeals. Such response encourages parents to be even more playful, creating an upward spiral of loving, fun-filled interaction, which further strengthens the emotional bond between baby and parent.

## SIX MONTHS TO EIGHT MONTHS

This is a period of tremendous exploration for babies, a time when they are discovering a whole world of objects, people, and places. Simultaneously, they are also discovering new ways to express and share feelings such as joy, curiosity, fear, and frustration with the world around them. Such blossoming awareness continues to open up new opportunities for Emotion Coaching.

Among the important developmental leaps that typically happen at about six months is the baby's ability to shift her attention while keeping in mind an object or person she is no longer looking at. In the past, she could only think about the object or person she was focusing on at the time. But now she can look at a toy clown, for instance, be amused by it, and then look at her parent, sharing her amusement over the clown. As simple as this accomplishment may seem, it presents a whole new world of possibilities for play and emotional interaction. Now she can invite you to play with the many objects that fascinate her. She can share her feelings about those objects with you.

To encourage the development of such emotional intelligence, accept your baby's invitations to play with objects, and imitate the baby's emotional reactions. This should spur more sharing, more emotional expression.

By eight months, babies typically begin crawling and discovering their environment. But the explorer is also learning to distinguish differences between the various people he encounters, which sets the stage for the first significant appearance of fear. You will see this demonstrated in bouts of "stranger anxiety." A baby who once smiled indiscriminately at folks in the grocer's checkout line now buries his face in his mom's shoulder. While he once leaned willingly into the waiting arms of a new baby-sitter, he now has formed "specific attachments" to his parents, and may cling desperately when they try to set him down in a new setting with strangers around.

At the same time, the baby is getting much better at understanding spoken words, which also helps with emotional communication. Although it will probably be several months before he begins to talk himself, he can understand a great deal of language and is able to follow instructions, such as, "Go get your white bear and hand it to me." I can recall holding my daughter, Moriah, during this time in her life and saying, "Sweetheart, you look tired. Why don't you put your head down on my shoulder and rest?" and Moriah would do just that.

All of these new developments—physical mobility, the ability to shift attention, the baby's special attachment to his parents, his understanding of spoken language, and his fear of the unknown—come together in a skill psychologists called "social referencing."

This is the baby's tendency to approach a particular object or event and then turn to the parent for emotional information. Approaching an unfamiliar dog, for example, a baby might hear his mother say, "No, don't go there!" The baby is able to read the combination of the mother's words, tone of voice, and facial expressions, and understand the concept of potential danger. On the other hand, the baby might approach a noisy toy robot, look back, and see his mother with a relaxed smile. Now he knows the robot is safe to play with. In this sense, the parent has acquired a unique role in the emotional life of the child, the role of "safe base." The baby feels free to explore, knowing he can return to this base periodically for reassurance.

When a baby practices social referencing with a parent, it's a sign that the two are emotionally connected and the child feels emotionally secure. As a result of imitative play learned early in infancy, the child has become proficient at reading his parent's emotional cues. He knows he can trust signals such as facial expressions, body language, and tone of voice. (Here's an interesting note about the way parental conflict may affect this process: Researchers Susan Dickstein and Ross Parke have discovered that babies do not practice as much social referencing with their unhappily married dads, although they continue to do so with unhappily married moms. We think this reflects the fact that men often withdraw emotionally from their children as well as from their wives when the marriage starts to fail. Unhappily married women, on the other hand, may withdraw from their husbands, but they tend to stay emotionally connected to their children.)

To strengthen the emotional bond with babies at this age, I encourage parents to be a mirror of sorts for their children; that is, to reflect back to the child the feelings they are expressing. This is an important part of early Emotion Coaching—helping your child put her feelings into language. Use words as well as your own facial expressions to say things like, "You feel sad (happy, scared, etc.) right now, don't you?" Or, "You're getting very tired now. Want to sit in my lap for a while?" If your perceptions are correct, the baby will understand you and show it. Don't worry, however, if you read your baby incorrectly from time to time. This is a common occurrence, and fortunately, babies are very tolerant.

Remember also that your baby is looking to you for emotional cues. You can use this to help him cope with stranger anxiety, which so commonly emerges at this age. If mom looks relaxed around the new baby-sitter, perhaps even giving the sitter a hug, baby may get the message that this new person is to be trusted.

## NINE MONTHS TO TWELVE MONTHS

This is the period when babies begin to understand that it's possible for people to share their thoughts and emotions with one another. The baby hands a broken toy to his dad, for example, and dad says, "Oh it's busted. That's too bad. You feel sad, don't you?" By nine months, the baby is beginning to comprehend that dad knows how she is feeling inside. Before, when a parent empathized with the baby, reflecting back the child's feelings with voice inflection, facial movement, body language, the child was learning about the world of emotional expression. But the baby was not aware that parent and child could actually have *the same thoughts and feelings*. Now she knows such sharing is possible, all of which strengthens the growing emotional bond between parent and child. This new understanding is an extremely important leap in terms of Emotion Coaching because it's what makes two-way conversations about feelings possible.

At the same time, the child is developing an understanding that the objects and people in his life have a certain amount of permanence or constancy. Just because a ball rolls under the chair and can't be seen anymore, doesn't mean it doesn't exist. And just because Mom has left the room and can't hear me, she's still part of my world and capable of returning.

As your child explores this concept of "object constancy," he may be fascinated with games that allow him to take small objects in and out of containers, hiding them and then making them reappear. Or, he may repeatedly throw his spoon off his high chair and out of sight, then ask you to fetch it for him again and again.

This budding understanding of the constancy of objects and people may be related to another important development in your baby's life: his growing attachment to specific people—namely, his parents. Now that he's sure you exist even when you're not around, he can miss you and demand that you stay. He may put up quite a fuss when he sees you putting on your coat, or otherwise senses that you're about to leave. When you're gone, he has a sense that you must be *somewhere*, but he doesn't know where, and he may find this upsetting. Also, he has very little sense of time, so it's hard for him to understand just how long you'll be gone.

Psychologists studying infant attachment have observed the way one-year-olds react to being taken care of by unfamiliar adults, to their parents' leaving, and to their reunions. They have found that babies who feel secure may be upset when their parents return, but they allow themselves to be comforted, molding to their parents' bodies as they are held and talked to. But babies who feel insecure about their parents' emotional availability respond to reunions differently, usually in one of two ways: One is a dismissing or avoiding style, where the child ignores her parents when they return and acts as if she is just fine. When her parents try to comfort her, she may push them away from her body instead of molding to them. The other style is anxious and preoccupied, where the baby clings to the parent upon the parent's return and seems hard to comfort. If your child shows such signs of insecurity, she may need for you to be more emotionally available when the two of you are together. In other words, she needs you to respond to her expressions of emotion with empathy, concern, and affection, all of which strengthen your emotional bond.

To help a child this age cope with the separation anxiety that typically occurs when parents have to leave, reassure him that you will return. Remember that although a one-year-old may not be able to speak well himself, he usually understands a great deal of your language, so your reassurances can help. Keep in mind also, that he's looking to you for emotional cues, so if you appear anxious or fearful about the parting, he may pick up on that emotion and feel it, too. Therefore, it's best to find a caregiver with whom you're comfortable, and make sure you and the baby have time to get acquainted with this person before you have to leave. This will make you feel more relaxed and so will the baby. And finally, you can help your child practice being apart from you by letting him explore separate spaces at home on his own. If he crawls off to another (baby-proofed) room, for example, let him go for a while before you check up on him. If you're together in one room and you have to go to another, tell him where you're going and that you'll be back momentarily. Gradually, he'll get the idea that parents can leave and nothing terrible happens, and that parents can be trusted to come back when they say they will.

Remember that you can help your child feel more secure, more emotionally bonded to you, by expressing your understanding of her thoughts and feelings. This can be done moment by moment as you care for her and play with her. Or, you can continue to invent games that encourage imitation and wide-ranging expressions of emotion. One game that my daughter, Moriah, and I invented when she was this age we called "The Guys." Each night I would take a pen and draw a different facial expression on each finger of one hand. The thumb would always look angry, the index finger sad, the middle finger fearful, the ring finger surprised, and the little finger happy. Then Moriah would crawl up on my lap and we would talk with "the guys" about how our day had been. The thumb might say, "Oh, I had a bad day. I'm so mad I could kick something." And the index finger would say, "Oh, I had a bad day, too, but I was sad today. I wanted to cry." Then they would turn toward Moriah and say, "What kind of day did you have?" She would think for a while and then grab the finger that was most like her day. This would give me a chance to help her label her feeling. "Oh, you had a sad day today." After she acquired more words, this gesture would be accompanied with her own words. She might say, "Missed Mommy." Then I might add, "Oh, you felt sad today because you missed Mommy after she went to work," which let me show her empathy. "I understand how you felt," I might add. "Sometimes when Mom goes to work I feel sad too because I miss her."

---

## THE TODDLER YEARS (AGES ONE TO THREE)

TODDLERHOOD IS A fun and exciting time as your child develops a sense of himself and begins to explore his autonomy. But there's a good reason that this period has also been dubbed the terrible twos. It's the time children become much more self-assertive and, for the first time, noncompliant. As your child practices his burgeoning language skills, the words you'll hear most often include, "No!"

"Mine!" and "Do by myself!" or "Me do!" Emotion Coaching becomes an important tool parents can use to help toddlers deal with their emerging sense of frustration and anger.

As in all stages of development, parents do well to look at conflicts and challenges from the perspective of the child. Because the toddler's primary developmental task at this age is to establish herself as an independent little being, try to avoid situations that make her feel that she has no power, no control. A woman in one of our parenting groups described trying to make her two-year-old take a dropperful of pink medicine prescribed for an ear infection. Using the tack she had employed since he was an infant, she swaddled him in a towel, held him down, and tried to force him to swallow the medicine. "But he fought like crazy and refused to take it," she explained. "Then my sister walked in, took the dropper out of my hand, and said to my son, 'Do you want to do it yourself?' My son nodded, took the dropper, squeezed the medicine into his mouth, and swallowed every drop." All he wanted was a little control over the situation.

It helps to give toddlers lots of little (but real) choices as you go through your day together. Rather than saying, "It's chilly outside. You must wear a coat," say, "What would you rather wear today? Your jacket or your sweater?" Keep your limit setting focused on issues of your toddler's safety and your peace of mind. Providing her with a stimulating, child-proofed environment makes this easier.

At the same time toddlers are grappling with matters of self-assertiveness, they are becoming increasingly interested in other children. In fact, from a very early age, they seem to be acutely aware of differences and similarities among people most like themselves. Research psychologist T. G. R. Bower showed that baby boys preferred looking at films of a young boy moving and baby girls preferred looking at films of a young girl moving. Amazingly, when Bower created a film showing only bright dots placed at the joints of the moving children (a dot at the knee, another at the elbow, and so on), he found that once again, baby boys preferred the "boy dot" films while baby girls preferred the "girl dot" films.

While toddlers may be extremely attracted to one another, they don't yet have the social skills needed to play well together. Indeed, attempts at cooperative play and sharing are often problematic, given the "toddler rules of ownership," which are: (1) If I see it, it's mine; (2) If it's yours and I want it, it's mine; and (3) If it's mine, it's mine forever. Parents should realize that such attitudes are not based on meanness; they are simply an expression of the toddler's developing sense of self. Children this age can only consider their own points of view and are incapable of understanding that others may feel differently. Consequently, the concept of sharing is meaningless to them.

There is a positive side to toddlers' conflicts over toys, and the emotional fireworks that usually result. Such episodes provide terrific opportunities for Emotion Coaching. Parents can help their toddlers by acknowledging and labeling the child's anger or frustration. ("You feel mad when somebody takes your doll," or, "You feel frustrated that you can't have that ball right now.") Parents can also begin to explore problem solving with the children by introducing them to the concept of taking turns. If a conflict deteriorates into a physical fight, let the perpetrators know that "we don't hit" or otherwise hurt our playmates out of anger, and then turn your attention to the victims, offering empathy and soothing.

Remember, also, to praise and encourage your toddler anytime you see him making even the slightest overture toward sharing, but don't expect it. Parallel play, where each child stays in his or her own space playing independently, is usually more successful at this age.

Toddlers' conflicts over belongings will never be completely eliminated. But for sanity's sake, you may want to minimize such episodes. This can be done by explaining to children that they should only take toys to a friend's house or to the child-care center if they intend to share them. And when your toddler is expecting playmates at his house, have him choose a few special belongings that will be off-limits to the visitors. Then, with some degree of ceremony, put them away before the outsiders arrive. This may give the child the sense of power and control that he is seeking.

In addition to his increasing awareness of himself as separate from others, another important social milestone is the toddler's developing interest in symbolic and pretend play. Sometime between the ages of two and three, children begin acting out behaviors they've observed earlier in other family members. What's new here is the child's ability to store memories of actions and events in their mind and then retrieve them for imitation at a later time. It's fun to watch a two-year-old pretend to cook, shave, sweep the floor, or talk on the telephone. And watching a child tenderly kiss her teddy bear good night or harshly scold her dolls for misbehaving may serve as a poignant reminder that children learn much about how to handle their emotions by observing those around them.

## EARLY CHILDHOOD (AGES FOUR TO SEVEN)

BY AGE 4, children are usually out and about in the world, meeting new friends, spending time in a variety of environments, learning lots of new and exciting things. Along with these experiences come new challenges: School is fun, but teachers soon expect you to be able to sit quietly in groups and pay attention to the matter at hand. You generally know how to get along with friends, but they still make you mad or hurt your feelings sometimes. And now that you're old enough to comprehend horrors like house fires, wars, burglars, and death, you've got to keep from being overwhelmed by fear of such things.

Mastering these challenges requires the ability to regulate your emotions, one of the major developmental tasks kids face in early childhood. By this, I mean children must learn to inhibit inappropriate behavior, focus attention, and organize themselves in the service of an outside goal.

Nowhere are children more likely to develop skills at regulating their emotions than in their relationships with their peers. It's here that they learn how to communicate clearly, to exchange information, and to clarify their messages if they are not understood. They learn how to take turns in talking and playing. They learn to share. They learn how to find a common ground in their play activities, to have conflicts, and to resolve them. They learn to be understanding of another person's feelings, wishes, desires.

Because friendship provides such a fertile ground for the emotional development of young children, I encourage parents to ensure that kids get plenty of one-on-one free time with one another. We now know that even a very young child can form strong and lasting attachments to other kids. And we know that these relationships should be taken seriously and respected by parents.

Play sessions for children this age usually work best in pairs. That's because four- to seven-year-olds often have a hard time figuring out how to manage more than one relationship at a time. As a parent, you may find this troubling, especially if you witness two children rejecting a third who tries to join the play. But it helps to keep in mind that the children's rejection isn't necessarily based in meanness. They simply want to protect the play they have managed to establish as a pair. Unable to express this in any terms that the third child would understand or accept ("I'm sorry, Billy, but the pair is the largest social unit we can handle at this point in our development"), the children usually resort to cruder, harsher tactics, like saying, "Go away, Billy. You're not our friend anymore!" Some children may do this with their parents as well, telling one, "Go away, Daddy! I don't love you anymore. I only love Mama!" What the child actually means is she was enjoying the intimacy she had established in the moment with mom. This being the case, dad should not take the snubbing to heart. Indeed, small children can be quite fickle. It's not unusual for two children to reject a third, only to switch gears and regroup moments later, now welcoming the rejected child into a new game or activity.

So what's the best way to react when you see your child excluding a third from play? I recommend offering the child some guidance on how to manage her social relationships graciously, especially if you think it's important to instill values of kindness and sensitivity for others' feelings. You might suggest simple words she can use to explain the situation to the third child. For example, she could say, "I only want to play with Jennifer right now. But I hope that you and I can play together later on."

If your child is the one who is being excluded, it's important to acknowledge your child's feelings, particularly if he or she is feeling sad or angry about the situation. Then you can help your child come up with ways to solve the problem, whether that means inviting another child to play, or finding something enjoyable to do alone. The conversation between Megan and her mother on page 95 provides an example of a parent who uses Emotion-Coaching skills to handle this situation effectively.

In addition to teaching important social skills, friendships among small children also invite fantasy play, allowing kids to soar to the heights of creativity, creating characters and acting out dramas at the same time. Young friends often use fantasy to help one another work through perplexing problems and to deal with the stresses of daily life. This suggests that pretend play facilitates the child's emotional development by helping them to access suppressed feelings in much the same way adults might use visualization or hypnosis. My former student Laurie Kramer discovered, for example, that fantasy play with another child was the best aid in helping a youngster adjust to the birth of a new sibling. By having their playmates take on the role of the newborn, the new "big brothers" and "big sisters" in her study were able to explore a wide range of feelings toward the baby, all the way from hostility to tenderness. In the parental role, they got the chance to play with the baby, teach it, scold it, and nurture it.

I have witnessed children in other studies as well reveal an amazing depth of feeling through fantasy play. We saw one small girl playing house turn to her playmate and say, "We don't have to take naps all the time like my mama and Jimmy (her mother's new boyfriend) do. We're not tired like they are." Then a little bit later, the child's friend asked, "What does your mama say when she closes the door?" The girl replied, "She says, 'Don't come in here.' " Not understanding why her mother excluded her, she added, "She doesn't want me around. She doesn't love me."

Knowing that fantasy can provide a door to a small child's thoughts and worries, Emotion-Coaching parents can use pretend play as a way to connect with their children at this age. Children commonly project ideas, wishes, frustrations and fears onto an object such as a doll or other toy. Parents can encourage the exploration of feelings and offer reassurances by simply reflecting on the lines the child's toy delivers, by taking on the role of another toy, or both. Here's a sample conversation. Notice how easily the parent uses the child's fantasy projection as part of the exchange:

*Child:* This bear is an orphan because its parents didn't want it anymore.
*Dad:* The bear's mom and dad just left?
*Child:* Yeah they went away.

*Dad:* Are they coming back?
*Child:* Never.
*Dad:* Why did they go away?
*Child:* The bear was bad.
*Dad:* What did he do?
*Child:* He got mad at the mama bear.
*Dad:* I think it's okay to get mad sometimes. She will come back.
*Child:* Yeah. Here she comes now.
*Dad* (picking up another bear and speaking in the voice of the mama bear): I just had to go take out the garbage. Now I'm back.
*Child:* Hi, Mommy!
*Dad:* You were mad but that's okay. Sometimes I get mad, too.
*Child:* I know it.

Encouraging children to pretend is a real skill, but once learned, it can be practiced in simple and fruitful ways. For example, your child may be wishing he was bigger and stronger, so he might say, "I used to be very little, but now I can lift the side of the couch. Did you know Superman can even fly?" It's almost as if the child is asking for permission to become Superman to explore such feelings of power and confidence. You can do your part to encourage the fantasy simply by saying, "Pleased to meet you, Superman. Are you going to fly now?"

Children may also intersperse conversations about real-life situations while playing pretend games with you. Don't be surprised if, in the midst of some Barbie doll or Power Ranger fantasy, your child suddenly says something like, "I'm afraid to stay with that baby-sitter again." Or, "How old am I going to be when I die?"

Although the genesis of such ideas may remain a mystery to you, it's obvious that something in the play has stirred up an emotion the child would like to share. The intimacy and spontaneity of pretend play has made her feel safe and close to you, so she lets this sensitive matter rise to the surface. Because she has suspended the pretend play momentarily to explore the emotion, it's probably best for you to suspend play as well, and to have a heart-to-heart talk about the fear she is experiencing.

One reason fantasy play is so popular among four- to seven-year-olds probably has to do with its utility in helping kids cope with a multitude of anxieties likely to peak in early childhood. While the number of fears young children face may seem endless, they are actually all based on a small set of factors:

FEAR OF POWERLESSNESS. I once overheard two five-year-olds discuss "all the things in the world that can kill you." They talked about "robbers, evil people, monsters," and their most dreaded fear of all—"the shark." They discussed all the ways they could destroy these scary things. Then they talked about how they used to be afraid of "silly things like the dark" when they were "babies." But now that they were big, the boys boasted, they were no longer frightened by such foolishness.

This conversation reminded me that even if we could somehow shield children from awareness of all the dangers that really exist in the world, they would invent their own monsters. That's because such fantasies help them cope with their natural feelings of powerlessness and vulnerability. While children are repelled and frightened by the power of monsters, they like to imagine conquering the things they fear. This helps them feel more powerful, less vulnerable.

Emotion-Coaching parents can do their part to help kids feel more powerful as well. As with toddlers, young children grow in self-esteem when they are given choices about what to wear, what to eat, how to play, and so forth. Another important strategy is to allow kids the autonomy to do the things they are ready to do. Whether they are learning to wash their hair or play a new computer game, children need their parents to offer encouragement and guidance without being intrusive. If your child get frustrated trying to tie his own shoe, for example, resist the urge to take over, a move that conveys your belief in the child's incompetence. Instead, offer words of understanding such as, "Long laces can be tricky sometimes." Then, even if the child ends up needing your assistance, you have acknowledged that you understand what he is experiencing.

FEAR OF ABANDONMENT. There is a natural reason why children this age are fascinated with stories like *Snow White*, where a father dies and leaves his daughter to the fate of a wicked stepmother, or *Oliver Twist*, where a youngster must fend for himself as an orphan, beggar, and thief. Such stories articulate a fear common to most children this age, that they could someday be abandoned.

Because this fear is so real and pervasive to children, I discourage parents from using it as a way to threaten, discipline, or even "joke" with their children. Whenever you hear your children expressing such fears, you can use your Emotion-Coaching skills to acknowledge their feelings. Reassure them that you will always see to it that their needs are met and that they will be loved and well cared for.

FEAR OF THE DARK. To children, the dark may represent the great unknown, the place where all their fears and monsters lie. With maturity, children learn that darkness need not be so frightening. But at this age, it's perfectly reasonable for kids to seek the comfort of light and the knowledge that you are nearby and accessible if needed.

Let go of the idea that a child needs to be made tougher by denying his fear of the dark. I know one dad who would not give in to his son's request for a light because he worried that the boy was becoming "a wimp." After several nights, however, the father sensed that his son was becoming even more anxious. In addition to his fear of the dark, the boy became worried about losing his dad's approval. He also became afraid that lying awake at night would leave him unable to function in school the next day. In time, the dad relented, installed a night light, and now the whole family is sleeping more peacefully.

FEAR OF BAD DREAMS. Nightmares are naturally frightening for most every child, but they can be especially scary to young children, who have trouble distinguishing such dreams from reality. If your child wakes up crying from a dream, try holding him and talking to him about the dream, explaining that it wasn't real. Stay with him until he calms down, offering him reassurances that the bad images are gone and that he is safe and secure.

In addition, children may be helped by hearing stories that explain the concepts of dreams and sleep. One particularly fine book is *Annie Stories*, by Doris Brett, who devised tales to help her daughter cope with nightmares. In it, Annie tells her mother about a mean tiger who has been chasing her in her dreams. The mother gives Annie an invisible magic dream ring to take with her to sleep. Then, when the tiger begins to chase Annie again, the girl remembers her ring and confronts the tiger. Finding out the tiger only wants to be her friend, Annie now has an ally with whom she can face her other fears.

When I told my own daughter, Moriah, the Annie stories, she decided to rename the main character Moriah. Later, I found her in the bathroom, standing on the toilet so she could tell herself the stories in the mirror. The strong fear she had about her nightmares changed very quickly after this. She still had them occasionally, but they were no longer so terrifying to her.

FEAR OF PARENTAL CONFLICT. As we discussed in Chapter 5, parental conflict can be very upsetting to children, who often sense that arguments between their folks may jeopardize their own security. As they grow older and become more aware of the consequences of parental fighting, children may also fear that their parents' conflict will lead to separation and divorce. In addition, children often take responsibility for the conflict, believing the problems are their fault. They may come to believe they have the power to solve the conflict; that it is their job to keep the family together.

Parents should remember, then, to keep kids from getting too involved in conflicts between mom and dad (see Chapter 5). Also, when your children witness an argument between you and your partner, help them by showing them the resolution to the conflict as well. As the work of psychologist E. Mark Cummings shows, young children may not understand verbal resolutions very well, but they can be comforted by seeing mom and dad share a genuine hug of forgiveness.

FEAR OF DEATH. Children this age know about death and they may ask you direct questions about it. It is important to be honest, and to let them know that you understand their worries, that you don't find them silly or trivial. If your child has lost a friend, relative, or pet to death, you can acknowledge their sadness about missing that person or animal, and offer hugs and comfort. Trying to ignore or minimize your child's feelings of grief and fear will not make them go away. It will only communicate to children that you are uncomfortable talking about death and it will prevent your child from bringing important feelings to you in the future.

WHATEVER YOUR CHILD'S fears, it's helpful to remember that fear is a natural emotion and it can serve a healthy function in young people's lives. While kids should not be so fearful that they don't explore and learn, they also need to know that the world is sometimes a dangerous place. In this regard, fear can serve to make children appropriately cautious.

Remember to use the basic techniques of Emotion Coaching when you talk to your children about their fears. This means helping kids to recognize and label fear when it surfaces, talking about their fears in an empathetic way, and brainstorming ways to cope with various threats. Talking about strategies for coping with real-life dangers like fire, strangers, or illness provides a good opportunity to discuss issues of prevention as well. If your child expresses fear of fire, for example, you might respond, "The thought of a fire in our house is scary. That's why we always have a smoke detector ready to warn us if something is burning."

Also keep in mind that children may talk about their fears in indirect ways. A boy who asks whether there are still orphanages probably isn't interested in a lecture on child welfare policy; he's thinking about his own fears of abandonment. Listen, therefore, to the emotion behind the question—especially when you hear your child query about topics that touch on scary issues like abandonment or death.

## MIDDLE CHILDHOOD (AGES EIGHT TO TWELVE)

DURING THIS PERIOD of childhood, kids are beginning to relate to a larger social group and understand social influence. They may begin to notice who is in and who is out among their peers. At the same time, children are developing cognitively, learning the power of intellect over emotion.

Because of your child's growing awareness of peer influence, you may begin to discern that one of his primary motivations in life is to avoid embarrassment at all costs. Children this age often become quite particular about the style of clothes they wear, the kind of backpack they'll carry, the type of activities they'll be seen doing. They'll go to great lengths to avoid calling attention to themselves, especially if it might lead to teasing or criticism from their friends. While this can be irritating to parents who want their children to be leaders, not followers, conformity at this age is quite healthy. It means that your child is becoming adept at reading social cues, a skill that will serve him well throughout his life. And in middle childhood, it's particularly important because children this age can be merciless in their teasing and humiliation. Indeed, teasing is the forge that forms many standards of behavior at this age. Girls tease as well as boys, although with boys, teasing may also extend to physical confrontation.

With the stakes so high, children soon learn that the best response to teasing is to show no emotional response at all. Protest, cry, tattle, or get angry when the ringleader is stealing your hat or calling you names and you risk further humiliation and rejection. Turn the other cheek and you've got a good chance at maintaining your dignity. Because of this dynamic, children perform an "emotion-ectomy" of sorts, cutting feelings out of the arena of peer relations. While most children master it, our studies found that the ones who master it best are those who learn, through Emotion Coaching, how to regulate their emotions earlier in childhood.

This "cool" attitude toward peer relationships may be confusing for parents who have been good Emotion Coaches for their children. In our parenting groups, we found that moms and dads often mistakenly think that all children this age need to do when they have a conflict with peers is to share their feelings with the other child and work things out. While this strategy may work in preschool, it can be a disaster in middle childhood, when expressing emotions is seen as a social liability. Emotion-Coached children are likely to have developed the social insight to know this. They'll be able to read their peers' cues and act appropriately.

At the same time children this age are trying to stifle their emotions, they are becoming more aware of the power of intellect. At around age ten or so, many experience a dramatic increase in their ability to reason logically. I like to compare them to *Star Trek*'s Mr. Spock, who shuns feelings, but revels in the world of logic and reason. They enjoy responding to the world as if their minds were computers. Tell a nine-year-old to "pick up your socks," for example, and he may lift each sock up and then put it down in place, explaining, "You didn't tell me to *put them away*."

Such sassiness and mockery of the adult world is typical of a child who is looking at life in terms of black and white, either-or, right and wrong. Suddenly aware of all the arbitrary and illogical standards operating in the world, a preteen may begin to perceive life as one big *Mad* magazine. Adults are seen as hypocrites, while mockery and contempt of grown-ups become the child's favorite "emotions."

Emerging out of all of this judgment and evaluation is a child's sense of his own values. You may notice your child becoming quite concerned at this age with what is moral and just. He may conceive of "pure worlds" where all people are treated as equals, where Nazism and war could never arise, where tyranny could never exist. He may become contemptuous of an adult world that could allow such atrocities as the slave trade or the Inquisition. He will begin to doubt, he will begin to challenge, he will begin to think for himself.

The irony, of course, is her simultaneous commitment to the arbitrary and tyrannical standards of her own peer group. At the same time she's espousing an individual's right to freedom of expression, she may limit her wardrobe to one and only one style of designer sweatshirt. At the same time she is deeply concerned about cruel treatment of animals by the cosmetic industry, she may be participating in an unkind plot to exclude a certain classmate from the basketball game at recess.

How, as a parent, should you react to such inconsistencies? My advice is to let them go, recognizing that this is a time of exploration. Know that children's total adherence to arbitrary rules in their peer world is part of a normal and healthy development. It reflects their ability to recognize standards and values in their peer world that are related to acceptance and avoiding rejection.

If you find out that your child is involved in some treatment of another child that you consider unfair, let your child know how you feel. Use it as an opportunity to convey your values regarding kindness and fair play. But, unless the incident was truly mean, I would advise against an overly harsh response or punishment. Cliquishness and the exertion of peer pressure is normal behavior for children this age.

If your child complains of being excluded or unfairly treated by peers, you can use Emotion-Coaching techniques to help him cope with feelings of sadness and anger. Then, help him brainstorm solutions to the problem at hand. Explore, for example, the ways a person goes about making and keeping friends. Don't trivialize a child's desire to fit in, to dress and act like other children in his age group. Instead, validate his desire for acceptance and be his ally in making it happen.

As for children's mockery of adult conventions, I advise parents not to take their children's criticisms personally. Sassiness, sarcasm, and contempt for adult values are normal tendencies of middle childhood. If you genuinely feel that your child has treated you rudely, however, tell him so in specific terms. ("When you make fun of my hairstyle, I feel like you don't respect me.") Again, this is a way to convey values such as kindness and mutual respect within the family. As always, children this age need to feel emotionally connected to their parents and they need the loving guidance that connection brings.

## ADOLESCENCE

THE TEEN YEARS are a period marked by great concern with questions of identity: Who am I? What am I becoming? Who should I be? Don't be surprised, therefore, if your child seems to become totally self-absorbed at some point in adolescence. His interest in family matters will wane as his relationships with friends take center stage. After all, it is through his friendships that he will discover who he is outside the familiar confines of home. And yet, even within his peer relationships, a teenager's focus is usually on himself.

While doing research on children's friendships, we once taped a conversation between two teen girls that epitomized the adolescent's concern with self. Having just met, one of the girls revealed that she had spent the summer as a counselor at a camp for emotionally disturbed children. Rather than asking her new acquaintance for details, the second girl simply used the revelation as a launch pad for her own self-exploration. "Wow, that's really interesting," the second girl said, "but I could never do that. I have no patience. My sister hands me her new baby and I think he's cute, but when he cries, I just hand him back like, 'No, thanks.' And I don't think I could ever be a mom. No way. I have no patience. I don't see how you could ever get the patience to be a counselor to those kids. I suppose I should be more like you, but I'm not sure I could be. Do you think I could?"

And so the monologue continued as the girl compared herself to her new friend, wondering aloud about her ability to change and grow, considering which characteristics in herself she admired and which she detested. If she allowed the spotlight to shift, it was not because she wanted to get to know her friend more intimately, but because she wanted to further see her friend as a foil to herself. As it is with most teenagers, her friendship served as a vehicle for exploring her own identity.

Although extreme, this example shows the motivation beneath adolescent self-absorption. Teens are on a journey of self-discovery and they are constantly steering, first in one direction and then another, trying to find a way that's true. They experiment with new identities, new realities, new aspects of self. Such exploration among teenagers is healthy.

Their way, however, is not always smooth. Hormonal changes may cause uncontrolled and rapid mood shifts. Unsavory forces in the social environment may exploit young people's vulnerability, putting them at risk for problems like drugs, violence, or unsafe sexual activity. Yet the exploration continues as a natural and inevitable part of human development.

Among the important tasks teens face in this exploration is the integration of reason and emotion. If middle childhood can be represented by *Star Trek*'s highly rational Mr. Spock, then the best symbol for adolescence may be Captain Kirk. In his role at the helm of the Starship *Enterprise*, Kirk constantly faces decisions where his highly feeling, human side is pitted against his penchant for logical, empirically based reasoning. Of course, the good captain always finds just the right balance so as to provide impeccable leadership for his crew. He uses the kind of judgment we can only hope our teenagers will exercise when placed in situations where the heart hears one call and the head hears another.

Teens seem most likely to face such decisions around issues of sexuality and self-acceptance. A girl finds herself sexually attracted to a boy she doesn't really respect. ("He is *so* cute. Too bad he has to open his mouth and ruin everything.") A boy catches himself spouting opinions that he once protested in his father. ("I can't believe it! I sound just like my dad!") Suddenly, the teen realizes that the world is not so black and white. It's made up of many shades of gray and, like it or not, all those shades may be encompassed within the teen himself.

If finding one's path in adolescence is difficult, so is being the parent of a teenager. That's because most of your teen's exploration of self must be done without you. As counselor and author Michael Riera writes, "Until this point you have acted as a 'manager' in your child's life: arranging rides and doctors' appointments, planning outside or weekend activities, helping with and checking on homework. You stay closely informed about school life, and you are usually the first person your child seeks out with the 'big' questions. Suddenly, none of this is applicable. Without notification and without consensus, you are fired from this role as manager. Now you must scramble and re-strategize; if you are to have a meaningful influence in your teenager's life through adolescence and beyond, then you must work your tail off to get re-hired as a consultant."

This, of course, can be an extremely delicate transition. A client doesn't hire a consultant who makes him feel incompetent or threatens to take over his business. A client wants a consultant he can trust, who understands his mission and offers solid advice that will help him reach his goals. And at this point in life, a teenager's primary goal must be achieving autonomy.

So how can you fulfill the role of advisor? How can you stay close enough to be an Emotion Coach while allowing your child the independence his development as a full-fledged adult requires? Here are a few pointers, based in large part on the work of psychologist and author Haim Ginott:

**Accept that adolescence is a time for children to separate from their parents** Parents must accept, for example, that teenagers need their privacy. Eavesdropping on your son's conversations, reading his journal, or asking too many probing questions gives him the message that you don't trust him. This, in turn, sets up a barrier to communication. Your child may begin to see you as the enemy rather than his ally during difficult times.

Along with respecting a child's privacy, you must respect his right to be restless and discontent at times. As poet and photographer Gordon Parks once wrote of his own adolescence, "In its pain-bred name, I was rapturously unhappy." Allow your child the space to experience this depth of feeling by avoiding obvious questions like, "What's the matter with you?" Your teenager may be sad or angry or anxious or despondent, and such queries only imply your disapproval of these emotions.

If, on the other hand, your teen freely opens his heart to you, try not to act as if you instantly understand. Because of their fresh perspective, teenagers often feel that their experiences are unique. They feel insulted when adults find their behavior transparent, their motivations obvious. Therefore, take time with your listening and hear your teen with an open mind. Don't assume that you already know and understand everything he has to say.

Because the teen years are a time of individuation, know that your teen may choose styles of dress, haircuts, music, art, and language that you don't care for. Remember that you don't need to approve of your child's choices, you only need to accept them.

By the same token, don't try to emulate your teenager's choices. Let his dress, music, gestures, and slang make a statement that says, "I'm different from my parents and I'm proud of it."

**Show respect for your teenager.** Think, for a moment, what it would be like to have your best friend treat you the way many parents treat their teenagers. How would it feel to be constantly corrected, reminded of your deficiencies, or teased about sensitive issues? What if your friend delivered long-winded lectures at you, telling you in judgmental tones what to do with your life and how to do it. You would probably feel as though this person did not have much respect for you, did not care about your feelings. In time, you would probably pull away, no longer trusting your friend with your heart.

While I won't say that parents need to treat their teenagers exactly as friends (the parent-child relationship is far more complex), I will certainly say that teens deserve at least as much respect as we afford our buddies. Therefore, I would encourage you to avoid teasing, criticism, and humiliation. Communicate your values to your child, but do it in a way that's brief and nonjudgmental. Nobody likes to be preached to, least of all teenagers.

When conflicts arise over your teen's behavior, don't use trait labels (lazy, greedy, sloppy, selfish) to talk about it. Talk instead in terms of specific actions, telling your child how what she has done affects you. ("When you leave without doing the dishes, I feel resentful because I have to do your work for you.") And certainly don't try to use reverse psychology—for example, telling your teen to do just the opposite of what you really want, anticipating that she'll rebel and you'll get your desired outcome in the end. Such strategies are confusing, manipulative, dishonest, and they rarely work.

**Provide your child with a community.** There is a popular saying that "it takes a whole village to raise a child." At no time is this more true than adolescence. That's why I advise you to get to know the people involved in your teenager's daily life, including her friends and her friends' parents.

I once heard a woman speak at her synagogue about the work her college-age daughter was doing to help with the resettlement of Ethiopian refugees. The mother acknowledged that the young woman's work was a great act of charity and kindness and that she thought her daughter was a fine human being. "As much as my husband and I would like to take credit for the way our daughter has turned out," the woman said, "I think the credit really belongs to this community." She went on to explain that there had been difficulties during the girl's teen years, times when the daughter was so upset she would not speak to her mom and dad. But during all the turbulence, the woman knew the girl was spending time in her friends' homes and talking with her friends' parents. And because they were all part of the same community, she knew their families shared the same values. "I trusted this community and, as a result, our daughter has grown to be a woman we're all proud of," the mother said. "But we didn't raise her alone. This whole community raised her."

Because we cannot be all things to our children—and especially not during adolescence—I advise parents to give their children the support of a caring community. It may be through a synagogue, a church, a school, or a neighborhood group. It may simply be through your extended family or an informal network of friends. The point is, be sure your kids have access to other adults who share your ethics and ideals. These will be the people your child can rely on when he inevitably and naturally distances himself from you, but still needs guidance and support.

***Encourage independent decision making while continuing to be your child's Emotion Coach.*** Granted, finding the right level of involvement in your teenager's life is one of the toughest challenges you may face as a parent. As always, encouraging autonomy means allowing kids to do what they are ready to do. Now is the time they'll be making decisions about things that matter. Now is also a good time to practice saying, "The choice is yours." Express confidence in your child's judgment and resist speculating about possibly disastrous outcomes as a warning.

Encouraging autonomy also means allowing your teen to make unwise (but not unsafe) decisions from time to time. Remember that teens can learn as much from mistakes as they can from their successes. This is especially true if they have a caring, supportive adult nearby—somebody to help them cope with their negative emotions over failures and to come up with ways to do things better in the future.

Remember, our studies indicate that success will come easier to young people whose parents practice Emotion Coaching. These are the teens who will be more emotionally intelligent, understanding and accepting of their own feelings. They will have had more experience solving problems on their own and with others. As a result, they will experience more success academically and in their relationships with peers. With such protective factors in hand, these teens will be buffered against the risks all parents fear as their children enter adolescence—risks like drugs, delinquency, violence, and unsafe sex.

Therefore I urge you to stay aware of what's going on in your child's life. Accept and validate your child's emotional experiences. When there is a problem, lend an ear and listen empathetically, without judgment. And be an ally when he comes to you for help with a problem. Although these steps are simple, we now know they form the basis of a lifetime of emotional support between parent and child.

# APPENDIX:

# RECOMMENDED

# CHILDREN'S BOOKS

READING ALOUD IS AN EXCELLENT ACTIVITY TO SHARE WITH your child from infancy through adolescence. It demonstrates to children that adults care enough to spend this intimate time with them. Also, books can be a great catalyst for conversation about feelings.

Below is a list of favorite children's books that deal with difficult emotions like anger, sadness, and fear. As you read them with your child, take time to talk about the books' themes and the emotions they elicit.

## BOOKS FOR INFANTS AND TODDLERS

*Feelings* by Aliki (Greenwillow, 1984)

A catalogue of emotions with great illustrations that can help young children form a vocabulary for feelings like sorrow, joy, love, hate, pride, fear, and frustration.

*Going to the Potty* by Fred Rogers, illustrated by Jim Judkis (Putnam, 1986)

Trust public television's Mister Rogers to help little ones sort through their feelings about a major life transition. Other books in this "First Experience" series include *Going to Day Care*, *Going to the Doctor*, and *The New Baby*.

*Holes and Peeks* by Ann Jonas (Greenwillow, 1984)

Peeking through buttonholes and other small spaces to see scary things makes them seem less harrowing.

*The Runaway Bunny* by Margaret Wise Brown, illustrated by Clement Hurd (Harper & Row, 1972)

Baby bunny fantasizes about running away from his mother. With each fantasy, mother reassures him that she'll always be there to find and protect him.

## BOOKS FOR EARLY CHILDHOOD

*Alexander and the Terrible, Horrible, No Good, Very Bad Day* by Judith Viorst, illustrated by Ray Cruz (Atheneum, 1972)

It all starts with a cereal box that has no prize and goes downhill from there.

The *Berenstain Bears* series by Stan and Jan Berenstain (Random House)

In each book, the Bear Family comes up with reasonable solutions to common problems of family life. Topics include nightmares, telling the truth, limiting television, getting along with friends, money woes, going away to camp, and more.

*Gila Monsters Meet You at the Airport* by Marjorie Weinman Sharmat, illustrated by Byron Barton (Macmillan, 1990)

A little boy's outrageous fantasies about moving to a new city provide an opportunity for families to talk about fears, real and imagined.

*Harry and the Terrible Whatzit* by Dick Gackenbach (Clarion, 1978)

A reassuring story about a little boy who follows his mom into the cellar to protect her from the monsters he imagines lurk there.

*The Hating Book* by Charlotte Zolotow, illustrated by Ben Schecter (Harper, 1969)

A brief story about the ups and downs of spending time with a close friend.

*Ira Sleeps Over* by Bernard Waber (Houghton Mifflin, 1972)

Ira must decide whether to bring his teddy bear when he's invited to spend the night at a friend's house.

*Julius, the Baby of the World* by Kevin Henkes (Greenwillow, 1990)
How Lily the mouse copes with her anger and jealousy over the arrival of a new baby brother.

*Little Rabbit's Loose Tooth* by Lucy Bate, illustrated by Diane deGroat (Crown, 1975)
One charming bunny's experience of this exciting milestone.

*My Mama Needs Me* by Mildred Pits Walter, illustrated by Pat Cummings (Lothrop, Lee & Shepard, 1983)
Before the arrival of his new sister, Jason is worried about his ability to be a good big brother. After the baby comes, he's relieved that she sleeps most of the time.

*My Mom Travels a Lot* by Caroline Feller Bauer, illustrated by Nancy Winslow Parker (Puffin, 1981)
A matter-of-fact outlook on the good and bad aspects of having a traveling mom.

*No Nap* by Eve Bunting, illustrated by Susan Meddaugh (Clarion, 1990)
A humorous book about a little girl with the manic energy of one who is very tired but will not sleep.

*Outside Over There* by Maurice Sendak (Harper, 1981)
In this richly illustrated book, Ida enters a dreamscape to rescue her baby sister, who's been kidnapped.

*Owen* by Kevin Henkes (Greenwillow, 1993)
Owen and his mother worry what he'll do with his security blanket when he goes to school for the first time.

*Shy Charles* by Rosemary Wells (Dial, 1988)
This timid little mouse has trouble with dance lessons and saying thank you to strangers, but can call for help in a real emergency. Once the crisis is over, he goes back to being his retiring self.

*The Something* by Natalie Babbitt (Farrar, Straus, 1970)

Afraid that "Something" might climb through his window at night, Mylo makes a clay sculpture of his frightening fantasy creature. Then, when he meets his creation in a dream, he's no longer intimidated by it.

*Uncle Elephant* by Arnold Lobel (Harper, 1981)
Separation anxiety is the theme of this book, which deals with a little elephant who fears his folks have been lost at sea.

*Where the Wild Things Are* by Maurice Sendak (Harper & Row, 1963)
A well loved book about Max, who is sent to bed without his supper and then dreams of wild, scary, but charming monsters.

*William's Doll* by Charlotte Zolotow, illustrated by William Pene du Bois (Harper, 1972)
William's father, brother, and friends discourage him from wishing for a doll. But the little boy's grandmother puts the matter in perspective for the whole family.

## BOOKS FOR MIDDLE CHILDHOOD

*Afternoon of the Elves* by Janet Taylor Lisle (Scholastic, 1991)
Issues of loyalty, friendship, and privacy are addressed in this tale of two fourth-grade girls, one a misfit who draws the other into her fantasy world of elves.

*Anne of Green Gables* by Lucy M. Montgomery (Bantam, 1908; reissued, 1983)
The adventures of eleven-year-old orphan Anne Shirley, whose hot temper and exuberant personality challenge her foster family on Prince Edward Island at the turn of the century.

*The Bear's House* by Marilyn Sachs (Dutton, 1987)
An ill-kempt ten-year-old, whose mother is sick and whose father deserts them, suffers the taunts of her classmates. To escape her pain, she retreats into the fantasy world of a classroom dollhouse.

*Best Enemies* by Kathleen Leverich, illustrated by Susan Condie Lamb (Greenwillow, 1989)
Second-grader Priscilla Robin learns to stand up for herself against a menacing classmate in ruffles.

*Call It Courage* by Armstrong Sperry (Macmillan, 1940)
A South Seas tale of a boy, teased by peers, overcoming his fear of the sea.

*A Gift for Tia Rosa* by Karen T. Taha, illustrated by Dee deRosa (Bantam, 1991)
Carmela adores her elderly Hispanic neighbor, Tia Rosa, who is teaching her how to knit. When the old lady dies suddenly, Carmela must find a way to demonstrate how much she loved her friend.

*The Hundred Dresses* by Eleanor Estes, illustrated by Louis Slobodkin (Harcourt Brace, 1944)
A sensitive Polish immigrant girl's struggles to fit in with her elementary school classmates.

*Matilda* by Roald Dahl, illustrated by Quentin Blake (Viking, 1988)
Brilliant and resourceful Matilda must cope with outlandishly cruel parents and a fiendish headmistress. She finds refuge through the friendship of a loving teacher.

*Sleep Out* by Carol Carrick, illustrated by David Carrick (Clarion, 1973)
Christopher and his dog conquer their fears to spend the night camping in the woods alone.

## BOOKS FOR OLDER CHILDREN AND TEENS

*Are You There God? It's Me, Margaret* by Judy Blume (Bradbury, Dell, 1970)
Nearly twelve, Margaret chats often with God as she faces her fears and anticipation about growing up.

*Maniac Magee* by Jerry Spinelli (Little, Brown, 1990)
This exciting story of a wise and kind twelve-year-old runaway orphan touches issues of racism, homelessness, and community violence.

*The Moonlight Man* by Paula Fox (Bradbury, 1986)
Catherine learns much about herself during the vacation she spends with her alcoholic father, shortly after her parents' divorce.

*My Brother Is Stealing Second* by Jim Naughton (Harper & Row, 1989)
The emotional story of a teenage boy's recovery after the accidental death of his brother.

*One-Eyed Cat* by Paula Fox (Bradbury, 1984)
Ned, a boy isolated from friends and family, must come to terms with his guilt over shooting out the eye of a wild cat.

*Scorpions* by Walter Dean Myers (Harper & Row, 1988)
A twelve-year-old boy from Harlem copes with pressures at home and school at the same time he finds himself becoming the leader of a street gang.

# NOTES

## 1 : EMOTION COACHING: THE KEY TO RAISING EMOTIONALLY INTELLIGENT KIDS

PAGE

20   *"Family life is our first school"*: Daniel Goleman, *Emotional Intelligence* (New York: Bantam, 1995), pp. 189–90.

20   *Working with research teams:* John Gottman, Lynn Katz, and Carol Hooven, *Meta-emotion: How Families Communicate Emotionally, Links to Child Peer Relations and Other Developmental Outcomes* (Mahwah, N.J.: Lawrence Erlbaum, 1996).

24   *By observing and analyzing:* Ibid.

25   *With more than half:* U.S. Bureau of the Census, "Live Births, Deaths, Marriages, and Divorces: 1950 to 1992," *Statistical Abstract of the United States: 1994* (114th Edition) (Washington, D.C., 1994).

25   *Our own research shows:* John Gottman and Lynn Katz, "Effects of Marital Discord on Young Children's Peer Interaction and Health," *Developmental Psychology*, Vol. 57 (1989), pp. 47–52.

25   *But when the Emotion-Coaching parents:* Gottman, Katz, and Hooven, *Meta-emotion*.

26   *28 percent of American children:* B. A. Chadwick and T. Heson, *Statistical Handbook on the American Family* (New York: Oryx Press, 1992).

28   *Between 1985 and 1990:* F. Landis Mackellar and Machiko Yanagishita, *Homicide in the United States: Who's at Risk*

(Washington, D.C.: Population Reference Bureau, February 1995).

28   *From 1965 to 1991:* Elena de Lisser, "For Inner-City Youth, a Hard Life May Lead to a Hard Sentence," *Wall Street Journal,* November 30, 1993.

28   *some 30 percent are:* National Center for Health Statistics, "Advance Report of Final Natality Statistics," *Monthly Vital Statistics Report,* Vol. 42, No. 3, Suppl. (Hyattsville, MD: Public Health Service, 1993).

28   *half of all new marriages:* U.S. Bureau of the Census, "Live Births, Deaths, Marriages, and Divorces: 1950 to 1992."

29   *around 28 percent:* Chadwick and Heson, *Statistical Handbook on the American Family.*

29   *half of the families living in poverty:* Census of Population and Housing, 1990: Guide (New York: Diane Publishing).

29   *Figures from the 1989 U.S. Census:* U.S. Bureau of the Census, "Child Support—Award and Recipiency Status of Women: 1981 to 1989," *Statistical Abstract of the United States: 1994* (114th Edition) (Washington, D.C., 1994).

29   *One study of children:* F. F. Furstenberg et al., "The Life Course of Children of Divorce: Marital Disruption and Parental Contact," *American Sociological Review,* Vol. 48 (1983), pp. 656–68.

29   *According to one Canadian study:* Martin Daly and Margo Wilson, "Child Abuse and Other Risks of Not Living with Both Parents," *Ethology and Sociobiology,* Vol. 6 (1985), pp. 197–210.

29   *the typical American family:* Juliet B. Schor, "Stolen Moments," *Sesame Street Parents,* July/August 1994, p. 24.

30   *One survey showed:* Juliet B. Schor, *The Overworked American: The Unexpected Decline of Leisure* (New York: Basic Books, 1991), p. 5.

31   *preschoolers typically demand:* Gerald R. Patterson, *Coercive Family Process* (Eugene, OR: Castalia, 1982).

31   *Psychiatrist Lloyd deMause:* Lloyd deMause, "The Evolution of Childhood," *The History of Childhood* (New York: Harper & Row 1974).

32   *Social psychologist Lois Murphy:* G. Murphy, L. Murphy, and

T. M. Newcomb, *Experimental Social Psychology* (New York: Harper and Brothers, 1931).

32   *an "authoritative" style of parenting:* Diana Baumrind, "Child Care Practices Anteceding Three Patterns of Preschool Behavior," *Genetic Psychology Monographs*, Vol. 75 (1975), pp. 43–88; and Diana Baumrind, "Current Patterns of Parental Authority," *Developmental Psychology Monograph*, Vol. 4 (1971).

34   *Haim Ginott:* Haim G. Ginott, *Between Parent and Child* (New York: Macmillan, 1965).

35   *Adele Faber and Elaine Mazlish:* Adele Faber and Elaine Mazlish, *Liberated Parents/Liberated Children* (New York: Avon, 1975); *How to Talk so Kids Will Listen and Listen so Kids Will Talk* (New York, Avon, 1980); *Siblings Without Rivalry* (New York: Norton, 1987); *How to Talk so Kids Can Learn—At Home and in School* (New York: Rawson, 1995).

3 : THE FIVE KEY STEPS FOR EMOTION COACHING

PAGE

77   *To find out if one gender:* Gottman, Katz, and Hooven, *Meta-emotion.*

102   *"accepting the childishness of children":* Haim G. Ginott, *Between Parent and Child* (New York: Macmillan, 1965) p. 110.

103   *I urge parents who use time-outs:* For more information on the effective use of time-outs, I recommend Carolyn Webster-Stratton's excellent book, *The Incredible Years: A Trouble-Shooting Guide for Parents of Children Aged 3–8* (Toronto: Umbrella Press, 1993). Her book provides step-by-step guides on dealing with discipline and control problems, and her intervention has been well researched and shown to be effective. For preadolescents and adolescents, I recommend two research-based books by Gerald Patterson and Marion Forgatch: *Parents and Adolescents Living Together: The Basics* (Eugene, Oregon: Castalia Press, 1987) and *Parents and Adolescents Living Together: Part 2* (Eugene, OR: Castalia Press, 1989).

103  *A 1990 survey of college students:* A. M. Graziano and K. A.
Namaste, "Parental Use of Physical Force in Child Discipline," *Journal of Interpersonal Violence*, Vol. 5(4) (1990), pp.
449–63.

103  *Only about 11 percent of parents in Sweden:* W. W. Deley,
"Physical Punishment of Children: Sweden and the U.S.A.,"
*Journal of Comparative Family Studies*, Vol. 19(3) (1988); R. J.
Gelles and A. W. Edfeldt, "Violence Toward Children in the
United States and Sweden," *Child Abuse and Neglect*, Vol.
10(4) (1986), pp. 501–10.

## 4 : EMOTION-COACHING STRATEGIES

PAGE

115  *"If you can't build ":* Christopher Hallowell, *Father to the Man:
A Journal* (New York: Morrow, 1987), p. 64.

119  *Imagine your spouse bringing home:* Faber and Mazlish, *Siblings
Without Rivalry*, p. 36.

134  *Following each item:* The first two items were suggested by Alice Ginott-Cohen.

## 5 : MARRIAGE, DIVORCE, AND YOUR CHILD'S EMOTIONAL HEALTH

PAGE

139  *Emotion Coaching can have a buffering effect:* Gottman, Katz
and Hooven, *Meta-emotion*.

141  *the rate of clinically significant mental health problems:* E. Mavis
Hetherington, "Long-term Outcomes of Divorce and Remar-
riage: The Early Adolescent Years," in A. S. Masten (chair),
"Family Processes and Youth Functioning During the Early
Adolescent Years," symposium conducted at the biennial
meeting of the Society for Research in Child Development,
New Orleans, LA (1993), cited by E. Mark Cummings and
Patrick Davies in *Children and Marital Conflict: The Impact of
Family Dispute and Resolution* (London: Guilford, 1994), pp.
131–32.

141  *"a preoccupied and/or emotionally disturbed":* E. Mavis Hether-

ington, "Coping with Marital Transitions: A Family Systems Perspective," *Monographs of the Society for Research in Child Development*, Vol. 57 (1992), p. 6.

142 *Research psychologist E. Mark Cummings:* E. M. Cummings, "Coping with Background Anger in Early Childhood," *Child Development*, Vol. 58 (1987), pp. 976–84; E. M. Cummings, R. J. Iannotti, and C. Zahn-Waxler, "The Influence of Conflict Between Adults on the Emotions and Aggression of Young Children," *Developmental Psychology*, Vol. 21 (1985), pp. 495–507.

142 *nonverbal stress reactions:* R. Shred, P. M. McDonnell, G. Church, and J. Rowan, "Infants' Cognitive and Emotional Responses to Adults' Angry Behavior," paper presented at the biennial meeting of the Society for Research in Child Development, Seattle, WA (1991), cited by Cummings and Davies in *Children and Marital Conflict*, pp. 131–32.

143 *"the great education tragedy":* Barbara Dafoe Whitehead, "Dan Quayle Was Right," *The Atlantic Monthly*, April 1993.

143 *Children carry such problems:* Nicholas Zill, Donna Ruane Morrison, and Mary Jo Coiro, "Long-Term Effects of Parental Divorce on Parent-Child Relationships, Adjustment, and Achievement in Young Adulthood," *Journal of Family Psychology*, Vol. 7 (1993), pp. 91–103.

144 *To find out how social stresses:* Howard S. Friedman et al., "Psychosocial and Behavioral Predictors of Longevity," *American Psychologist*, Vol. 50 (1995), pp. 69–78.

147 *Emotion Coaching not only protects:* J. M. Gottman, *What Predicts Divorce?* (Hillsdale, N.J.: Lawrence Erlbaum, 1994).

148 *what kind of marital interactions predict:* John Gottman, *Why Marriages Succeed or Fail* (New York: Simon & Schuster, 1994).

154 *kept track of their pulse:* To take your heart rate, gently press your right index and middle fingers against your right carotid artery, which is two to three inches below your earlobe and under the jawbone. You should be able to feel your pulse. To calculate your pulse rate per minute, count the number of pulse beats you feel in fifteen seconds and multiply by four. To determine your average, baseline rate, take your pulse

three different times while you're sitting comfortably. Although individual pulse rates vary widely, most women clock in at between 82 and 86 beats per minute, while men average between 72 and 76 beats per minute.

158 *children often displayed aggression:* E. M. Cummings and J. L. Cummings, "A Process-Oriented Approach to Children's Coping with Adults' Angry Behavior," *Developmental Review,* Vol. 8 (1988), pp. 296–321.

158 *the degree of resolution mattered:* Cummings, "Coping with Background Anger in Early Childhood."

6 : THE FATHER'S CRUCIAL ROLE

PAGE

166 *One long-term study:* R. Koestner, C. E. Franz, and J. Weinberger, "The Family Origins of Empathic Concern: A 26 Year Longitudinal Study," *Journal of Personality and Social Psychology,* Vol. 58 (1990), pp. 709–17.

166 *By age forty-one, study participants:* C. E. Franz, D. McClelland, and J. Weinberger, "Childhood Antecedents of Conventional Social Accomplishment in Midlife Adults: A 26 Year Prospective Study," *Journal of Personality and Social Psychology,* Vol. 60 (1991), pp. 586–95.

167 *In 1960, only 19 percent:* David Popenoe, "American Family Decline, 1960–1990: A Review and Appraisal," *Journal of Marriage and the Family,* Vol. 55 (August 1993), pp. 527–55.

168 *"Such change has rendered":* Robert L. Griswold, *Fatherhood in America: A History* (New York: Basic Books, 1993).

168 *Between 1960 and 1987:* Popenoe, "American Family Decline, 1960–1990."

168 *among first-time marriages:* A. Cherlin, *Marriage, Divorce, Remarriage* (Cambridge: Harvard University Press, 1981).

168 *Birth to single mothers:* U.S. Bureau of the Census, "Births to Unmarried Women, by Race of Child and Age of Mother: 1970 to 1991," *Statistical Abstract of the United States: 1994* (114th Edition) (Washington, D.C., 1994).

168 *A recent survey of medium to large U.S. businesses:* S. L. Hyland, "Helping Employees with Family Care," *Monthly Labor*

*Review*, Vol. 113 (1990), pp. 22–26; K. Christensen, *Flexible Staffing and Scheduling in U.S. Corporations* (New York: Conference Board, 1989).

169   *custody is awarded to moms:* Griswold, *Fatherhood in America,* p. 263.

169   *One researcher estimates:* Michael E. Lamb, "Introduction: The Emergent American Father," in Michael E. Lamb, ed., *The Father's Role: Cross-Cultural Perspectives* (Hillsdale, N.J.: Lawrence Erlbaum, 1987), pp. 3–25.

170   *five-month-old baby boys:* F. A. Pedersen, J. Rubinstein, and L. J. Yarrow, "Infant Development in Father-Absent Families," *Journal of Genetic Psychology*, Vol. 135 (1979), pp. 51–61.

170   *one-year-old babies cried less:* M. Kotelchuck, "The Infant's Relationship to the Father," experimental evidence, in M. E. Lamb and S. K. Bronson, "The Role of the Father in Child Development: Past Presumptions, Present Realities, and Future Potential," paper presented to a conference on Fatherhood and the Male Single Parent, Omaha, November 1978.

170   *Observing parents with their newborns:* M. Yogman, S. Dixon, E. Tronick, H. Als, and T. B. Brazelton, "The Goals and Structure of Face-to-Face Interaction Between Infants and Fathers," paper presented at the biennial meeting of the Society for Research in Child Development, New Orleans, LA, March, 1977.

171   *Studies of three- and four-year-old children:* K. MacDonald and R. D. Parke, "Parent-Child Physical Play: The Effects of Sex and Age of Children and Parents," *Sex Roles*, Vol. 7–8 (1986), pp. 367–79.

172   *"Just as men of the Baby Boom generation":* Ronald F. Levant, with Gini Kopecky, *Masculinity Reconstructed: Changing the Rules of Manhood—At Work, in Relationships, and in Family Life* (New York: Dutton, 1995), p. 107.

173   *projects like Levant's Fatherhood Project:* Levant's work with the Fatherhood Project is summarized in Ross D. Parke, *Fatherhood* (Cambridge: Harvard University Press, 1996).

174   *women whose husbands participated:* W. J. Hennenborn and R. Cogan, "The Effect of Husband Participation on Reported Pain and the Probability of Medication During Labor and

Birth," *Journal of Psychosomatic Research*, Vol. 19 (1975), pp. 215–22.

175 *a dad who shows a high interest:* D. R. Entwisle and S. G. Doering, *The First Birth* (Baltimore: Johns Hopkins University Press, 1981).

175 *fathers who begin diapering:* R. Lind, "Observations After Delivery of Communications Between Mother-Infant-Father," paper presented at the International Congress of Pediatrics, Buenos Aires, October 1974.

176 *Even among newborns:* A. N. Meltzoff, and M. K. Moore, "Newborn Infants Imitate Adult Facial Gestures," *Child Development* (1983), pp. 54, 722–29.

176 *mothers' attitudes toward fathers' participation:* A. Beitel and R. D. Parke, "Maternal Attitudes as a Determinant of Father Involvement," Unpublished manuscript, University of Illinois (1993).

177 *The importance of fathers' accessibility:* R. W. Blanchard and H. B. Biller, "Father Availability and Academic Performance Among Third Grade Boys," *Developmental Psychology*, Vol. 4 (1971), pp. 301–5.

178 *"Having a competent father":* H. B. Biller, *Father, Child and Sex Role* (Lexington, MA: D.C. Heath, 1971), p. 59.

178 *"It's by performing":* Ronald F. Levant, with Gini Kopecky, *Masculinity Reconstructed*, p. 197.

181 *A British study of scientific workers:* R. A. Lee, "Flextime and Conjugal Roles," *Journal of Occupational Behavior*, Vol. 4 (1983), pp. 297–315.

181 *workers on flextime:* H. Bohen and A. Viveros-Long, *Balancing Jobs and Family Life: Do Flexible Work Schedules Help?* (Philadelphia: Temple University Press, 1981).

181 *research on egalitarian marriages:* Pepper Schwartz, *Peer Marriage: How Love Between Equals Really Works* (New York: Free Press, 1994), p. 14.

181 *fathers working as air-traffic controllers:* R. L. Repetti, "Short-Term and Long-Term Processes Linking Perceived Job Stressors to Father-Child Interaction," *Social Development*, Vol. 3 (1994), pp. 1–15.

181 *when dads have more independence:* M. L. Kohn and C.

Schooler, *Work and Personality: An Inquiry into the Impact of Social Stratification* (Norwood, N.J.: Ablex, 1983); D. R. Miller and G. E. Swanson, *The Changing American Parent* (New York: Wiley, 1954).

182 *90 percent of whom live apart:* Robert L. Griswold, *Fatherhood in America* (New York: Basic Books, 1993), p. 263.

183 *75 percent of all women:* P. C. Glick, "Remarried Families, Stepfamilies and Stepchildren: A Brief Demographic Profile," *Family Relations*, Vol. 38 (1989), pp. 24–47.

## 7: EMOTION COACHING AS YOUR CHILD GROWS

PAGE

187 *"The Still Face Game,":* M. K. Weinberg, E. Z. Tronick, "Beyond the Face: an Empirical Study of Infant Affective Configurations of Facial, Vocal, Gestural, and Regulatory Behaviors," *Child Development* (1994), pp. 65, 1503–15.

187 *Babies with depressed moms:* T. Field, B. T. Healy, and W. G. LeBlanc, "Sharing and Synchrony of Behavior States and Heart Rate in Nondepressed Versus Depressed Mother-Infant Interactions," *Infant Behavior and Development*, Vol. 12 (1989), pp. 357–76.

187 *And if a mother's depression continues:* T. Field, J. Pickens, N. A. Fox, T. Nawrocki et al., "Vagal Tone in Infants of Depressed Mothers," *Development and Psychopathology*, Vol. 7 (1995), pp. 227–31.

187 *The period between ages three months:* Ibid.

188 *Using this technology:* G. Dawson and K. W. Fischer, *Human Behavior and the Developing Brain*, (New York: Guilford, 1994).

188 *Further studies in Field's labs:* N. M. Palaez, T. Field, M. Cigales and A. Gonzalez et al., "Infants of Depressed Mothers Show Less 'Depressed' Behavior with Their Nursery Teachers," *Infant Mental Health Journal*, Vol. 15 (1994), pp. 358–67; Z. Hossain, T. Field, J. Gonzalez, J. Malphurs et al., "Infants of 'Depressed' Mothers Interact Better with Their Nondepressed Fathers," *Infant Mental Health Journal*, Vol. 15 (1994), pp. 348–57.

189 *parents fail to read:* E. Z. Tronick, and J. F. Cohn, "Infant-Mother Face-to-Face Interaction: Age and Gender Difference in Coordination and the Occurrence of Miscoordination," *Child Development*, Vol. 60 (1989), pp. 85–92.

192 *babies do not practice as much:* S. Dickstein and R. D. Parke, "Social Referencing in Infancy: A Glance at Fathers and Marriage," *Child Development*, Vol. 59 (1988), pp. 506–11.

196 *baby boys preferred looking:* T. G. R. Bower, *The Rational Infant* (New York: W. H. Freeman & Co., 1989).

200 *fantasy play with another child:* Laurie Kramer and John Gottman, "Becoming a Sibling: With a Little Help from My Friends," *Developmental Psychology*, Vol. 28 (1992), pp. 685–99.

203 *One particularly fine book:* Doris Brett, *Annie Stories: A Special Kind of Storytelling* (New York: Workman, 1986).

204 *young children may not understand:* E. M. Cummings, "Coping with Background Anger in Early Childhood."

210 *"Until this point":* Michael Riera, *Uncommon Sense for Parents with Teenagers* (Berkeley: Celestial Arts, 1995).

210 *"In its pain-bred name":* Gordon Parks, "Adolescence," *Whispers of Intimate Things* (New York: Viking Press, 1971).

# INDEX

abandonment, fear of, 202–3
adolescence, 73, 104, 140
  autonomy and, 213
  Emotion Coaching and, 208–13
  networks of emotional and com-
    munity support for, 158–59, 212
  respectful treatment of, 211–12
  as time of individuation, 210–11
adult situations, child's experience
  seen in terms of, 118–19
advice, unsolicited, 119–20
agendas, parental, 113–16, 134–37
aggression, 25, 32, 61, 104, 139, 140
Allen, Woody, 169
allies, parents as, 73, 94
anger, 25, 41, 53, 57, 61, 63, 78
  children's stress reactions to, 142
  communication of, 80–81
  concealing of, 79
  Emotion Coaching and, 130
  girls and, 49, 60
  parental, 35, 56, 66, 130
  parents as targets of, 117–18
  parent's reaction to, 21, 52, 54
  self-test for, 82–85
*Annie Stories* (Brett), 203–4
apologies, parents and, 66–67, 81, 118
*Atlantic Monthly,* 143
authoritarian parents, 32
autonomic nervous system, 38–39,
  142

baby talk, 186
base of power, 125–26
Baumrind, Diana, 32

bed wetting, 92
behavior zones, 102–3
betrayal, 150
*Between Parent and Child* (Ginott),
  34–35
Biller, Henry, 177–78
Blanchard, Robert, 177–78
Bly, Robert, 166
body language, 94–95, 143
bonding, 21, 27, 66, 67–68, 72, 113,
  144
  father-child, 166
Bower, T. G. R., 196
boys:
  absent fathers and, 166
  involved father's effect on, 170
  as toddlers, 196
brainstorming, 75, 81, 105, 106
Brazelton, T. Berry, 170
Brett, Doris, 203

California, University of, at River-
  side, 144–45
case histories, children:
  Alex, 62
  Andrew (nine-year-old), 114
  Becky (four-year-old), 30, 56
  Ben (four-year-old), 64, 65–66
  Cameron (five-year-old), 58
  Carly (seven-year-old), 90–91
  Charley, 59
  Emily (seven-year-old), 19
  Heather, 53
  Jennifer (five-year-old), 21, 63–64,
    66